Ethnic and Minority Cultures as Tourist Attractions

ASPECTS OF TOURISM

Series Editors: **Chris Cooper** (*Oxford Brookes University, UK*), **C. Michael Hall** (*University of Canterbury, New Zealand*) and **Dallen J. Timothy** (*Arizona State University, USA*)

Aspects of Tourism is an innovative, multifaceted series, which comprises authoritative reference handbooks on global tourism regions, research volumes, texts and monographs. It is designed to provide readers with the latest thinking on tourism worldwide and push back the frontiers of tourism knowledge. The volumes are authoritative, readable and user-friendly, providing accessible sources for further research. Books in the series are commissioned to probe the relationship between tourism and cognate subject areas such as strategy, development, retailing, sport and environmental studies.

Full details of all the books in this series and of all our other publications can be found on http://www.channelviewpublications.com, or by writing to Channel View Publications, St Nicholas House, 31-34 High Street, Bristol BS1 2AW, UK.

ASPECTS OF TOURISM: 65

Ethnic and Minority Cultures as Tourist Attractions

Edited by

Anya Diekmann and Melanie Kay Smith

CHANNEL VIEW PUBLICATIONS
Bristol • Buffalo • Toronto

Library of Congress Cataloging in Publication Data
A catalog record for this book is available from the Library of Congress.
Ethnic and Minority Cultures as Tourist Attractions/Edited by Anya Diekmann and
Melanie Kay Smith.
Aspects of Tourism: 65
Includes bibliographical references and index.
1. Culture and tourism—Case studies. 2. Ethnic neighborhoods—Case studies.
3. Tourism—Social aspects—Case studies. I. Diekmann, Anya, editor of compilation.
II. Smith, Melanie Kay.
G156.5.H47E75 2015
338.4'791–dc23 2014033161

British Library Cataloguing in Publication Data
A catalogue entry for this book is available from the British Library.

ISBN-13: 978-1-84541-483-2 (hbk)
ISBN-13: 978-1-84541-482-5 (pbk)

Channel View Publications
UK: St Nicholas House, 31-34 High Street, Bristol BS1 2AW, UK.
USA: UTP, 2250 Military Road, Tonawanda, NY 14150, USA.
Canada: UTP, 5201 Dufferin Street, North York, Ontario M3H 5T8, Canada.

Website: www.channelviewpublications.com
Twitter: Channel_View
Facebook: https://www.facebook.com/channelviewpublications
Blog: www.channelviewpublications.wordpress.com

The policy of Multilingual Matters/Channel View Publications is to use papers that
are natural, renewable and recyclable products, made from wood grown in sustainable
forests. In the manufacturing process of our books, and to further support our policy,
preference is given to printers that have FSC and PEFC Chain of Custody certification.
The FSC and/or PEFC logos will appear on those books where full certification has been
granted to the printer concerned.

Typeset by Deanta Global Publishing Services Limited.
Printed and bound in Great Britain by Short Run Press Ltd.

Contents

Contributors

Anya Diekmann is professor in tourism at the Université Libre de Bruxelles (Belgium). Her research focuses on different aspects of urban cultural and slum tourism in India and Europe. Her publications include work on social tourism and cultural tourism with a particular focus on heritage, urban and ethnic tourism. In 2011, she co-authored with Kevin Hannam *Tourism and India: A Critical Introduction* (Routledge) and she is co-editor with Scott McCabe and Lynn Minnaert of the book *Social Tourism in Europe: Theory and Practice* (Channel View), and she co-edited with Kevin Hannam, *Beyond Backpacker Tourism: Mobilities and Experiences* (Channel View), in 2010.

Melanie Smith has extensive experience of researching and writing about urban culture and communities, as well as working with policymakers, planners and regeneration agencies. Her doctoral research (2002–2009) focused on the role of local communities in the cultural regeneration of Greenwich in London, UK. This included numerous ethnic communities. She is the author or editor of several books about cultural tourism, including two editions of *Issues in Cultural Tourism Studies* (2003, 2009) and *Tourism, Culture and Regeneration* (2006). Much of her recent work in Budapest, Hungary, has been in the field of urban cultural tourism, and is now focusing on the politically and ethically contentious status of Roma, Jewish and other ethnic or minority cultures in central and eastern Europe.

Nimit Chowdhary is professor with South Asia's most prestigious tourism school – the Indian Institute of Tourism and Travel Management (IITTM). Nimit heads the school operations for North India at its campus in Delhi-NCR. He divides his energies between training, research and consultancy besides teaching at master's level and on doctoral programmes. He has authored 6 books and more than 100 papers besides addressing more than 100 conferences, seminars and conclaves as keynote speaker or session chair. His most recent book *Handbook for Tour Guides* has been well received and has become a 'must-read' for tourist guides. Nimit travels extensively for research projects and on-site training. His current research interests include tour guiding, rural tourism, entrepreneurship and destination management. He advises different governments, policymakers and industry on tourism issues.

Isabelle Cloquet is research fellow at the Université Libre de Bruxelles. Her research interests focus on tourism and entrepreneurship, more particularly in sub-Saharan Africa. Her additional fields of interest include heritage interpretation and nature-based tourism. As part of the LITOTeS team, she also worked on studies pertaining to city branding and urban tourism in ethnic quarters.

Jock Collins is professor of social economics in the Management Discipline Group at the UTS Business School, Sydney, Australia. He is co-director of the Cosmopolitan Civil Societies Research Centre at UTS. His research interests centre on an interdisciplinary study of immigration and cultural diversity in the economy and society. His recent research has been on Australian immigration, ethnic crime, immigrant and indigenous entrepreneurship, immigrant youth, ethnic precincts and tourism, multiculturalism, the Cronulla Beach Riots, global teachers, immigrants and the built environment and immigrants in regional and rural Australia and the social use of ethnic heritage and the built environment. He is the author or co-author of 10 books, the most recent of which is *Global Teachers, Australian Perspectives: Goodbye Mr. Chips Hello Ms. Banerjee* (with Carol Reid and Michael Singh), published by Springer Press in 2014.

Nelson Graburn was educated in the classics and natural sciences at The King's School, Canterbury, and he earned his BA in social anthropology at Cambridge (1958). He attended McGill (MA 1960) and the University of Chicago (PhD 1963). After postdoc at Northwestern doing research on Inuit-Naskapi/Cree interethnic relations (1963–1964), he was hired at UC Berkeley where he has taught anthropology for 50 years. He has served as curator of North America in the Hearst Museum since 1972 and co-chair of Canadian studies since 1976. He has held visiting positions in Canada, France, the UK, Japan and Brazil and has lectured at more than 20 universities in China. He has lived in 22 Inuit communities (1959–2014) in the Canadian Arctic (and Greenland and Alaska) doing research on kinship, cultural change, art and identity, and he has carried out research on domestic tourism, multiculturalism and heritage in Japan (since 1974) and China (since 1991). Among his books are *Ethnic and Tourist Arts* (1976); *Japanese Domestic Tourism* (1983); *The Anthropology of Tourism* (1983); *Tourism Social Sciences* (1991); *Multiculturalism in the New Japan* (2008); 旅游人类学论文集 [*Anthropology in the Age of Tourism*] (2009); *Tourism and*

Glocalization: Perspectives in East Asian Studies (2010); and *Tourism Imaginaries: Anthropological Approaches* (2014).

Bianca Freire-Medeiros is senior lecturer of sociology at Getulio Vargas Foundation (Rio de Janeiro, Brazil). Bianca Freire-Medeiros was a visiting fellow at the Center for Mobilities Research (CeMoRe) at Lancaster University. She has published extensively in several languages on urban sociology, mobility studies and visual culture. Since 2005, she has investigated tourism activities in different segregated spaces. Her latest publication is *Touring Poverty* (Advances in Sociology Series, Routledge, 2013).

Márcio Grijó Vilarouca is lecturer of political science at the Getulio Vargas Foundation (Rio de Janeiro, Brazil). Since 2011, he is responsible for the FGV-Survey, a department that develops research related to the favela, residents' perceptions about the presence of the State and the Pacifying Police Units in their community.

Omar Moufakkir was born in Morocco. He completed his primary and secondary education in Casablanca, undergraduate studies in France, graduate studies in the Netherlands and obtained his PhD from Michigan State University, USA, in park, recreation and tourism resources. His research focus is on the relationship between tourism and peace, cross-cultural understanding and the impact of immigration on destination image and travel propensity. He is the editor-in-chief of the *Journal of Tourism and Peace Research* (www.icptr.com). He is now affiliated with the School of Hospitality Business at Saxion University of Applied Sciences, The Netherlands.

Yvette Reisinger is professor of marketing in the College of Business Administration, Gulf University for Science and Technology (GUST), Kuwait. She has a long-standing research interest in tourism, culture and communication, particularly in the area of cultural influences on tourist behaviour and destination marketing. She has conducted extensive cross-cultural studies of China, Indonesia, Japan, Korea, Thailand and Australia, and received several articles of excellence awards for her work on cultural differences among Asian tourist markets. Her other research interests include tourism experiences and human transformation through tourism. She is the author or editor of several books and more than 150 academic papers. Her books *Cross-Cultural Behaviour in Tourism: Concepts and Analysis* (2003), *International Tourism: Cultures and Behaviour* (2009) and two parts of *Transformational Tourism* (2013, 2014) provide a path to very important fields of tourism study in a global world and the first account of tourism research in these areas. She is now focusing on the multicultural aspects of tourism and the influence of globalisation on ethnic and minority cultures.

Joshua Schmidt is a social researcher at the Ramon branch of the Dead Sea and Arava Science Center under the joint auspices of the Israeli Ministry of Science, Technology and Space and Ben-Gurion University of the Negev and a post-doctoral affiliate in the Department of Foreign Languages and Linguistics at Ben-Gurion University of the Negev. His multidisciplinary research interests include contemporary Israeli popular and peripheral culture, ethnolinguistics, ethnomusicology, tourism and wellness, cultural archaeology and visual ethnography. In 2011, he received his doctorate in anthropology from Ben-Gurion University of the Negev. His thesis combined ethnography with sign-oriented linguistics to analyse the uses and functions of electronic dance music among secular and religious Israeli youth. Schmidt is currently conducting an ethnolinguistic analysis of words used in conjunction with the transformation of Mitzpe Ramon from a peripheral mining town to an international tourist destination.

Stephen Shaw (PhD) is director of the Creative Industries Research Centre (CIRCa) in the Faculty of Business and Law, London Metropolitan University, where he is Reader in Business and Management. He has published a wide range of papers, which in recent years have focused on tourism-led regeneration, especially in city regions that have a rich cultural heritage and clusters of creative industries with transglobal influences. In particular, he has been principal investigator for cross-disciplinary research to explore opportunities through which urban spaces can be made more accessible, safe and welcoming for visitors and local people alike. This includes the development of more effective approaches to community engagement for improvements to public spaces and walking environments. Under the auspices of the British Association of Canadian Studies, he chaired the Canada–UK Cities Group (2008–2011), and from 2011 to 2013 he chaired the Cultural Tourism Committee of ICOMOS-UK (UNESCO World Heritage).

Esti Venske is a senior lecturer in the Department of Tourism and Events Management at the Cape Peninsula University of Technology where she is extensively involved with the social upliftment of previously disadvantaged, marginalised communities through service learning and community engagement event management projects. She completed her master's degree with a focus on the development of ethnic and cultural tourism products in South Africa and she has extensively researched indigenous South African cultures as a marketing mechanism for tourism. Her current doctoral studies focus on sociocultural event management and leadership and include aspects related specifically to gay events. She has presented and co-published international papers on culture as a tourism product as well as gay tourism and the development of Cape Town's post-apartheid gay village.

Anita Zátori is a lecturer at Corvinus University of Budapest and a research assistant at the Institute of Tourism and Catering, University of Applied Sciences, Budapest. She has recently completed her PhD, which focused on tourist experience, its co-creation and management issues, and tour guiding. Urban cultural tourism, creativity, and issues of representing cultural heritage, living culture, and minority culture in sightseeing tours are key concepts in her recent research activity, which are also partly connected to her doctoral research.

Acknowledgements

We would like to thank all of our contributors to this book for their interesting chapters. Thank you to all of our contacts and interviewees who helped to provide information and data for the book. Thank you also to our publishers at Channel View, especially Elinor Robertson and Sarah Williams.

Preface

We have both been working in the field of cultural tourism for many years now and indigenous and ethnic, migrant and minority cultures and communities have always been a great source of fascination to us. Many anthropologists have produced excellent work on indigenous cultural tourism around the world, especially in remote and developing regions. Less attention has perhaps been given to ethnic communities living in urban environments. This subject is somehow closer to us as we both lived (or live) in two multicultural and ethnically diverse cities, London and Brussels. Melanie's PhD focused on urban cultural planning in the 2000s and when she was researching cultures and communities in the London borough of Greenwich, there were around 44 ethnic groups listed in that borough alone! Since then, many more immigrant groups have chosen London as their temporary or permanent home. Brussels on the other hand has not only residents coming from all the member states of the European Union, but it also attracts many African immigrants, particularly from Congo and the Maghreb region. Both cities have become in parallel, but at a different level, major tourism destinations in the world today. London has become one of the top, if not the most popular destination in the world, while Brussels slowly but surely is managing to shake off the boring image of an administrative capital and is becoming a more vibrant and multicultural city which attracts a broader range of tourists. This, we believe, is no coincidence. The same is true of many other cities around the world. Diverse ethnic cultures and an atmosphere of tolerance are attractive qualities in a city, not only socially but economically too, as emphasised by Richard Florida in his seminal works.

However, this book is also set against a backdrop of the rise of far right-wing parties in many European countries whose rhetoric is generally anti-immigration at best, and racist and/or homophobic at worst. Economic recession and social discontent often lead to the scapegoating of ethnic minorities, irrespective of their role in the current crisis. So this book has been written at a time when ethnic and minority cultures are of great interest culturally and touristically, especially in cosmopolitan cities, but also at a time when the communities have relatively little political and social support. With this book we hope to cast the spotlight on ethnic and minority cultures and communities at a time when positive promotion of those rich and diverse cultures is more important than ever. We hope that this book will go some small way to increasing understanding of and appreciation for their lives and traditions.

Melanie Smith, Budapest
Anya Diekmann, Brussels
March 2014

Introduction

In recent years, the populations of many countries have become much more ethnically diverse as a result of immigration and facilitated mobility. Many subcultures have grown, especially in cosmopolitan cities. The percentage of ethnic minorities in the population of today's cities can be as much as 40% or 50%. Florida's (2002, 2005) seminal work on creative cities clearly emphasises the importance of diversity (including a Gay Index) in determining the economic and social success of cities. Positive aspects of contact with other cultures include developing understanding, respect and mutual appreciation, and reducing stereotypes, prejudices and racial tensions. For tourism developers, ethnic diversity can also be one of the most important attributes of a destination. The expectations of exotic experiences and sights of 'Otherness' are potential sources of economic revenue for a destination (Ooi, 2002). However, there are also negative aspects of ethnic cultures living in proximity to one another or within a majority culture that can lead to social tension, discrimination and racism (Council of Europe, 2014). Tourism can sometimes be a social force because of its transformative capacity (Higgins-Desbiolles, 2012; Reisinger, 2013) contributing to improving intercultural relationships.

ı Many migrant and ethnically diverse districts are marked by deprivation and degradation with poor urban planning, social exclusion and what is sometimes described as a 'ghetto' economy (Hoffmann, 2003).ı Therefore, these districts are not necessarily considered as an asset, but more as a problem to deal with. However, in recent years, many of these quarters were subject to regeneration, often through gentrification or tourism or both. The problem occurring then was that many of the original migrant population had to leave the area to move to more affordable parts of town, 'leaving' their culture in the area that transformed into an ethnic commercial belt. However, the maintenance of specific cultural services and commercial supply forged the identity of the area. Examples are global. From the Americas to Australia, Singapore, Europe and many Asian and African countries, ethnic and cultural minorities shaped the urbanscape contributing largely to the representation of multicultural societies.

With growing demand for the diversification of tourism supply in cities, cultural and ethnic communities themselves and/or the tourist authorities discovered an opportunity to place them on the tourism map as a tourist asset highlighting the diversity of the destination. Chinatowns, Little Italies, Jewish quarters, African quarters, etc. all became a tool for attracting visitors looking for something different from the classic urban heritage. The paradox lies in the segregation for tourism purposes of migrant communities who may wish to be integrated. Over the past few years, tourism research has focused more and more on the diversification of the tourism market, on niche products and the growing desire among consumers for new and exciting experiences. In the urban tourism context, there has been a growing interest in the 'fringe' or 'alternative' areas of cities, often incorporating everyday life, cultural events or special celebrations of diverse social and ethnic groups. Maitland (2007) suggests that many tourists, especially repeat visitors to destinations, are seeking alternative experiences that are based on the authenticity of local areas. Some of these are surprisingly ordinary, but the fact that they are based in 'fringe' areas of cities inhabited by local residents and characterised by more organic developments means that they are appealing to visitors. This implies that sometimes the 'true' cultures of cities are more desirable than purpose-built attractions. They offer elements of surprise while helping to maintain a sense of place. This can include ethnic quarters or ethnoscapes.

Ethnic tourism as a form of tourism practice is often considered to be just another subsector of cultural tourism (Diekmann & Maulet, 2009; McKercher & Cros, 2002; Smith, 2006). Cave *et al.* (2007: 436) state that 'Globally, ethnic communities are asserting their ownership of intellectual and cultural property through cultural tourism'. The cultural politics of tourism has been discussed by many authors (Hall & Tucker, 2004; Hollinshead, 2004; Smith, 2003; Smith & Robinson, 2006), especially in the context of the anthropology of tourism (e.g. Macleod & Carrier, 2010) and indigenous tourism (e.g. Butler & Hinch, 1996, 2007; Zeppel, 2006). Of course, in the field of cultural studies, racial and ethnic issues have been central to debates since the mid-1980s, with identity construction and representation being recurrent themes (e.g. Stuart Hall). Many years before this, philosophers and writers were already questioning the objectification of the 'other' and discussing marginality and 'alterity', for example Jean-Paul Sartre wrote about Jews and anti-Semitism in the 1940s, Simone de Beauvoir penned *The Second Sex* about women and feminism in 1949 and Frantz Fanon wrote about colonisation and the ethnic other in the 1950s. Many of their arguments centred on resistance, freedom and existential authenticity. Although some of these arguments are slightly beyond the scope of this book, central to all of these and later debates are theories of politics, power and ideology, which question hegemonic, Eurocentric and ethnocentric approaches to the representation of the culture of 'others'. These issues are especially relevant to ethnic and cultural communities in the context of tourism, including immigrant and diasporic groups who have increasingly become part of the tourist landscape in many Western cities. Cave *et al.* (2013) discuss how tourism is a powerful agent of marginalisation, which can include physical, economic, technological, political and social marginalisation. This can be redressed through community-developed projects or appropriate 'third sector' interventions. However, the paradox may be that cultures and communities are commodified, appropriated or changed as a result of wanting to develop for the purposes of cultural consumption and tourism.

For the purposes of this book, a distinction is made between indigenous cultural tourism and ethnic cultural tourism. The former refers to the lifestyles and traditions of small communities and tribal groups living in fragile and remote environments, often in postcolonial developing countries, whereas the latter refers to the lives and culture of ethnic minority groups, immigrants and diasporas living largely within post-imperial Western societies and predominantly in cities. In many cases, ethnic communities have clustered in certain geographical areas of a city to form Chinatowns, Little Italies or similar. Some cultural quarters develop organically and can lead to an enhanced sense of community for diasporic groups or immigrants in search of a common identity in a new or foreign environment. However, often the clustering is based on economic factors such as cheap rents, affordable or available land on the margins of cities (e.g. slums, favelas) or are the consequences of political oppression (in the case of former Jewish ghettos or South African townships). It is therefore more common that such areas are referred to pejoratively as slums or ghettos than ethnoscapes or ethnic quarters. However, the increasing fascination of tourists is leading to a certain degree of romanticisation of such areas and the application of more 'appealing' labels especially for marketing purposes.

The quarters in which ethnic communities tend to live are usually highly multicultural with a broad variety of stakeholder groups. This makes the organisation and promotion of tourism and other leisure and cultural activities somewhat complex. The diversification process of the tourism supply is often combined with a necessity for the regeneration of certain urban areas. Trying to improve the social conditions of specific communities by emphasising their distinctiveness through the commodification of their lives and cultures is a contentious process which must be handled sensitively to avoid appropriation and disempowerment. While there are ongoing discussions in many countries all over the world about the integration of migrant populations, there is also a turn towards more protective nationalist convictions. This makes the social and political status of minorities and otherwise excluded communities more uncertain, even though their social or ethnic appeal may be growing in the eyes of tourism developers.

Several authors (Chang, 1999; Hoffmann, 2003; Reisinger, 2012; Santos *et al.*, 2008, etc.) have discussed the complexity of tourism development for host communities with all of its economic, social, cultural and ethical implications in an urban environment with a particular focus on North

America and Singapore. This book broadens the cultural and geographical scope and examines various aspects of the tourism development process concerning minorities, cultural and ethnic, as well as excluded communities. Sociologists, anthropologists, economists, urban planners and tourism researchers from different countries tackle the complex development issues from various perspectives. The authors examine the different ways in which such groups react and respond to the promotion of their lives and culture(s) in the context of leisure and tourism and offer solutions, recommendations and examples of good practice in how to implement policies, plans and strategies for the mutual benefit of all stakeholders in urban contexts.

Communities Under Scrutiny

One of the key terms that needs to be defined at the beginning of this book is the term 'community'. This word has almost as many definitions as the word 'culture'. Indeed, community and the recognition of a multitude of different communities are inherent to power relations and socioeconomic distinctions and developments. Sociological or anthropological definitions of community can help to determine and understand the linkages that exist between the host community, tourism stakeholders and authorities as well as guests. These linkages may depend on the type of community and the sense of community under scrutiny. McMillan and Chavis (1986) distinguish between the territorial and geographical notion and the relational notion among community members. Emotional attachment is underlying to both notions. In line with numerous sociologists, Berger (1998: 324) compares community to society:

> Community is tradition; society is change. Community is feeling; society is rationality. Community is female; society is male. Community is warm and wet and intimate; society is cold and dry and formal.

This statement can provide, to a certain extent, an explanation of the development and success of communities as destinations for tourists, in that communities, at least in terms of emotional attachment and the relational notion, are based upon common culture, family and closeness. Bruhn (2004: 30) summarises Tönnies' concept of an idealised community as an entity with a 'simple, familialistic, intimate, private way of life where members were bound together by common traditions and a common language and villagers experience a sense of "we-ness"'. While this romanticised vision of community might be meaningful for some, it is not for others as we will see later in the book. Indeed, there are many communities that are created involuntarily, such as the slum community or some other 'ethnic' districts, places where migrants had to settle when they first came to a country that developed later mostly into commercial belts, like the case of Matonge in Brussels (discussed in Chapter 2).

Although communities are often promoted as ONE community belonging to ONE specific area (quarter/district), the term 'community' should then not necessarily be understood with a specific spatial attachment. For Craven and Wellman (1973), communities are indeed social networks and do not necessarily depend on whether the people live in the same neighbourhood (Wellman & Gulia, 1999). In fact, ethnic or cultural quarters are multicultural spaces composed of locals, immigrants, residents and users (Chang, 1999) with often one specific culture shaping the area through their shops and/or restaurants. In most cases, however, the locality has, at some point, been meaningful to the community for various reasons, mainly as a host area for migrants or as a ghetto.

The residents of a community quarter are thus not necessarily (and less and less) members of the community but are either members of the middle class gentrifying the area or, on the contrary, are new migrants with less income. In both cases, community members who formerly lived in the area had at some point been forced to seek other areas to live in. However, the services and goods provision stayed in the previous location, becoming a commercial ethnic belt (McLaughlin & Jesilow, 1998). The reason for this lies in the fact that community members do not move collectively into another area but settle in different economically accessible areas. The commercial ethnic belts provide services, food and beverages for either community members or community tourists, and for external tourists from the country's/continent's dominant culture as an exotic setting (Conforti, 1996; Selby, 2004).

The situation is comparable in gay quarters, where food and beverage provision targeting one specific group of society attract 'community' members from outside the area and only very few community members live in the area itself. In all these examples it is as much the provision of specific goods and services, which are (also) consumed by incoming 'community' members that shape the place and make it attractive for the external tourists (Figure 1).

Li (2009: 1) also discusses a new model of contemporary ethnic community which is termed 'the ethnoburb': 'Ethnoburbs are multiethnic communities in which one ethnic minority group has a significant concentration but does not necessarily constitute a majority'. This model differs from others in that it consists of (often) upwardly mobile immigrant communities who may already be second or third generation, many of whom have never lived in an inner city but instead inhabit suburbs. Here, they are well integrated into mainstream society although they keep their distinct community and multifaceted identity. This model is typical of many Chinese communities in North American cities, for example, who no longer inhabit or never inhabited Chinatown(s). A distinction is made

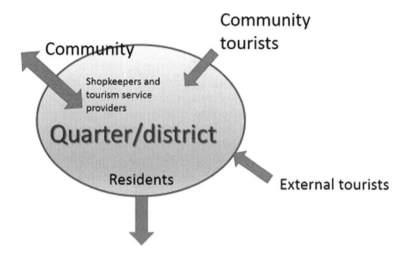

Figure 1 Community and visitor flows
Source: Adapted from Diekmann and Maulet (2009)

between ethnoburbs and ghettos or enclaves, as segregation is not forced and conflicts with other groups are non-existent or minimal.

Community's Spatial Link with Promoted Spaces in Ethnic and Cultural Districts

In the case of slums, the communities' common feature is poverty independent of their identity. Unlike other distinctive quarters, the service provision here is less important than the living places of the given community and here the 'community' is actually the residents of the visited districts. However, there is usually also a cultural 'added value' and a specific identity to the commodified poverty in the favelas and townships. In the case of the favelas, it is the culture of salsa dancing, for example, and in townships it is the symbolism of the freedom fight and the hardship of black African communities under the apartheid regime in South Africa. For the community, township tourism 'brings visitors to the sites of significance to the anti-Apartheid movement as well as improving tourists' understanding of poverty issues of historically oppressed communities' while adding experiences of 'the conditions of life in the former "black townships" created under Apartheid' (Nemasetoni & Rogerson, 2005: 201).

Beeton's (2006) term 'destination communities' describes the phenomenon best. All different types of communities are considered whether they are either willingly or involuntarily promoted or exploited as a tourism asset by either public or private tourism agencies. Yet, a distinction can be made between the different communities under scrutiny. Ethnic and minority communities are clearly not homogeneous and have to be researched on a community-by-community basis, although there are some common characteristics:

- They tend to be socially marginalised or the victims of prejudice.
- They are not homogeneous – there are many subgroups with different cultural practices and viewpoints.
- They often live in areas of deprivation (although this cannot be generalised for some areas like Little Italies, Jewish and gay quarters).
- They are often diasporic or displaced from their original homeland (but not applicable to gay citizens).
- Their culture may be based more on intangible than tangible elements.
- Their arts and festivals are often valued more than their economic or social contribution.

Table 1 provides a summary of the main communities who are considered in this book. It is recognised that there are thousands of ethnic and indigenous minorities who could have been the focus of the work; however, the aim was to provide examples of those who typify common issues and challenges across many cities and countries. For example, there are Gypsy communities all over Europe who suffer from the same social prejudices as the Hungarian Gypsies; many European cities have Jewish quarters where the Jewish community is partly absent because of the Holocaust legacy; several cities across the world have gay quarters which are becoming more popular with heterosexual tourists; ethnic quarters like Chinatown, Little Italies and Banglatowns are a common feature of many cities which had extensive immigration at one time or another; favelas, slums and townships across numerous countries (e.g. Brazil, India, South Africa) are comparable because of their socio-economic characteristics.

Segregation plays an important role in tourism development, for the uniqueness of the community in the spatial and cultural context is justification for the display of diversity of a destination. Yet, as we will see later, the segregation is often artificial and ambiguous in the sense that the protagonists are well integrated into the broader urban society but consume community goods within a specific area or quarter in a city. Other communities are integrated into economic life and are even a central feature of it, but become excluded through poverty or origin from basic services and a lack of recognition or respect from more mainstream others. This is the case for slum dwellers who are active either inside or outside the slum (outside they are not necessarily identified as belonging to the slum community). On the other hand, ethnoburb dwellers may be fully integrated into mainstream society and political, economic and social life (Li, 2009).

Table 1 The communities focused on in this book

Type of communities	Main characteristics	Typical tourist attractions
Jewish communities	• Relatively wealthy and educated • Do not usually live in the 'Jewish quarter(s)' • Holocaust heritage prominent in Europe • In some countries victims of reappearing anti-Semitism	• Tours of the Jewish quarter • Jewish festivals • Synagogue visits • Museums and Holocaust memorials
Gypsy communities	• Culturally diverse (many groups) • Traditionally nomadic • Very little material culture • Socially marginalised, victims of prejudice and often very poor	• Gypsy festivals • Music and dance • Colourful costumes
African communities	• Diverse in character (e.g. from different African countries) • Diasporic or displaced • Little material culture • Sometimes victims of racism and anti-immigration rhetoric • Valued more for their music and dance than for their social or economic skills	• African quarters or villages • Shops and markets • Restaurants and cafés • Festivals and music events
Slum and township dwellers	• Extremely poor and deprived • Diverse in socio-economic characteristics • Perceived as 'joyful' celebrators of culture despite their poverty	• Slum, favela and township tours • Arts, crafts and cultural events

Chinese ethnic communities	• Traditional lifestyles • Colourful costumes • Perceived as exotic by urban Chinese and international tourists alike	• Rural villages often artificially preserved for tourism purposes • Urban 'theme park' replicas of villages • Cultural activities and events which are often 'improved' for tourists
Ethnic communities in 'ethnic quarters' of cities (e.g. Chinese, Indian, Italian)	• Diasporic but may be second or third generation • Often run businesses in the ethnic quarter but do not always live there • Commercially orientated and used to tourism • May be integrated into mainstream society but face some prejudice or stereotyping	• Ethnic quarters • Restaurants, bars and cafés • Cultural festivals • Shops and markets • Tours
Gay communities	• Relatively wealthy • More likely to be White • Usually do not live in the so-called 'gay quarter' • Perceived to be cultured and enjoy the arts • Perceived to be lovers of evening entertainment, clubs, parties and festivals	• Gay Pride Festival • Gay quarters • Gay pubs, bars and clubs

In terms of culture, people in migrant communities are usually social-ised in both the majority and mainstream contexts, a process which is both fluid but also sometimes conflicting (Cave *et al.*, 2007). Both global and local influences are simultaneously pervasive, especially in cosmopoli-tan cities or 'megalopolises'. Giulianotti and Robertson (2007) discuss in detail the role of immigration in the process of so-called 'glocalisation'. They distinguish four kinds of glocalisation projects:

Relativisation or the preservation by social actors of their pre-existing ideas and practices, thus contributing to the differentiation of the host culture.

Accommodation or the absorption by social actors of the meanings and practices associated with other societies.

Hybridisation or the mixing and blending by social actors of their own and other sociocultural representations and habits to produce distinctive new forms.

Transformation or the abandonment by social actors of their own tradi-tions on behalf of those associated with other sociocultural systems.

The extent to which immigrant culture is 'glocalised' may determine its attractiveness for tourism. If a complete transformation takes place, this may diminish the interest for tourists who perceive the culture to be little different from the culture of mainstream society (for example, this is the case of some Hungarian Gypsy groups in Chapter 3). Hybridisation may be seen as an exciting process for many (e.g. locals), but also as a destroyer of traditions and perceived authenticity for tourists.

Tourism developments

In recent years, there has been a growth in the development of tour-ism in poor ethnic quarters, often called 'human safari', 'poverty' and 'slum' tourism. For example, Conforti's (1996) 'Whites on Safari' relates to the bus visits of Harlem by White American tourists. 'Voyeurism' and 'poverty porn' refer to the visit of slums and shanty towns in developing countries. The latter is an example where socially weaker groups become a destination for travellers because of their distinctiveness. The topic operates according to a north/south gradient and stresses the boundaries between the rich and the poor becoming objects of pity and/or compas-sion. It questions the commodification of poverty into a tourism product. In Chapter 7, Freire-Medeiros and Grijó Vilarouca refer to the growing number of 'incursions into territories of supposed dirt, danger and despair' and describe how 'that modality of tourism offers a peculiar juxtaposition of amusement and fear, leisure and guilt, emotional expression and exploi-tation'. The 'success' of these areas, however, is increasing, for instance, with the favela of Rocinha in Rio de Janeiro being the third most impor-tant attraction of the city with 300,000 visitors per year (Freire-Meideros,

2009a). When analysing the history of ethnic districts in the Western world and their exposure as tourist destinations, it seems that while the press hardly ever questions the visiting of ethnic quarters like Harlem, it judges harshly the visiting of impoverished areas in other countries, questioning the motivations of both visitors and hosts (Selinger & Outterson, 2009). This book will therefore focus in some detail on the ethics of slum tourism in addition to ethnic quarters as it is a hotly debated theme in much of the recent literature.

Research so far

Research in urban ethnic destinations started mainly in the 1990s when Conforti (1996), Chang (1999), Lin (1995), Li (2000) and others looked into the development of ethnic quarters, analysing the display of 'otherness' and looking into the importance of preserving ethnic precincts for the community that moved to other places, but stayed attached for community identity and nostalgic reasons (Conforti, 1996). Most of the case studies focused on tourism development in the US and Canada. Later on, research shifted to an analysis of the post-Fordist debate in the context of tourism development in ethnic districts (Hoffmann, 2003) and a broader analysis of the phenomenon of promoting ethnic districts (Aytar & Rath, 2012; Rath, 2007). Yet, the number of studies is relatively low considering the global phenomenon of urban ethnic tourism development.

Slumming is not new even though extensive multidisciplinary research has only existed for 10 years or so. 'Slumming has played a central role in the formation of the modern city in Europe (London) and the US (New York), and prior research has indicated how slumming experiences came to transform political and cultural discourses in the 19th-century city' (Steinbrink, 2012: 101). Nuissl and Heinrichs (2013: 106) describe slums as 'places whose otherness has always been a source of fascination to bourgeois society'. They describe how the word slum first appeared in English writings at the beginning of the 19th century as an area of poor housing, unsanitary conditions, a refuge for marginal activities including crime and drug abuse; it is also seen to be squalid and overcrowded. In the early 20th century, middle- and upper-class society went slumming in quarters such as Harlem for racial and sexual encounters (Heap, 2009). Around 2000, Harlem developed into an urban ethnic tourism destination dwelling on the Afro-American heritage and its music culture to become a 'hip' destination off the beaten tracks. In the early 20th century, Harlem represented an opportunity for escaping traditional bourgeois life. The difference, however, is that nowadays the community is responsible for the tourism development and power relations are taking place at a different level.

Nuissl and Heinrichs (2013) cite the UN Habitat (2003) research that examined definitions of slums in 29 cities of the world, which proved to be very different. It is also interesting that pejorative associations especially with poverty did not feature as strongly as might be expected from the academic and tourism literature. Slum tourism discourse tends to centre on poverty but it is valorised as such and is almost expected by the tourists as part of the experience. Burgold *et al.* (2013: 100) suggest that 'An overtly negative semantic field surrounding the category of "slum" is predominant'. On the other hand, there is also a certain degree of romanticisation as a result of novels, films and media (e.g. *City of Joy* and *Slumdog Millionaire*), which perpetuate the idea that slums are also full of hope and joy. Ghettos and slums are frequently associated with music and dance, for example, but their global valorisation becomes increasingly disconnected from the living conditions from which they emerged. Burgold *et al.* (2013: 103) state that 'the moral charging of slum tourism as bad, i.e. voyeuristic, and exploitative or good, i.e. educational and helpful, depends on the interpretation of slums and townships as either places of hardship and despair or places of development of hope'. Of course they are simultaneously both and neither.

Since the 1990s, a 'revival' of slum tourism has reappeared with the organised visit of the favelas in Brazil. Today, there are numerous tours, bed and breakfasts and hostels in the favelas. Slum tourism also developed in Africa and India and other Asian countries. Slum tourism is often assimilated with township tourism. However, one major point distinguishes the two: while tourism in townships, such as Soweto, is very much related to identity and symbolism for the freedom fight of the black community, slums generally do not have any other symbolic significance than to be a 'forgotten' part of a city, full of migrants coming in from the countryside in the hope of a better life. They are areas with extremely poor living and social conditions. So, a good question is why would tourists want to visit these places? The defenders of visiting slums express the wish to understand the 'reality' of the slum and its living condition in contrast to the 'classic' tourist sites. However, Dyson (2012) and Diekmann and Hannam (2012) illustrate how subjective 'reality' is represented and consequently perceived in the case of Dharavi in Mumbai.

The subject of this book has gained some topicality with recent redevelopment projects of, for instance, Little Italies in various cities such as San Diego where descendants of former Italian migrants attempt to revalorise the area where their ancestors lived after their arrival in the States. Moreover, a recent report published by the Asian American Legal Defense and Education Fund (AALDE, 2013) of Chinatowns in Boston, New York and Philadelphia highlighted the threats of gentrification. According to Andrew Leong 'China Towns are turning into a sanitised ethnic playground for the rich to satisfy their exotic appetite for a dim sum and fortune cookie fix' (BBC, 2014). The study of AALDE, co-authored by Andrew Leong, shows how the districts are reduced and encircled by neighbouring districts. The report states that:

> Local governments drove areas of accelerated gentrification and have encouraged and assisted the gutting of China Towns. Government policies have changed these traditionally working class, Asian, family household neighborhoods into communities that are now composed of more affluent, White, and non-family households. (AALDE, 2013: 3)

Also, slum tourism is at a critical point of development. All over the world, slums are turned into tourist destinations. The aim is not necessarily to improve the residents' living conditions but to commodify poverty and to gain benefits. More and more private companies are developing all sorts of tourism within the poorest urban areas.

Main Themes of the Book

The book will focus on a number of key issues, including the following:

- Theoretical developments in relation to the 'tourist gaze' and 'the other'.
- The role of the 'everyday life' of 'the other' in the tourist experience.
- The social, economic and political status of ethnic, minority and segregated groups.
- The historical and contemporary development of ethnic quarters of cities and 'fringe' areas.
- The development of culturally and ethnically diverse attractions and events.
- Past and present models of urban policy and planning which deal with minorities, segregated and ethnic communities.
- Advances in community-based tourism and cultural planning.
- The quest for new and alternative experiences among tourists or 'guests'.
- Perceptions of and levels of involvement in tourism development of 'hosts'.
- The role of governments, policymakers, urban planners and other stakeholders in developing ethnic and minority tourism.
- Recommendations for urban policy, planning, cultural and tourism development which focus on ethnic and minority communities.

Structure of the Book

The book aims to take a global and holistic view on tourism development in the ethnic and minority communities under scrutiny, whereas previous books have generally dealt with only one aspect of this phenomenon. This includes those areas which have thus far been under-researched in the field, e.g. host community perspectives. For reasons of clarity and user-friendliness, the book is divided into four parts. The parts relate to the socio-economic and cultural characteristics of ethnic and cultural communities, the development policies needed to plan for ethnic and minority cultural tourism and issues that are pertinent to both hosts and visitors. Each part is introduced separately and illustrated by two or three case-study chapters.

Part 1: Sociocultural Developments

The first section refers to the sociocultural developments that lead to the 'touristification' of community districts or quarters and how far minorities, ethnic or otherwise socially excluded communities become the scope of attraction for tourists. This is very much related to the ways in which the postcolonial tourist gaze highlights 'otherness' and questions whether the binaries of host/guest and self/other are an oversimplification. This section looks at the perceptions of ethnic and minority communities from a majority society perspective, as well as self-identity and image, and some of the challenges that are faced by not only the communities themselves, but also the intermediaries who attempt to develop tourism products based on their cultures. This includes questions of appropriation, encroachment, objectification and exclusion.

The chapters in this section explore firstly the development of ethnic quarters in London, UK, followed by an analysis of the African quarter of Brussels, Matonge, and finally a discussion of the socio-economic challenges of developing Roma or Gypsy tourism in Budapest, Hungary.

Steve Shaw's chapter on ethnic quarters examines both the positive and negative aspects of developing tourism in such quarters, emphasising the need for appropriate urban policy and planning. He suggests that there has often been a generic approach to the development of such quarters resulting in a 'formulaic sameness'. Instead of creative fusions being formed, products can become quite standardised. Worse still, the ethnic communities may still find themselves to be the object of a White, middle-class, postcolonial gaze and a form of valorisation through tourism development which masks social and economic inequalities. His case studies focus in particular on Asian communities in London in areas whose trajectories have been quite different, highlighting the divergences that can exist even within one city.

Isabelle Cloquet and Anya Diekmann discuss Matonge, the so-called African quarter of Brussels in Belgium. In 2005, the tourism authorities decided to put Matonge on the tourism map in order to diversify the tourism offer of the city, and to highlight its multicultural cosmopolitism. Today, a variety of guided tours can be booked to visit Matonge and 'admire the exotism' of the place. Guides take visitors around, focusing on a broad variety of themes from the history of the former Belgian colony to presenting specific goods and services of the African community. However, many community members feel scrutinised and gazed at, emphasising their difference and exoticism. The chapter looks into 'misguided' tours, examining the critics of the community members towards these kinds of visits and tackling the difficult relationship through an analysis of the various stakeholders involved in organising the tours. It aims at stressing the fine balance between voyeurism, interest and education.

Anita Zátori and Melanie Smith consider the social, economic and political status of the Roma communities in Budapest. The areas of the city which are inhabited by concentrations of Roma communities tend to be socially and economically deprived and many of these were traditionally considered to be 'no-go' areas for locals and tourists alike. However, there have been considerable efforts to regenerate these areas and improve not only the socio-economic status of communities, but also the visual and aesthetic dimensions of the neighbourhoods. The trend of regenerating 'alternative' or 'fringe' areas of cities which tend to attract tourists who are interested in the lifestyles and activities of the people there is gradually starting to happen in Budapest too, where several tour guiding agencies are promoting 'alternative' tours. These focus for example on 'the hidden backyards of Gypsy families'. In addition to tours, there is also a discussion of the existing or potential appeal of Roma arts, festivals and food. It is suggested that cultural and ethnic tourism may be able to highlight some of the positive aspects of Roma community life and traditions and help to mitigate the social and political prejudice that still exists today.

Part 2: Community Perceptions

The second section refers to community perceptions of tourism development, including a discussion of the different terminology used to describe those people who live and work in an ethnic quarter or slum. Whereas some may be indigenous to the area, the majority are immigrants, even second or third generation or more. On the other hand, in some cases, the workers do not reside in the district and there may also be many people who help to 'form' the community who visit regularly and use the space and services, but they live elsewhere. Diasporic tourists may also see themselves as somehow belonging. This adds to the complexity of generalising about 'the community' and their perceptions of developments or visitation. However, the active support of the local communities is essential for the successful management of tourism. There should also be some economic and other tangible benefits. Without this, communities will start to feel disempowered, exploited or worse. On the other hand, surprisingly it is often the case that local communities are more enthusiastic about tourism development than many researchers might imagine.

The chapters in this section explore the host gaze upon international tourists in a number of different countries and contexts, followed by a case study of Mitzpe Ramon in Israel where multiple community groups co-exist with increasing numbers of tourists, and finally an analysis of the reactions to tourists of slum dwellers and workers in Dharavi, Mumbai.

Yvette Reisinger and Omar Moufakkir's chapter examines the host gaze upon international tourists in various geographical regions and nations. The host gaze refers to perceptions and experiences as well as cultural observations made by hosts and the cultural stereotypes and assumptions embedded in these observations and comments. The Western/non-Western locals gazes upon Western/non-Western tourists are analysed. The chapter seeks to understand how host gazes vary depending on different types of tourists. The specific sociocultural and historical aspects of the host gaze are discussed. The chapter highlights the importance of the host gaze as a valuable mechanism that can potentially help hosts to better understand guests, accommodate their needs, resist stereotyping, define themselves and enjoy the intercultural exchange between locals and tourists and thus experience positive aspects of working in tourism. Since there is a fast-growing population of non-Western tourists travelling to non-Western destinations, the chapter also sheds an important light on the non-Western host gazes upon non-Western tourists that emerge in specific cultural contexts.

Joshua Schmidt's chapter examines the multiple interpretations that different inhabitants can have of the same environment. His case study is that of Mitzpe Ramon, a small but ethnically diverse town situated in the remote Israeli Negev desert. He also analyses the perceptions and the degree of involvement of these communities in the development of ecotourism in the region. This is an interesting example of where the actual location which is deemed to be peripheral further exacerbates some of the communities' already existing feeling of marginality within the country. It means that they are unengaged and even disinterested in the conversion of a nearby crater landscape into a biosphere which is becoming interesting for tourists. This perception is somewhat different in the case of secular, middle-class newcomers to the area. Many of these are also creative entrepreneurs who are starting to provide tourism services and hospitality. Even the nomenclature of districts and the associations may be very different for newcomers and tourists and the original or older inhabitants, who feel somehow excluded from these new developments.

Anya Diekmann and Nimit Chowdary present a case study of slum tourism in Dharavi in Mumbai, India, where daily slum tours are now taken to observe the lives of those who live and work in the slums. The authors firstly question the ethics of such a form of tourism and the extent to which it is intrusive in the lives of local inhabitants. While some authors and researchers defend the idea that slum tourism and slum tours may help to fight poverty and bring economic benefits, others are convinced that it is purely voyeuristic and a form of 'poverty porn'. However, the research on this phenomenon from the perspective of the host communities has been very limited. This chapter therefore attempts to redress this gap and presents the results of interviews with slum dwellers and other stakeholder groups in Dharavi. The results are perhaps surprising in that they suggest a more positive reaction to tourism on the part of slum dwellers and workers than may have originally been expected.

Part 3: Visitor Experiences

The third section looks at visitors' motivations, experiences and expectations. The introduction considers the extent of existing research on some of the communities considered in this book and identifies some markers that characterise the visitors of slums and ethnic quarters. It shows that the individual background and education can shape a romanticised vision and discusses the commodification of slums and favelas. It also highlights the desire of tour operators not to show poverty but to shift the image from poverty to the dynamic character of the visited spaces. Furthermore, the section introduction analyses the changing demand for urban tourism, including the diversity of the visitors and the importance for the quarters of community (e.g. diasporic) visitors compared to international tourists.

The two chapters in this section firstly focus on the perceptions of Brazilian and international visitors of the favelas in Brazil, followed by an analysis of tourist experiences in Chinatowns in Australia.

Bianca Freire-Medeiros and Márcio Grijó Vilarouca discuss the results of a research project on the potentialities of Rio de Janeiro favelas as tourist attractions carried out in 2011. This includes analysing the major findings of a survey conducted with 900 (450 foreigners and 450 Brazilians) visitors to the city. The authors identify their socio-economic and demographic profile; examine how familiar they are with the experience of favelas as tourist destinations and their opinion about it;

and confront them with the possibility of being a favela tourist. Taking into account that poverty tours offer a peculiar juxtaposition of misery and leisure, suffering and fun (Freire-Medeiros, 2009a, 2012), their goal was to identify preconceptions and moral concerns that are potentially present and influence the promotion of different favelas as regular tourist destinations.

Jock Collins discusses how Australia has more immigrants than most Western societies today. Major cities like Sydney and Melbourne are vital cosmopolitan global cities with a strong immigrant minority presence evident on the built landscape and social environment. Ethnic precincts such as Chinatowns have emerged in Sydney, Melbourne and other Australian cities sites where national and international tourists mingle with local residents and workers to enjoy Chinese food and attractions and attend ethnic festivals. At the same time, smaller regional centres, like Griffith in New South Wales (NSW), have a strong minority immigrant presence that led to the building of museums and the establishment of festivals that attract national and international tourists. Drawing on fieldwork in a number of urban and regional sites, this chapter explores some of the links between ethnic minority communities in large cosmopolitan cities and smaller regional towns and national and international tourism in Australia. It probes the role of immigrant communities and government authorities in the development of 'ethnic tourism' and looks at the contradictions that often emerge.

Part 4: Development Policies

The final section examines development policies which have started to place culture and communities at the centre of regeneration and tourism initiatives, for example cultural planning. Urban planning theorists increasingly recognise the need to integrate multiple stakeholders and alternative voices into the narratives and practice of city planning. Bottom-up and grassroots initiatives in urban policy and planning may be somewhat rare in the case of ethnic and minority groups, who tend to lack critical mass, but their voices are heard through cultural and arts initiatives and events, which help to attract tourists. In slums, favelas and townships, there may need to be more of a focus on poverty alleviation or pro-poor tourism, although it is recognised that the economic and social benefits of tourism can only be minimal.

The chapters in this section focus on the challenges of developing ethnic tourism in China, the management and promotion of Jewish quarters in Europe, especially Budapest in Hungary, and managing a gay quarter in Cape Town in South Africa.

Nelson Graburn shows how urban tourists, both international and Chinese, are fascinated by poor ethnic minorities who are deemed exotic. In some Chinese metropolitan regions, 'folk culture villages' have been developed which are like life-size models of rural villages complete with folk cultural performances. These are something like an ethnic theme park and serve those tourists who may not be able to gain access to remote rural villages. Unlike European models of heritage and authenticity, Chinese developers actively encourage communities to preserve their villages to make them more 'picturesque' and devise ways of 'improving' their culture for the purposes of attracting tourists and being more commercially successful. These attitudes are engrained in the notion of professionalism and entrepreneurship. This is a form of 'customized authenticity'. Graburn notes that the representation of culture in many of the urban theme parks (and indeed elsewhere) is based on a somewhat idealised nostalgic past, and the 'authenticity' of minority village cultural expressions has no value except as a source of inspiration for entertaining and commercial performances.

Melanie Smith and Anita Zátori analyse some of the challenges of managing so-called Jewish quarters in European cities, especially in those countries where Jewish communities suffered significantly during the Holocaust. This has sometimes led to the Jewish quarters being abandoned for many years or redeveloped (some might say appropriated) by non-Jewish developers. Some of these areas were also former ghettos, for example in Budapest, Hungary, so there is the added challenge of balancing sensitive issues of remembrance and memorial with the development of tourism and entertainment. The case study of Budapest suggests that there is significant interest among Jewish and non-Jewish tourists alike not only in Holocaust heritage, but also in contemporary expressions and representations of Jewish culture, such as festivals, music and food. This is leading to the positive promotion of contemporary Jewish life which is increasingly flourishing, but without forgetting some of the darker events of the past and the circumstances which led to them.

Esti Venske's chapter focuses on the post-apartheid era in South Africa and the situation of the gay community in Cape Town. Interestingly, the country became the first in the world to include the protection of sexual orientation in the equality provision of the country's post-apartheid con-stitution. This led to the showcasing of gay culture in the form of festivals and events and the promotion of Cape Town as a gay-friendly destina-tion (e.g. the South African Gay and Lesbian Travel Alliance [SAGLTA]). Esti examines some of the tensions when gay quarters are located close to other residential areas which may be relatively conservative, for example in the case of the De Waterkant gay village in Cape Town next to where a Malay/Muslim community also resides. Tourism in the Bo-Kaap is mainly centred around cultural tourism activities with a strong link to the community's Muslim heritage. Venske emphasises the need for socio-cultural responsiveness and collaboration for responsible tourism development in both ethnic and gay quarters of cities.

Part 1: Sociocultural Developments

Introduction

This section provides an overview of some of the social and cultural issues that are pertinent to ethnic and minority communities, including the way in which they are perceived by others and the way in which they perceive themselves. Many ethnic encounters are viewed through the lens of postcolonialism, whether it is visiting an indigenous group in their homeland, a diasporic group in an urban ghetto or displaced urban dwellers in a city slum. The relationship of power is an unequal one in most cases and poverty may be an integral, even essential part of the tourist encounter. In other cases, the communities or their cultures may even be absent; in eastern European so-called Jewish quarters, for example, where many Jewish communities perished during World War II. In the case of Roma or Gypsies, the culture may be largely intangible and somewhat elusive, especially if the communities are still nomadic. Gay quarters tend to attract well-heeled, middle-class tourists who may or may not be gay, but assume that their presence will be a welcome addition to the evening economy or a cultural event. Questions of appropriation, invasion and so forth may not feature in the personal narrative of the tourist, which predominantly relates to their own quest for new and unique experiences.

> The relationship between ethnic groups and tourism brings together the quest for the authentic on the part of the tourist and the rationalised and demonstrated ethnicity of the host, especially where economic gain on the latter is both paramount and sought. (Duval, 2004: 61)

The gaze upon displaced or diasporic ethnic communities in cities may be somewhat different from the often romanticised and mythologised gaze of those tourists on colonial 'safaris' around the(ir) former empires (e.g. as discussed by Wels, 2004). On the other hand, Graham *et al.* (2000) state that much of the world's colonial (and often dissonant) heritage can be found in the centre of cities. Still, it is much harder to idealise or fossilise one's perception of the 'Other' in a fast-moving, global city where multiple influences affect and alter culture, irrespective of tourism. As stated by Hall and Tucker (2004: 188), there is a need to recognise 'the emergent nature of culture and identity, and to acknowledge and celebrate cultural hybridity and transnationalism rather than lamenting the loss of some *a priori* notion of cultural tradition'. Hollinshead's (2004) work on the notion of hybridity and Thirdspace using the work of Bhabha explores this notion of new and emergent identities which can be extremely useful for conceptualising ethnic tourism and diasporic tourism (Coles & Timothy, 2004).

The construction of ethnic and minority identities is closely connected to the interpretation of the past and heritage. As stated by Tunbridge and Ashworth (1996):

> The shaping of any heritage product is by definition prone to disinherit non-participating social, ethnic or regional groups, as their distinctive historical experiences may be discounted, marginalised, distorted or ignored. This, it has been argued, is an innate potentiality and a direct consequence of the selectivity built into the concept of heritage. Choice from a wide range of pasts implies that some pasts are not selected, as history is to a greater or lesser extent hijacked by one group or another for one purpose or another. (Tunbridge & Ashworth, 1996: 29)

Gathercole and Lowenthal (1994) suggest that indigenous and ethnic minorities tend to cherish their monuments and sites as being bastions of community identity, especially as they have usually been forced to relinquish their land, religion, language and autonomy under colonial rule. However, many immigrant and diasporic groups are no longer in their birthplace or homeland and may therefore have left most of their material culture behind. Many artefacts may also have been destroyed by invaders or in deliberate campaigns of ethnocide (e.g. the Nazis during World War II). Some ethnic groups also tend to value intangible heritage above tangible artefacts or built heritage.

Perceptions of Ethnic Minorities

Ruethers (2013) suggests that ethnic groups, immigrants and diaspora have often been treated as 'boundary figures' from the 'borderlands' or 'tourist borderzones'. Some of the communities are in the unfortunate position of being labelled 'socially undesirable' by the majority population. This is true of the majority of immigrants, at least for the first generation, as well as for those of a different ethnic group especially when identified by skin colour. Different religious practices (e.g. Jewish or Muslim) or cultural norms (e.g. Gypsy nomadism) may also lead to marginalisation by the majority population. Although many people from these communities may choose not to self identify, their identities may be betrayed by their physiological differences (e.g. dark skin and hair), their accents or their attire. They may also be geographically concentrated within a city, for example, in slums or ghettos. However, the communities may ironically not even inhabit the quarters to which they give their name. For example, Ruethers (2013) refers to 'Jewish spaces' as those areas of cities which had none or very few remaining

Jews and were controlled by non-Jews (e.g. Jewish quarters in central and eastern Europe). On the other hand, 'The notion of Jewish culture without Jews may well be a deeply discomfiting one. Yet neo-Judaic activities may be useful in maintaining a space for public curiosity and discourse in the face of otherwise overwhelming cultural forgetfulness and public silence'.

Linke (2012: 296) describes how 'propelled by variable capitalist interests, the iconicity of "shanty town" or "ghetto" is circulated as a popular commodity form throughout Europe's metropolitan centres'. Ethnic quarters or ethnoscapes form part of the 'imaginaries' of tourism which are frequently based on nostalgia, romance or idealisation (Salazar, 2013). For example, Ruethers (2013: 684) states that 'Jewish and Gypsy spaces are themed spaces, staging the past or the romanticised present. They are "out of time", about dead Jews and the timeless Gypsy, emphasising tradition and the exotic, pre-modern Other. The spaces are separated from the places of living Jews and Gypsies'. Much of the tourist interest in ethnic quarters, slums and ghettos comes from the global popularity of 'ghetto-style' fashion, music or other forms of culture which have become disconnected from the living realities in which they arose. Linke (2012: 299) suggests that 'global appropriations and enactments of the ghetto-look may be experienced as libratory by mainstream consumers of American popular culture'. 'Selective visualisation' of slums, ghettos or ethnic quarters can also help to conceal socio-economic inequalities (Burgold et al., 2013).

Motivations to visit ethnic quarters or ethnoscapes may be relatively simple (unlike the more complex motivations of those who visit slums or townships). Shaw et al. (2004) suggest that:

> quests for knowledge and understanding of other cultures co-exist with more mundane quests for take-away food and drink. Some visitors are attracted by colourful street markets, festivals, world music and other performance art; others by bars, clubs and late-night entertainment in quasi-exotic settings. (Shaw et al., 2004: 1997)

Visitors to slums might be attracted not only by the poverty of the communities, but also by their perceived vibrancy. Burgold et al. (2013) suggest that in popular culture, imaginaries of slums highlight industry, culture, creativity and community.

One irony is that many groups are accepted and revered culturally for their music, dance or arts (e.g. Gypsy violin music and dance, Jewish Klezmer music, African-American blues or jazz), but they are still socially, economically and often politically marginalised. Mainstream societies may desire such communities to behave as human zoos or travelling circuses, but their self-perception is very different. Macleod (2013) discusses the concept of 'cultural configuration', which involves the intentional manipulation of culture to present only certain aspects. Hitchcock (2013) also suggests that authenticity can be a matter of choice for many communities, who can decide quite how far they adapt or even exaggerate their culture for tourists. Ethnic communities may have some control over this, for example the Gypsies who distinguish between domestic cultural practices and outward display in their musical performances (Ruether, 2013). This goes back to MacCannell's (1976) idea of the 'frontstage' and 'backstage'. However, this is all assuming that ethnic communities are autonomously empowered to make such decisions, and in the case of Jewish communities, the original inhabitants may be largely absent.

Reisinger (2013) questions the simplification of binaries like global and local and/or homogenisation and heterogenisation in the context of culture, arguing that it is more interesting to think in terms of cultural innovation, recontextualisation or fusion. This is especially relevant to ethnic communities who are rarely homogeneous and who are often not specifically local either, being immigrants, diaspora or displaced people. There may be different subgroups (e.g. there are at least three different types of Gypsy in Hungary; Jewish people may be secular, orthodox or ultra-orthodox; many people are mixed race in cosmopolitan cities). Those who are not self-identifying (and even those who are) may be fully or partially integrated into the mainstream society or aspiring to be. Such groups may not perceive or want to perceive themselves as different, special or unique. Shaw *et al.* (2004) stated that:

> Ironically, the sign-posting of difference will produce an anodyne and relatively homogeneous culture of consumption, disconnected from the social life of the local population. In time, this will create an isolated, tourism-oriented enclave; a sharp and cruel contrast to the poverty of adjacent inner-city areas that are less appealing to the gaze of visitors. (Shaw *et al.*, 2004: 1997)

Tourist Experiences of the Ethnic 'Other'

Tourists are often keen to reaffirm their idealised view that the Other is not in such a bad situation. Burgold (2013: 102) stated that 'one can for example observe that many tours tend to culturalise poverty, which then leads the tourists to trivialise the tenuous living conditions of the slum dwellers' ('It's not that bad at all.'). Defining oneself as being somehow closer to the 'Other' (the narrative that 'they are more similar to us than I thought') or playing down economic, social or political problems is maybe a way of assuaging postcolonial and middle-class guilt of being richer, more privileged or even alive (e.g. when faced with life-threatening poverty or a past Holocaust). Of course, many ethnic quarters have become fairly gentrified as the inevitable consequence of urban regeneration processes and the slums which are visited by tourists are generally 'richer' than those that are not and would not even qualify as being zones of extreme poverty (Frenzel, 2013).

Host and guest may be indistinguishable from each other in some contexts especially in multi-ethnic cities, and Robinson (2013) even questions the usefulness of terms like host–guest where the differentiation between local resident and tourist is becoming increasingly blurred. Hannam and Roy (2013) argue that it is becoming harder to distinguish between tourism and other mobilities. This is certainly true of large multi-ethnic cities. Many tourists are trying to engage in forms of tourism which bring them closer to local residents. Russo and Qualieri-Dominguez (2013) discuss how many bohemian or creative tourists have become almost indistinguishable from local populations in destinations like Barcelona. Richards (2011) notes that today's cultural tourist is just as likely to be in search of 'popular', 'everyday' 'low' or 'street' culture as they are likely to visit a heritage site or museum. Wolfram and Burnill (2013) suggest that the term 'tourist' has become quite pejorative for many people. They use the term 'tactical tourists' for those who somehow want to become a part of the destination and the everyday life of its people, especially those activities which take place in 'backstage' or fringe areas. The tourists' desire to discover 'authentic' experiences in cities is becoming as strong as it is among backpackers in remote destinations. Tourists also want to help shape their own experiences in a process of so-called 'prosumption' or 'co-creation' and engage in self-development. Creative tourism is one way of providing this. Depending on how it is defined and executed, creative tourism can provide small-scale, sustainable experiences for local communities, although Richards (2013: 302) warns that 'The use of creativity to develop tourism (also) runs the risk of strengthening the tendency towards colonization of the lifeworld by the forces of commerce'.

Robinson (2013) observes that some tourists may experience angst if they are forced to go beyond the 'script', but for others, it can be extremely liberating especially in terms of cross-cultural encounters and spontaneous intercultural dialogue. The problem is that most tourist experiences are heavily mediated. Tourists are rarely conscious of their own 'performances' in tourism, which are usually foregrounded by historical, social and cultural education or even indoctrination, as well as media representations and images (Meethan, 2013). Salazar (2013) emphasises tourists' overexposure to representations of places and experiences, and Smith and Richards (2013) suggest that tourists have always been over-directed in their experience of cultural tourism. However, going beyond the script can be challenging. Firstly, there may be no access to certain ethnic communities without a tour or guide (in slums and townships it is certainly recommended and most guidebooks advise against wandering into 'ghettos'). Safety and security play a major role (even if it is more perceived than real). It is also true that tourists are selective in their choices, often as a result of media representations, advice from guidebooks or tour guides and TripAdvisor and other social media reviews. For example, Ruether (2013) notes that tourists in France and Spain enjoy Gypsy performances but would never visit a Roma neighbourhood. The cultural or artistic is clearly privileged over the social. This is no different to those indigenous tourists in Australia who happily enjoy Aboriginal art trails but who would be dismayed to see an Aboriginal person living in squalor as an alcoholic.

The 'Touristification' of LGBT Space

The literature about lesbian, gay, bisexual, transgender (LGBT) tourism has proliferated exponentially in the past few years. This book does not attempt to provide a comprehensive analysis of the whole spectrum of LGBT tourism, just focuses on those areas of cities which have commonly become known as 'gay quarters' or similar. Events are not a main focus either, as these are usually not confined to one space and have more temporal limits (i.e. most occur only once a year). Their importance is recognised, however. For example, Waitt and Markwell (2006) claim that when gays gather for gay events, they feel that they are a majority, which is not the way they feel in everyday life. LGBT minorities do not have a physical or geographical homeland that authenticates group identity (Blichfeldt et al., 2013), so quarters of cities may develop which provide them with a safe space in which to be themselves with less fear of prejudice from the wider society. Pritchard et al. (2000) argue that gay spaces (in opposition to 'heteronormal space') provide a sense of freedom as well as community. Blichfeldt et al. (2013: 473) describe gay spaces as 'first and foremost, places that are "enacted" and "used" by gays – both at home and when on holiday' in which 'gays can be part of a community; be open about their sexuality; be with people like themselves and feel safe from prejudices and discrimination' (Blichfeldt et al., 2013: 474). Pritchard et al. (1998: 274) suggested that gay spaces not only enable the display of behaviour and affection, 'they are sites of cultural resistance with enormous symbolic meaning, providing cultural and emotional support for a political movement comprised of an increasingly diverse and geographically scattered community'.

However, Howe (2001) states that gays are often seen as just another attraction of a city, which straight people can gaze at in the distance. Rather than finding a sanctuary from heteronormativity, gay visitors may feel that they are reduced to a tourist attraction that straight people gaze upon in much the same way that they gaze at exotic animals in a zoo (Blichfeldt et al., 2013). For this reason, Visser (2007) asserts that gay space is not essential to the creation of gay identities as some gay people do not feel a need (or wish) to frequent gay spaces or places in order to feel different or gazed upon differently.

According to Florida (2002) who developed a 'Gay Index' for cities, there are close connections between economic development and business growth, and high numbers of gay residents. The strength of the so-called 'pink pound' has been discussed by many researchers, including in a tourism context. Hughes (2002) discussed how several market research studies highlighted higher travel propensity, income and spending than heterosexual markets. Some destinations are known to be homophobic and not conducive to the development of gay-friendly tourism. Hughes (2002) notes that there is often a clear desire to avoid places that are likely to be homophobic; however, not that many gay tourists wish to go on a 'gay-specific' holiday. On the other hand, cosmopolitan and multicultural cities like London, Amsterdam, New York, San Francisco, Sydney, Madrid, Barcelona and increasingly the cities of South America such as Rio and Buenos Aires are popular with gay residents and visitors alike. Boyd (2011) describes how 'San Francisco's Castro district has become a vital aspect of San Francisco's tourist economy, and the neighbourhood has become a huge money-making enterprise, both for the city of San Francisco, in the form of tax revenue, and for gay business-owners who managed to secure space along the Castro's commercial strip'. Even smaller cities have popular gay villages, such as Manchester in the north of England whose gay village has become the main focus of the city's vibrant nightlife (see Hughes, 2002; Pritchard et al., 2002), and Brighton, a seaside town, is also known to be one of the gay-friendliest places in the UK. The same is true of Sitges in Spain. Markwell (2002) suggested that many local authorities were keen to court the pink dollar for entertainment purposes at a time of financial strain and that cities started to be promoted as the 'gay capital' of somewhere. Waitt and Markwell (2006) define gay space as a metropolitan area, often composed of bars, restaurants, cafés, shops and residential areas. Hughes (2002) suggests that the gay mens' market has been identified as particularly interested in urban tourism because they tend to be at the 'cutting edge' of life, are more style conscious and individualistic than other markets, have sophisticated tastes and a strong interest in arts and culture.

On the other hand, it should not be assumed that just because gay quarters of cities become a lucrative focus of city policy and marketing and tourists infiltrate gay spaces and events that this necessarily leads to greater tolerance in everyday life. As stated by Markwell and Waitt (2009: 152), 'people who fail to conform to the socialized heteronormal practices of sexual citizenship may still be subjected to physical and emotional violence as they go about their everyday lives'. They go on to discuss how in the late 1990s the image of gay lifestyles and identities that were depicted in gay parades such as pride marches or Mardi Gras somehow wallpapered over social inequalities and intolerance. They cite Croome (1998) as saying:

lying just beneath the dazzle of the Mardi Gras and white, inner-city, middle-class gay and lesbian life there is injustice, poverty, powerlessness, alienation and a mountain of resentment. (Croome, 1998: 10)

One question posed is whether pride marches are a celebration of gay culture or an expression of anger or defiance: 'discourses of protest and dissent are still very evident in the festival spaces' (Markwell & Waitt, 2009: 163). The same has sometimes been said of African-Caribbean carnivals, originally a rebellion against, as well as a celebration of freedom from slavery. Either way, the presence of outsiders such as tourists may serve to dilute or obscure this message.

Tourists and non-gay residents are frequently attracted to gay spaces for a multitude of reasons, including curiosity. The so-called 'de-gaying' of space or 'heterosexual encroachment' can lead to the environment becoming more threatening for gay people, or creates resentment that their only space is being invaded when heterosexuals have access to the whole city. LGBT people often become the object of the gaze, especially if they are obviously transvestites or transsexuals. Many do not call for segregation but feel that a sanctuary is needed. As stated by Pritchard et al. (2002: 118) 'Gay and lesbian spaces have emotional and psychological importance as empowering places in a "straight" world'. Hughes (2002: 159) shows that in Manchester's gay village in the UK, the space is 'diluted as a centre of empowerment and cultural strength and gay people no longer feel "ownership"'. Gay-only door policies may be needed for bars but this cannot work for the streets or events.

Smith et al. (2009) note that because the 'tourist gaze' is directed from the dominant perspective of the white heterosexual European male, the marketing in LGBT tourism tends to be dominated by the perspective of the white European homosexual male. This has been discussed in more depth by Waitt and Markwell (2006), for example. This means that certain groups may still be excluded or marginalised based on their age, gender, nationality or skin colour. Hughes (2002) adds to this that gay spaces might not appeal to all gay people nor be 'open' for all, and that gay spaces are sometimes accused of being dominated mainly by white, wealthy, young and handsome gay men (Howe, 2001). Markwell and Waitt (2009) also state that 'Pride festival spaces have been increasingly critiqued for prioritizing particular understandings of gayness framed as affluent, white, stylish, monogamous and clean-cut'. Pritchard et al. (2002) suggest that the experiences of lesbians have also been marginalised and that notions of a homogeneous gay community and gay spaces can obscure gay mens' oppression or exclusion of lesbians. Lesbians face double discrimination in society. Their spaces are also frequently 'invaded' by heterosexual women who often feel more comfortable in gay male spaces than they do in heterosexual ones. Manchester's gay village in the UK was criticised for not catering to women except for one women-only bar. Blichfeldt *et al.* (2013) also emphasise the masculine domination of gay space.

Esti Venske's chapter on Cape Town in this book follows on from the work of Visser (2003) which considers an interesting case study and a lesser known one perhaps, although it is promoted as 'Africa's Gay Capital'. Given South Africa's history of apartheid, this is one city in which the 'ethnic male' plays a significant role as space is no longer racially segregated as it once was. However, the dominance of relatively wealthy, white, homosexual males has been very prevalent in the past. Visser (2003) describes how:

> Whereas homosexual lifestyles fell beyond the parameters of apartheid heteropatriarchy, white, middle-class gay men – by virtue of their privileged race and class position in this societal framework – claimed and asserted their identity through leisure and tourism consumption within this spatial structure. As a consequence, a White middle-class gay leisure space economy developed in most of South Africa's main metropolitan areas. (Visser, 2003: 169)

Post-apartheid, the constitution became more liberal and tourism flows increased. However, the dominance of white, homosexual males continued as stated by Visser (2002) in the context of Cape Town's De Waterkant:

> The historically disadvantaged communities remain excluded from the consumption of this area, largely due to the supply of gender-, race- and class-specific facilities and services. This exclusion cuts across the whole spectrum of South African society –poorer white males/lesbians as a whole/black South Africans, as well as most of the 'coloured' community. (Visser, 2002: 19)

Elder's (2005) work also suggests that the development of Cape Town's gay tourism spaces seems to cater more to elite, white gay men than to lesbians of any colour or poor black gay men.

Conclusion

Although the chapters in this section do not cover all of the issues mentioned above in detail, they touch on many of them. Stephen Shaw's chapter considers the postcolonial gaze in a range of contexts and communities. He emphasises the need for development policies and planning which also address social and economic equalities, not only privileging the cultural, artistic and gastronomic (the latter being of more interest and benefit to tourists than to locals). This is something of a pervasive theme throughout this book, including the tendency of visitors to romanticise the cultural ethnic experience which can mask the reality of the actual living conditions of communities. Cloquet and Diekmann partly focus on another theme which is central to this book – that of appropriation and (lack of) consultation. They show how this can result in local populations' discomfiture with the experience of 'othering' that takes place through guided tours and other tourist activities in their living and working quarters. The notion of 'encroachment' is important here too, which is the unwelcome visitation and (temporary) colonisation of a local space by non-local visitors. Similarly to Shaw, Zátori and Smith emphasise the social and economic reality of many communities' living spaces in cities, suggesting that positive representations through culture and tourism may help to improve perceptions of ethnic and minority groups, but accepting that they are not replacements for proper political, social or financial support.

1 Negotiating Asian Identities in London and Other Gateway Cities

Stephen J. Shaw

Introduction

Colourful images of streetscapes and festivals associated with ethnic and cultural minorities have increasing prominence in tourist guidebooks and websites for cities such as London that are gateways to immigration and settlement. In the language of place promotion, such localities may offer a 'cosmopolitan' ambience for visitors who want to explore them on foot, savour ethnic cuisine or enjoy the more hedonistic pleasures of their nightlife. An optimistic take is that 'ethnic quarters' showcase the contribution of immigrant communities to the cultural as well as economic life of cities; a welcome development especially when compared to the interracial tensions, disinvestment and visible neglect that prevailed in minority neighbourhoods of gateway cities in the not too distant past. In some cases, they nurture creative fusions between different cultures, especially in food, fashion and the performing arts. A more pessimistic interpretation is that the re-presentation of streetscapes in particular neighbourhoods for leisure and tourism consumption debases their former significance to the communities concerned: a mask that disguises the more widespread alienation, exclusion and poverty of subaltern groups.

The first section of this chapter considers the development of places associated with immigrant communities that have cultural roots in Asia. It highlights the diverse origins of 'Oriental' enclaves in different world regions, and the ways in which their streetscapes have been gazed upon by visitors from the dominant or majority culture through to the present day. From the 18th century, imperial power was marked out within trading posts such as Singapore into areas known to this day as *Little India*, *Kampong Glam* and so on. From the 19th century, a corollary of mass migration by White Anglo-Saxon Protestants (WASPs) to North American cities was the marginalisation of *Chinatowns*, *Japantowns* and other non-WASP neighbourhoods. In the second half of the 20th century, migrants established *Little*

Saigons in Australia and *Little Istanbuls* in Germany, while in the UK people from former Asian colonies inscribed their identities in the streetscapes
of cities that were former hubs of empire. In these very varied geographical contexts, places associated with Asian communities are being reconstructed – both physically and aesthetically – to appeal to contemporary
global audiences.

The second section reflects on the marked dichotomy between the
'idealistic' versus 'cynical' interpretations of this phenomenon (Germain
& Radice, 2006). The former portrays the development of ethnic quarters as a catalyst for cultural exchange and mutual understanding. The
latter 'camp' foregrounds appropriation and commodification of cultural
symbolism. Ironically, the commercial success of such initiatives has led
to formulaic sameness in their presentation of diversity. The author suggests that a more nuanced approach is required to comprehend the complex and often contradictory trends in the transformation of particular
streetscapes of immigration and settlement into spaces for 'consumption'
by visitors. Some evolving frameworks for interpreting local–global interactions and identity in contemporary societies may offer a way forward from
the *impasse* of polarised arguments; of particular relevance are Robertson's
(1992) concept of 'glocalisation' and Appadurai's (1997, 2001, 2003) insights
into 'ethnoscapes' and 'translocalities'.

The chapter concludes with a discussion of local–global interactions
that have shaped the development of three commercial streets in London
that reconstruct postcolonial associations with the Indian subcontinent.
The main case study examines the evolving streetscape of Brick Lane in
London's East End from the 1990s and its high profile but controversial
rebranding as *Banglatown* to rival the West End's *Chinatown*. Today, over
60 curry restaurants generate badly needed employment, but more recent
promotion has sought to play down overt stereotyping (Shaw, 2012;
Shaw *et al.*, 2004). Over the same period, Green Street, Newham, has consciously eschewed formulaic place promotion around a single ethnic brand.
Instead, it emphasises diversity and togetherness through cultural fusions
between East and West, especially in jewellery and fashion clothing. And,
in a west London suburb, Southall Broadway capitalises on its proximity to
Heathrow Airport to promote a business gateway to the rising 'tiger' economies of Asia. The author argues for a greater appreciation of geographical
and temporal context, and highlights the value of comparative and longitudinal studies to shed light on such diverging presentations of exotic identity,
even within a single city.

'Orientalism' for Contemporary Global Audiences

The ethnic quarters discussed below are in neighbourhoods that
were established by Asian communities who migrated not only to cities

elsewhere in Asia, but also to North America, Australasia and Europe. Within the constraints of regulations imposed by the city governments of the areas where they settled, migrants adapted streetscapes and public places and recreated activities such as festivals that in various ways reflected the distinctive cultures of their homelands (Shaw, 2007a, 2007b; Shaw et al., 2004). In many cases, they occupied the least desirable low-rent districts. The 'exotic spectacle' often provoked hostility, but in some cases it also attracted curious visitors from the dominant or majority culture. In the 21st century, streetscapes of particular ethnic quarters – some historic, others more recent developments – have become significant attractions for local as well as co-ethnic visitors. Increasingly, city governments showcase them as high-profile destinations for new global flows of tourists, promoting them to contemporary global audiences.

Edward Said's (1978) influential historical analysis foregrounds the ways that European societies have imagined and represented the material culture, landscapes and streetscapes of 'territories in the Orient'. In the postcolonial era, gateway cities have sought not only to refocus the gaze to represent more closely the national vision of their governments, but also to reposition themselves in world markets to satisfy domestic tourists and visitors from other Asian cultures, along with those of European origins. A notable example is Singapore, which has reframed the surviving architecture of former colonial quarters along with historic ethnic enclaves as flagship attractions: showpieces that enrich the tourism offering and provide visible evidence of the city state's commitment to 'official multiculturalism' (cf. Henderson, 2008; Tan & Yeoh, 2006). Further tourism-led regeneration and celebration of cultural diversity is anticipated in Malaysia, following the inscription of Melaka and George Town, Penang, as a World Heritage Site in 2008: two cities that developed through 'over 500 years of trading and cultural exchanges between East and West in the straits of Malacca' that endowed them with 'a specific multicultural heritage' that evolved during colonisation by the Portuguese, Dutch and British (UNESCO World Heritage List, 2012).

In other world regions, 'Oriental' enclaves of gateway cities have been gazed upon through different cultural lenses. Historical evidence suggests that the phenomenon of urban ethnic tourism in North America has its origins in New York, Chicago, Los Angeles and San Francisco, in the last half of the 19th century when it became fashionable among middle-class Bohemian WASPs to go 'slumming' or 'rubbernecking' in Chinatowns and other non-WASP districts, the disapproval of others no doubt adding to the *frisson* of the experience (Cocks, 2001; Gilbert & Hancock, 2006; Lin, 2011). Unfortunately, by the mid 20th century, historic Chinatowns and other minority districts had been bulldozed to 'modernise' American cities such as Philadelphia. However, as civil rights and other urban social movements gathered broader-based support, such wholesale clearance was resisted with varying degrees of success. By the 1976 Bicentennial, voluntary and public support for 'ethnic heritage recovery' included symbolic renovation of land-mark buildings that highlighted the valuable contribution of Asian and other minorities, e.g. the Chinatown History Museum in New York and *Little Tokyo* in Los Angeles (Pearlstone, 1990). By 2010, despite the dispersal of Chinese American communities, the rejuvenated streets in the *Chinatowns* of Lower East Side New York and Los Angeles had become showpieces for cultural heritage, and in the latter case a lively contemporary arts scene (Lin, 2011).

Such revalorisation of 'exotic' streetscapes has its counterparts in gate-way cities where the development of ethnic quarters is a comparatively recent phenomenon. These include Sydney, Australia, where the majority of settlers originated from Britain until the second half of the 20th century. Collins and Kunz (2007: 206) note that since the 1960s, Sydney's suburban precincts have diversified with a *Little Vietnam*, a *Little Turkey* as well as a downtown Chinatown: 'ethnic enterprises, clustered together. Formally or informally, they "adopt the symbolism, style and iconography of that group in their public spaces"' (Collins & Kunz, 2007: 207) to create a pleasing spec-tacle for visitors from the majority culture as well as co-ethnic, co-cultural and other minority groups. Elsewhere in the Pacific Rim, a street in Osaka has been reimaged as *Korea Town* to enhance its appeal to Japanese shop-pers. Hester (2002: 182–183) notes that initially such 'theming' was deeply contested by non-Korean residents in the locality. Nevertheless, the project was implemented to rejuvenate a thoroughfare that was showing signs of decline, to create a cosmopolitan retail offering and to demonstrate a new civic ideology of 'international co-operation'. Festivals and other events offer alternating displays of traditional national arts which highlight differences between Koreans and Japanese cultures, while at the same time promoting mutual respect in the spirit of 'living together' (Hester, 2002: 186).

The ethnic and cultural identities that feature in the tourism offerings of European gateway cities have been shaped by national immigration poli-cies, liberalisation of cross-border movement of people between member states of the European Union, as well as the unique circumstances of par-ticular gateway cities. For example, *Klein-Istanbul* in the Kreuzberg district of Berlin has become a significant tourism attraction, an ethnic minority enclave which developed from the 1960s when Turkish 'guest workers' were invited to fill Cold War labour shortages in a divided city. Along with other minorities – including Indian, African and Latin American – performances of music and dance of Turkish origin feature in the German capital's annual *Karnivale der Kulturen* 'carnival of the cultures' (Bloomfield & Bianchini, 2004: 88–89). In British cities, a few minority enclaves existed in the 19th century, e.g. Chinatown in Limehouse, Port of London. However, it was not until the 1950s and 1960s that the UK government encouraged large-scale immigration from former colonies, including the Indian subcontinent. In Birmingham, interracial tensions resurfaced periodically in the former

'Workshop of the World' (Rex & Moore, 1967). Nevertheless, as Henry *et al.* (2002) demonstrate, postcolonial, post-industrial Birmingham now capitalises on its ethnic diversity, e.g. British *Bhangra* music and dance, and cuisine that features the Birmingham *Balti* and *halal Chinese*.

Ethnic Quarters, Global Villages and Translocalities

The positive outcomes described above may well suggest a benign synergy between emerging visitor economies and a wider appreciation of ethnic heritage; a trend that should encourage mutual understanding and respect for diversity. This interpretation fits well with Hannerz's (1996: 103) ideal of cosmopolitanism as a 'willingness to engage with the Other', and Beck's (2002) notion of global villages stimulated by artistic intermediaries and merchants who move around with ease and negotiate their way between different worlds. Open-minded global villages are also central to Sandercock's (2003, 2006) vision of a tolerant *cosmopolis* that fosters an evolving hybridity. Landry and Bianchini (1995: 28) welcome opportunities for people with diverse cultures and lifestyles to interact productively, casually and without friction (cf. Ferdinand & Shaw, 2012; Shaw, 2007a: 189), an argument for *inter*culturalism that is further developed by Wood and Landry (2008). From this viewpoint, ethnic quarters provide valuable assets for well-connected global hubs such as Singapore. More altruistically, they may stimulate innovation through creative fusions: a democratising 'globalisation from below' (Henry *et al.*, 2002).

A more critical reading is that markers of difference extracted from other societies, such as material objects and street festivals, are decontextualised, transformed and homogenised to create desirable objects of consumption. Szerszynski and Urry (2002: 461–462) note the influential critique by Marx and Engels [1848] (1952: 46–47) of the systematic appropriation of marketable features of other cultures. A contemporary observer may conclude that astute capitalists continue to select, adapt and commercialise elements of Otherness that are valued by the privileged elite, and that the sociocultural impact is demonstrated not only in the appropriation of objects and festivals, but also of the street itself. Judd and Fainstein (1999: 36) comment critically on the serial reproduction of a successful formula: 'tourist bubbles' that are 'more likely to contribute to racial, ethnic, and class tensions than an impulse toward local community' (cf. Bell & Jayne, 2004; Binnie *et al.*, 2006; Jayne, 2006; Sorkin, 1992; Zukin, 1995). More recently, Hannigan (2007) has highlighted the sophisticated 'controlled edge' that satisfies the desire of young professionals for a visibly gritty street panorama without the danger: a safe adventure in neo-bohemia.

The two prognoses are clearly very different, but both envisage unilinear trajectories. In contrast to these polarised positions, Robertson (1992: 173–174) foregrounds ambiguity in the evolving concept of 'glocalisation':

the co-presence of *universalizing and particularizing* tendencies of local–global exchange that may feature *altruistic as well as commercial* characteristics. As Lin (2011: 48–50) points out, the former is illustrated in social movements that make reference to universal human rights to protect the identity of particular groups. These, in their turn, have inspired a wider 'roots' movement with an increasing interest in discovering, conserving and celebrating the rich heritage of ethnic and cultural minority groups such as those described above. The commercial dimension refers, in particular, to branding strategies through which global products are customised to stimulate consumption in national or local markets. However, the process may work in the opposite direction where selected features of particular exotic cultures are adapted for wider markets, in some cases for global consumption. The promotion of ethnic quarters provides an interesting variation, in that ethnic minority entrepreneurs, such as restaurateurs, adapt their products to the tastes of mainstream markets and international tourists.

From the perspective of social anthropology, Appadurai (1997, 2001) develops insights into global circulations of people, media images, technologies, money and ideas, and considers their implications for local–global interactions: 'the central problem of today's global interactions is the tension between cultural homogenization and cultural heterogenization' (Appadurai, 1997: 32). Distancing himself from the claims of grand narratives, he proposes an 'elementary framework' to explore an 'overlapping disjunctive order' (Appadurai, 1997: 33). He uses the suffix '*-scape*' to convey the idea that they are gazed upon from diverse perspectives: multiple *imagined* worlds. In this context, '*ethnoscape*' describes the 'landscape of persons who constitute the shifting world in which we live: tourist, immigrants, refugees, exiles, guest workers, and other moving groups and individuals' (Appadurai, 1997: 33). For these people on the move, the warp of relative stabilities – communities and networks, including kinship, friendship, work and leisure – are 'everywhere shot through with the woof of human motion, as more persons and groups deal with the realities of having to move, or the fantasies of wanting to move' (Appadurai, 1997: 33–34).

Later, Appadurai (2003) expands the argument to situate ethnoscapes in the local–global space:

> ...what little we do know suggests many such locations create complex conditions for the production and reproduction of locality, in which ties of marriage, work, business and leisure weave together various circulating populations with various kinds of 'locals' to create localities that belong in one sense to particular nation-states but are, from another point of view, what we might call *translocalities*. (Appadurai, 2003: 339)

Examples of translocalities that 'require serious attention' include tourist sites and free trade areas, border zones, refugee camps, migrant hostels and neighbourhoods of guest workers.

With reference to ethnic quarters that often combine several of these functions in one location, the author argues for greater appreciation of the temporal and geographical context, and for longitudinal and comparative studies to shed light on such diverging presentations of exotic identity, even within one metropolitan area.

Changing Asian Identities in London

Places that fit the descriptor 'translocality' are now well established on the tourist map of London; the local–global interactions of many actors and audiences have shaped their development. Those that are in various ways branded as 'Asian' quarters have generally been initiated by minority traders who 'glocalise' products such as the Birmingham *Balti* discussed above. However, the sustainable development of a visitor economy requires collaboration between the traders, other stakeholders and public agencies to create a street environment that is accessible, safe and welcoming for the 'host community' as well as visitors. In the main case study below, an emerging ethnic quarter has been nurtured in London's East End. Since the late 1990s, this has traded on its 'exotic' associations with Bangladesh. Over the same period, Green Street in Newham and Southall Broadway have also promoted their respective links with the Indian subcontinent. In each case, the vision for regeneration has embraced both altruistic and commercial strands, but the pattern of development has been different. Significant factors that have shaped their outcomes include location relative to centres of demand, the sociocultural structure of their communities and the configuration of streets and land uses. The policies and practices of city government have also been important influences, especially through transport planning and urban design, land use controls and other regulatory powers.

Brick Lane in Spitalfields – less than two miles (three kilometres) east of central London – has been a hub for the commercial, social and religious activities of successive waves of immigrants. As the long-established Jewish community moved away in the 1970s, the neighbourhood became home to newcomers from Bangladesh, and its Great Synagogue was converted to become the *Jamme Masjid* (Great Mosque). At first a mainly bachelor society, many of the young men found work in textile factories owned by co-ethnic entrepreneurs, but global competition led to closures and rising unemployment. Further, the street attracted unwelcome visitors from race-hate groups, and violent scenes of conflict were broadcast through news media. Somewhat against the odds, by the mid-1990s a handful of Bangladeshi-owned cafés were attracting non-Asian customers and a few adventurous tourists. The area attracted artists who lived and worked in the locality, and the street acquired a certain *shabby chic*. The London borough of Tower Hamlets (LBTH) in partnership with public, third-sector and commercial agencies secured government funding for regeneration to stimulate wealth creation and employment and improve the streetscape, notably through the Cityside Partnership 1997–2002 (Shaw, 2012).

The LBTH and Cityside gave strong support to the expanding trade in Asian cuisine and its supply chain through supply-side interventions that included a relaxation of planning control to create a 'Restaurant Zone' (LB Tower Hamlets, 1999), grants for restaurant façades, business advice and marketing support. Streetscape enhancements included ornamental arches and lamp posts with 'Asian style' motifs. Somewhat controversially, place promotion included rebranding the locality as *Banglatown*, a new rival to *Chinatown*, and two 'multicultural' festivals were established: the Brick Lane Festival (autumn) and *Baishakhi Mela* (spring). In its final report, Cityside (2002: 7) stressed the complementarity of 'the strengths of London's cultural diversity' and economic regeneration: 'many new restaurants have opened... over 100 new local jobs have been created'. Indeed, a survey they had commissioned (Carey, 2002) showed spectacular growth: 'from just eight in 1986 to over 40 by 2002, whose customers were "overwhelmingly White", with around 70% in the 25–34 age group' (Carey, 2002: 4). Further developments included nightclubs, boutique-style clothing shops, design studios and exhibition space (Shaw, 2008).

Nevertheless, the transformation of Brick Lane had been deeply controversial. Debate over the vision for *Banglatown* had reached something of a turning point in 2000 when a group of restaurateurs lobbied the LBTH to give the visitor economy a further boost by closing the street to traffic and creating a pedestrian mall for outdoor dining and drinking. However, the authority dropped its support for the scheme after a stormy public meeting, and the extensive consultation that followed (2000–2002) highlighted the wider concerns of residents, small businesses and community organisations (Shaw, 2011: 392). These included:

(1) Loss of convenience shops and displacement of local users.
(2) Inappropriate juxtaposition of street festivals and religious worship.
(3) Noise, nuisance and crime associated with the night economy.

By the early 2000s, conversions to restaurant uses in the central area of Brick Lane had largely been completed, there was further loss of local shops elsewhere. Festival organisers became increasingly sensitive to worshippers at the Great Mosque, and pressure to extend licensing hours for bars and restaurants has been resisted. Unintended consequences of the night economy continue to present challenges for security and policing, especially in controlling drug dealing and prostitution. The revised scheme that followed the consultation was implemented in stages from 2002–2006, and featured traffic calming and pavement widening rather than a pedestrianised mall. Its design eschewed overt markers to associate the street with a single ethnic group. Richard Simon, the urban designer who oversaw the revised scheme, reflected on the public engagement (Shaw, 2010: 391), commenting on the concerns that: 'it would become a sort of Bengali ghetto.... We felt that you could create a *Banglatown* identity without the obvious use of permanent features such as brightly coloured paving and highways'.

Six miles (nine kilometres) east of central London, Green Street in the London borough of Newham served a mainly White British population until the 1970s, when the closure of the nearby docks and factories caused a sharp downturn in business for local retailers. The area became more ethnically mixed. In the 1990s, a few Asian businesses developed a jewellery trade marketed to wealthier Asians from across London (Shaw *et al.*, 2004), and Green Street became something of a showcase for fashion clothing and jewellery that fuses Asian and Western influences. Place promotion highlights the street's diversity and streetscape enhancements symbolise 'togetherness', while festivals include the *Runga Rung* and a range of 'multicultural' events including Afro-Caribbean music, tea dances for the older White British community and central European music (Shaw & Bagwell, 2012). Since the 1970s, Southall Broadway in the London borough of Ealing, 11 miles (17 km) west of central London, has been an important shopping and entertainment centre, especially for Punjabi communities. The 'Southall experience' attracts non-Asians, for example to purchase spices. However, a campaign in the 1990s to brand it 'Punjabi Bazaar' was not successful. Instead, the *Southall Town Centre Strategy 2002–12* has promoted it as an 'international gateway for excellence in multiculturalism and commercial development' linked to London Heathrow Airport and Asia's rising 'tiger' economies (Shaw & Bagwell, 2012: 45–47).

Conclusion

Two opposing 'camps' of 'open-minded engagement' versus 'trading on difference' have voiced their very different understandings of the re-presentation of ethnic quarters as spaces of consumption. However, the complex and often contradictory processes of development in different spatial contexts are hard to explain by grand narratives of convergence, whether the prognosis is optimistic or pessimistic. The development ('place-production') of Asian quarters in gateway cities has varied origins and histories; they attract visitors with very different expectations of what they have to offer ('place-consumption'). The transformation of areas associated with past or present-day migrant communities into spaces of consumption appears to be a multifaceted phenomenon. As illustrated in Brick Lane, expectations of altruism and commerce may intertwine in an uneasy coexistence.

The discussion above makes reference to some emerging frameworks for investigating the dynamic interplay between the diasporic intercontinental linkages of migrant communities and their attachment to particular localities, including the commercial and social hubs of their dispersed communities in gateway cities. The concept of 'glocalisation' originally described the customisation of globally branded products and their re-presentation to markets in a particular country or locality (Robertson, 1992), but it can also mean the adaptation of culturally specific products to appeal to broader markets, such as those that arise from the presence of visitors in areas that are developed and promoted as ethnic quarters. Many such as Brick Lane offer exoticised goods and services, especially food, drink and entertainment that appeal to mainstream markets among the majority culture, and in some cases international tourists. Nevertheless, as illustrated in the examples of Green Street and Southall Broadway, their products may also be designed to appeal to markets that are co-ethnic and/or culturally mixed, with little reference to the mainstream. The concepts of 'ethnoscape' and 'translocality' derived from Appadurai's (1997, 2003) thesis of local–global interactions in postmodernity foreground transglobal flows of humanity, the geography of lifeworlds that fleetingly intersect, disjunctive interactions, divergence and uncertainty of outcomes.

Each locality has been shaped by its spatial and historical context: a set of circumstances and influences in a particular place, at a particular time. In Banglatown, the ethnic quarter has been branded to attract higher-spending target groups from the majority culture, especially from the nearby City of London. To stimulate economic recovery, city governments may do little to hold back the realisation of such commercial opportunities; the rationale of urban policies may highlight the imperative of rejuvenating the local economy as well as more idealistic visions of a city that is open-minded, cosmopolitan and inclusive. Social tensions may arise where aims are contradictory, highlighting the importance of deeper and more meaningful consultation to take account of other stakeholders, especially the smaller voices of less-privileged communities: critical issues for local development policies. Green Street and Southall Broadway illustrate the possibility of more sustainable approaches to resolve the tensions inherent in the local–global meeting grounds of ethnic villages.

2 Discovering or Intruding? Guided Tours in the Ethnic District Matonge in Brussels

Isabelle Cloquet and Anya Diekmann

Introduction

In the face of saturated traditional markets and heightened global competition, post-Fordist economies have sought to develop niche markets, requiring a more flexible specialisation (Hoffmann, 2003). Cultural consumption, symbols and creativity have thus become central to urban development in post-industrial economies. Multiculturalism and diversity have become an asset that public authorities have increasingly capitalised on to revitalise and reimage declining and/or degraded urban districts (Aytar & Rath, 2012). Ethnic neighbourhoods play an integral part in this vision of 'the city of quarters' (Roodhouse, 2006). They have gradually been integrated into the projected image of post-Fordist cities as their very presence has epitomised the positively connoted cosmopolitan aspect of gateway cities (Fainstein & Campbell, 2002; Law, 2002; Zukin, 1998). Brussels decided to follow the trend a few years ago, and started to include Matonge and its African-tinted atmosphere in its tourism development strategy. The present chapter intends to analyse and discuss tourism development in Matonge by examining the way that the quarter is currently valorised and the types of tourist experiences that are proposed to visitors. The first section of the chapter analyses issues highlighted by scholars as regards the tourist valorisation of ethnic quarters elsewhere. As guided tours are the main form of mediation in Matonge, the second section addresses the roles of guides as the link between the tourists and the visited community in the construction of the tourist experience. In the light of the theory, the chapter then provides an analysis of the guided tours proposed in Matonge.

Tourist Valorisation of Ethnic Quarters: A Complex Task

The idea of cosmopolitanism is based on a desire for mutuality that, paradoxically, starts from the assumption that people(s) are different (Salazar, 2010: 181). While multiculturalism and diversity have been seen as an opportunity in post-industrial cities, notably, for tourism development (Hoffmann, 2003), the valorisation of ethnic quarters is a complex and sensitive task, as multiple questions need to be addressed regarding the representation(s) it offers of the ethnic minorities and the tourist experience. While tourist valorisation of ethnic quarters can take various forms, e.g. guided tours, events and shopping, and pertain to various elements, e.g. traditions and folklore, heritage, arts and crafts, cuisine and lifestyle, empirical studies show that ethnic quarters are mainly marketed for their exoticism. Tourist valorisation most often emphasises 'otherness' rather than 'togetherness' (Hoffman, 2003; Santos *et al.*, 2008; Shaw, 2012; Shaw, this volume). This is not really surprising. As highlighted by Salazar (2006), world views and imaginaries conveyed in the language of tourism often accentuate exoticism in order to seduce potential tourists. Based on works by Pratt (1992), Said (1994) and Torgovnick (1990), Salazar (2006: 834) recalls that 'tourism tales are heavily influenced by the mythologized visions of "Otherness" from the travel literature and academic writings in disciplines like anthropology, archaeology, art, and history'.

In certain quarters, the focus on otherness can raise some issues, as exposed by Hoffmann (2003: 294) concerning tourism development in Harlem and how it was experienced by some hosts as 'racial voyeurism'. Those problems can be particularly acute when the valorised minority group is historically marked by the domination of the majority culture, i.e. slavery, ostracism and colonisation. Tourism valorisation can then contribute to perpetuating colonialist binaries of colonised/coloniser and traditional or primitive/modern (Amoamo & Thompson, 2010). Santos *et al.* (2008) stated in their study of Chinatown, Chicago, that tourism discourses would tend to laud and celebrate ethnic differences that were once feared and negatively perceived by the dominant group. On the one hand, the language of tourism seeks to reassure tourists by 'mollify[ing] the effects of strangeness' associated with a trip to an unfamiliar destination (Salazar, 2006: 843). On the other hand, stressing on aspects such as convenience, safety and friendliness participates in the 'othering' of the hosts, implying a hierarchical relationship between visitors and supposedly 'dangerous' even 'uncivilised' hosts.

Tour Guides and Their Role in the Creation of the Tourism Experience

The main form of tourist valorisation in Matonge consists in guided tours. Guides play a significant role in how tourists and hosts experience tours (Ap & Wong, 2001; Jennings & Weiler, 2004; Moscardo, 1999; Reisinger & Steiner, 2006; Salazar, 2010; Yu et al., 2002). Drawing on Cohen's (1985) study of the tourist guide, most scholars distinguish four sets of functions of tour guiding (Reisinger & Steiner, 2006; Salazar, 2010). The first two sets relate to instrumental and social leadership; guides are pathfinders responsible for organising tours and providing safe access to geographical and social points of interest, and they also are animators of their touring parties (Cohen, 1985). The remaining functions pertain to social and cultural mediation between tourists and hosts (e.g. local communities, institutions, sites, tourism facilities) (Cohen, 1985).

The mediatory aspect of guiding is of particular interest for the present study as it addresses the roles and responsibilities of guides, hence guided tours, in connecting tourists with hosts and the environment. Based on their literature review, Yu et al. (2004) suggest that the scope of mediation is at least threefold and includes access, encounters and information. Guides mediate access by 'determining which part of the local environment, heritage and culture is exposed to tourists and which is hidden' (Yu et al., 2004: 4). They mediate encounters by acting as an intermediary between parties and individuals and by displaying the appropriate behaviour, respect and empathy for the cultures of tourists and hosts (Yu et al., 2002). Guides also mediate information, enabling tourists to understand the significance of the visited place and to develop emotional and intellectual connections with it (Yu et al., 2004). Interpretation and cultural brokering are closely related to the latter aspect of mediation.

The mediatory role of tour guides has been the subject of debate as certain authors argue that tour guides' interpretation might be superfluous in authentic tourism (Reisinger & Steiner, 2006). Based on Heidegger's (1996) concepts of understanding and interpretation, Reisinger and Steiner (2006) suggest that tour guides should no longer be viewed as informants or organisers who de facto impose their interpretation on visitors. Instead, tour guides would stimulate authentic tourism if they acted as resourceful companions and helped tourists find meaning in what they experience (see Zátori & Smith, this volume). According to the authors, to play such a role, tour guides would ideally need to be close in age and cultural background to the groups they lead, as well as being able to draw knowledge from a number of disciplines other than tourism, including the social psychology of identity (Reisinger & Steiner, 2006). While this view is of interest as it emphasises the active role of tourists in creating a meaningful and emotional tourism experience, it fails to address issues of power within the tripartite system (i.e. tourist–host but also tourist–guide and guide–host). Imaginaries and positionality affect the relationships between hosts, guest and tour guides.

Not only have tour guides responsibilities towards stakeholders, but they are also subjected to their direct or indirect influences. Tour guides' position as intermediary implies that they are exposed to multiple tensions between themselves, as individuals, and other stakeholders, i.e. local people, institutions, the tourism industry, tourists (Jennings & Weiler, 2004; Salazar, 2010). For instance, Dahles (2002) pinpointed the influence that the Indonesian political authorities exerted on the discourse of official tour guides in the Suharto era. Salazar showed how local tour guides in Tanzania deliberately reproduced in their discourse the global language of tourism marketing and imaginaries (see Dann, 1996), using content and linguistic techniques to 'make sure that tourists experience exactly the kind of things that they expect and that were sold to them by tour operators or travel agencies' (Salazar, 2006: 841–842). Brin and Noy (2010) highlighted how guides' 'belonging to a national reference group' influenced tours offered in the Qatamon neighbourhood in Jerusalem.

The Case of Matonge in Brussels

Brussels is mainly known as the European capital and place where (unpleasant) political decisions are taken, shaping an image of a bureaucratic city. Aiming at overthrowing this image, in 2005 the tourism authorities developed new tourism strategies based on diversifying the tourism offer of the city through the promotion of 'new' districts. The seven new districts include among others a quarter with numerous African shops and restaurants, so-called Matonge. Indeed, the precinct plays an important role for the central African community in Belgium and its surrounding countries (Diekmann, 2012). The choice of the authorities to promote Matonge as a tourist attraction correlated with the freshly chosen cosmopolitan image for Brussels. Strangely enough, the concerned community (or its representatives) has never been officially informed that their quarter had been put on the tourism map of Brussels. Three years after the decision to promote Matonge, more than 60% of the shopkeepers were not aware of their new status as a tourist attraction (Diekmann & Maulet, 2009: 99). Indeed, the tourism authorities never consulted the host community. However, with increasing interest from visitors, independent organisations developed guided tours in Matonge. Before examining those guided tours, the history and current sociocultural and spatial context of Matonge are stressed in order to provide an understanding of its multifaceted significance, not only for the African community, but also for Brussels.

Matonge: Evolution of a quarter through colonial, post-independence, Fordist and post-Fordist eras

The non-administrative neighbourhood, called Matonge since the 1970s, has its origins in the 1950s a few streets from its present location, in the upmarket south-east fringe of Brussels (see map). At the time, Congo was still a Belgian colony. The quarter was known for hosting most colonial institutions and archives relating to Congo (Catherine, 2006). It was highly frequented by colons who spent their free time in bars and jazz clubs, an atmosphere tinted with African and Caribbean musical influences (Opsomer, 2008; Stevens, 2012). In 1952, the colonial institutions started to authorise a larger number of 'Congolese'[1] visitors in metropolitan Belgium. Those visitors were mainly wealthy students who came to Brussels and other cities to receive a higher education (Cornet, 2004). In Brussels, those students enjoyed the atmosphere of the 'colonial' quarter, which was easily accessible from the university and schools they attended. With their presence in the neighbourhood, some bars started to allow blacks in, and certain associations, such as the anti-colonialist Présence Africaine and the student residence for African students, the Maison Africaine, settled in the quarter. However, the incidents following the declaration of Independence in Congo severely impacted on the relationships with ex-colons; racism increased in Belgium and in the neighbourhood (Opsomer, 2008; Steven, 2012).

The neighbourhood regained its vitality a few years later when an increasing number of Africans, mainly Congolese, set up shops and bar-restaurants in the Galerie d'Ixelles, which is still the core of its present location (Demart, 2007; Stevens, 2012). In the 1970s, the quarter became an import–export platform between Congo and Belgium. Benefiting from a prosperous post-independence era and eased visa procedures, Congolese visitors brought goods to Belgium and returned home with Western luxury and trendy products they bought in Brussels (e.g. abacosts, high-quality wax fabric, Afro-American haircare products and clothes) (Oyatambwe, 2006; Stevens, 2012). Some of those visitors, namely those who were part of the Mobutian elite and musicians, exhibited ostentatious behaviours, spending large amounts of money in bars and nightclubs and showing off in designer clothing from Parisian and Italian haute couture (Demart, 2007; Stevens, 2012). The neighbourhood became a trendy centre for the Congolese musical sphere and a symbol of the West for the Congolese (Oyatambwe, 2006; Stevens, 2012); the influence of Congolese music spread the reputation of Brussels in other African countries. At that time, the quarter received its name 'Matonge' by its Congolese users.

'Matonge' comes from a bar-restaurant that served as a central meeting point in the neighbourhood and it also refers to a vibrant quarter in Kinshasa (Stevens, 2012).

Since the late 1980s, Matonge has experienced severe deterioration. The economic and political instability in former Belgian colonies (Congo, Rwanda and Burundi) led to a socio-economic decline as in the profile of Matonge's consumers. Indeed, the number of wealthy visitors dropped and were replaced by destitute refugees and illegal immigrants who were driven to Matonge by the idealised representations of the West partly constructed from the Congolese music (De Clercq, 2001). Consequently, the exquisite boutiques gradually closed and were transformed into less-expensive shops, providing very specific services such as import–export and money transfer, travel agencies specialising in African destinations, groceries selling African food, cosmetics, fabrics and music, African hairdressers and African pubs and snack bars (Stevens, 2012). Matonge increasingly became a transnational and multicultural space, attracting tourists of various sub-Saharan African origins who came from Belgium, France, Germany, the Netherlands and other countries in northern Europe. Those tourists visited the quarter to access African goods and services as well as to meet and share with people from their own cultural background (Diekmann, 2013; Diekmann & Maulet, 2009). For several years, Matonge has been facing issues such as real estate speculation, urban decay and criminality (Corijn et al., 2003 as cited in Stevens, 2012: 118; Demart, 2007; Oyatambwe, 2006; Paolillo, 2012). Safety issues have particularly impacted upon the image of the quarter and thereby the still remaining upmarket clientele; they have also tarnished the image that Westerners have had of the neighbourhood and of the whole African community (Demart, 2007; Diekmann & Maulet, 2009a).

Despite the aforementioned issues, Matonge entered travel guidebooks in the 1990s. Descriptions focused either on its (post)colonial history or on its 'exotic' African touch (Diekmann & Maulet, 2009a). Yet, the quarter had not attracted the interest of the public authorities until the municipal elections of 2002. One of the reasons for this lack of interest was that most African shopkeepers actually live outside the neighbourhood. The population of the quarter is indeed multicultural with more than 30 nationalities (Corijn, 2003 as cited in Stevens, 2012: 118). With the desire to secure the quarter, the new government engaged in a regeneration policy; to this end, it held talks with the African community. Those actions resulted in the creation of a police station in the quarter and in the setting up of a series of social and cultural associations. When in 2005, Brussels tourism authorities launched the new branding and tourism strategy of diversification, the 'exotic' aspect of Matonge fitted perfectly. In the last few years, Matonge has appeared in a city walk promoted by the official tourist board and in urban signage, e.g. a bus stop or bus stops and in underground stations (Demart, 2007; Paolillo, 2012). Security has improved but urban degradation still remains an issue. The quarter has also been exposed to growing pressures on its spatial delimitations from the neighbouring prosperous quarters. At present, the African-tinted atmosphere is concentrated on a very few streets while other influences – mostly Indian, Pakistani and European – have gradually extended and changed the cultural profile of other streets in the neighbourhood.

Guiding Tours in Matonge

Guided tours started in the late 1980s in Matonge (Paolillo, 2012). They were organised by associations external to the African host community. The latter soon criticised the paternalistic approach of some tours and disapproved of the way that tourists gazed at them, as if they were animals in a zoo. In response to the dissatisfaction of community members, one of the associations decreased the number of participants per group and implemented a participative approach, involving shopkeepers in their guided tours. Certain shopkeepers started to receive tour groups and introduce them to the foods, goods and services of their shops (Paolillo, 2012). According to key informants, the situation had not changed much in 2012–2013: the African community and the shopkeepers still disapprove of the tourist gaze; the discourse of some guides keeps on adopting a paternalistic tone; and most shopkeepers who have participated in tours are disappointed by the low benefits they derive from them. These negative reactions from the hosts invite us to scrutinise the approaches followed by tour providers as key actors in the tourist valorisation and mediation of Matonge.

Analytical framework and data collection

Adopting a postcolonial stance, the authors focus their analysis on tour providers and the way they currently integrate the aspects discussed in the introduction into their approach of valorisation and mediation; those aspects shaping the tourist experience. To be able to offer visitors a cosmopolitan experience, mediators – in the present case, tour providers and tour guides – would have to succeed not only in meeting the expectations of tourists and fostering respect for hosts but also in building a 'tourist third space' where communication transposes the binaries them/us into you/me, enabling a hybridisation of the self (Bhabha in Amoamo & Thompson, 2010; Van der Duim et al., 2005) (see also Introduction of this book). The analysis thus seeks:

- To identify the stakeholders involved in the tourism planning process of tourist valorisation and mediation of Matonge, and classify them in the tripartite system governing host–guest interactions (van der Duim et al., 2005): the hosts, the mediators (brokers) and the tourists.
- To determine if and how the hosts were involved in the planning process of tourist valorisation and mediation of Matonge.
- To characterise the mediation approach adopted by tour guides according to the following dimensions:
  - Logistics used: modes of transport, duration of tours and mediatory tools (non-human elements such as signage, quizzes, etc.), languages, choice of points of interest, etc.
  - Main features of the mediators; in the case of Matonge, mediators are human guides, are they insiders or outsiders of the host community?
  - Main features of discourse/narratives; does the discourse emphasise otherness or togetherness?
  - The making of a – even though temporary – 'third space', which could enable interpersonal interactions between hosts and brokers and/or tourists, conducive to cosmopolitan, hybridised formations, by addressing the position of power of stakeholders in the production of the hosts/guests experience (e.g. construction of the tourist discourse).

Most data used in this study were collected between February and April 2012 through semi-structured interviews with three providers of guided tours – well known for being key informants – in Matonge. The interviews were held and recorded by Paolillo (2012) in the context of her master's thesis. To complement the data, the authors of the chapter content analysed the websites of tour providers in June 2013. The aim of data collection was to gather information on tourism valorisation and mediation in Matonge. In order to address the content of the tours, the authors analysed the short descriptions of the tours displayed on the websites of tour providers. Giving the pitch of each tour, those descriptions enabled the authors to grasp the main focus of each tour, the aspects that are emphasised by each tour provider in their tourist discourse about Matonge. For that part of the analysis, four categories were inductively determined:

(1) 'colonial' includes all narratives about the colonial past of the quarter/ the Congolese people;
(2) 'exotic' encompasses all narratives focusing on particularities attributed to 'African' or 'Congolese';
(3) 'multicultural' narratives insist on the fact that either the quarter or Brussels hosts a high number of nationalities, and invites visitors to experience the cultural specificities of the visited ethnic groups (e.g. gastronomy);

(4)   'fusion' narratives stress globalisation in the quarter, the 'melting pot' created by the presence and interactions of diverse cultures in the quarter, their living together and their common future.

The analysis was complemented by Paolillo's notes as regards her participant observation of one guided tour and the content analysis of an educational guide edited jointly by two tour providers. The booklet targets teachers and guides as they plan to visit the quarter with groups of children. Both sources are complementary as they focus on different aspects of the quarter. While the former stresses the colonial and exotic dimensions of Matonge, the latter insists on multicultural, intercultural and globalised elements. ·

Stakeholders and involvement of the hosts in the planning process

The host community in Matonge that is put forward by the tours is mainly composed of shopkeepers, hairdressers and the owners or tenants of bars and restaurants, which address the specific needs of a clientele with African origins. The owners of those businesses are of diverse origins: essentially African and Pakistani. Apart from Brussels tourism authorities, the mediators comprise a range of tour providers. Thirteen of them have been identified as being the most active in the quarter (Paolillo, 2012). As shown in Table 2.1, nine are Brussels based while the others have their companies' headquarters in Flanders (Mechelen, Grimbergen, Ghent and Antwerp). Eleven are non-profit organisations and seven are subsidised by the Flemish government. Three are cultural centres (TP2, TP6, TP13), two providing leisure and educational activities to the youth; the remaining organisations are specialised in the provision of guided tours, mostly in Brussels. Seven offer a wide variety of themed tours and one focuses its interpretations on social issues (immigration, poverty, etc.). The clientele of the different tours is mainly composed of groups from associations, schools and enterprises. Most visitors are Belgian and Flemish in particular (see Table 2.2). This can be explained by the high ratio of Flemish organisations among tour providers (10 out of 12).

Since the mid-2000s, efforts have been made by the local cultural centres to involve the hosts in the valorisation and mediation schemes of the quarter. Taking into account the remarks of the hosts, TP2 revised the proceedings and narrative of its guided tours with the aim to limit the negative effects of the tourist gaze upon the hosts, and shopkeepers in particular. The tour now starts with a video that gives an overview of the history and current dynamics of the quarter. The visitors are then led through the neighbourhood, and they are invited to pass by the shop windows in small groups. Interpretation is also limited on the street. Realising that

Table 2.1 Profiles of tour providers active in Matonge

Name	HQ	Type of organisation	Public subsidies	Positioning	No. of tours in the quarter
Brukselbinnen-stebuiten TP1	Brussels	NGO	• Government of Flanders • Flemish public authorities in Brussels	Dynamics of urban development; architecture	120/year
Elzenhof TP2	Brussels	NGO	• Government of Flanders • The local authorities of Elsene	Cultural centre covering the whole municipality administrative area	25–30/year
Jes TP3	Brussels	Non-profit organisation	• Government of Flanders	Leisure and tourism for the youth	(No data)
KET-Toeren in Brussel TP4	Brussels	Sole proprietorship	No	General: Themed tours	
Klare Lijn TP5	Brussels	Non-profit organisation	(No data)	General: Themed tours	12/year
Kuumba TP6	Brussels	Non-profit organisation	Government of Flanders	Flemish centre that promotes African cultures	144/year
Le Bus Bavard TP7	Brussels	Non-profit organisation	Local authorities	General – themed tours	(No data)
Pro Vélo TP8	Brussels	Non-profit organisation	Government of Brussels; government of Wallonia, others	Bike tours – themed tours	10% of their bike tours
Tochten van hoop TP9	Brussels	Non-profit organisation	Government of Flanders	Brussels' social issues	40/year
Jeugd en vrede TP10	Mechelen	Non-profit organisation	Government of Flanders	Leisure and tourism for the youth	480/year

Polymnia TP11	Grimbergen	Non-profit organisation	(No data)	General themes mixed with culinary tastings + tours for people with intellectual disabilities	5/year
Vizit TP12	Ghent	Limited liability company	No	General by quarters + some themed tours	108/year
VtbKultuur TP13	Antwerp	Non-profit organisation	Government of Flanders	Fosters cultural consumption – general: themed tours	200/year

Source: Adapted from Paolillo (2012)

Table 2.2 Main features of guided tours in Matonge

Name	Languages	Guides: Insiders versus outsiders	Name of the tours[a]	Main aspects of discourse	Length	Origin of customers	Main customers	Contact with shopkeepers
Brukselbinnen-stebuiten TP1	Dutch French English German	Outsiders and insiders (partly uses guides from TP6)	From Congo to Matonge	Colonial Exotic	3h00–3h30	Flanders	Adults	No
Elzenhof TP2	Dutch	Outsiders and insiders (partly uses guides from TP6)	Is this Matonge? Matonge's past and future, the quarter and the world	Exotic Multicultural Fusion	2h30	Flanders and Brussels	Enterprises, associations	Sometimes
Jes TP3	Dutch	(no data)	Matonge: Going abroad while remaining at home	Exotic Multicultural	(no data)	(no data)	Schools	(no data)
KET-Toeren in Brussel TP4	Dutch	(no data)	Matonge: Mini-Kinshasa	Exotic	2h00	(no data)	Adults, seniors	(no data)
Klare Lijn TP5	Dutch English	Outsiders and insiders (partly uses guides from TP6)	Walking to Congo	Exotic	3h00	Flanders	Associations, seniors, schools	In a bar
Kuumba TP6	Dutch French	Insiders	Matonge: An African mist above Elsene	Colonial Exotic Multicultural	1h00–1h30	Flanders	Tour providers	No
Le Bus Bavard TP7	French Dutch English	Outsiders	Colourful Brussels	Multicultural	(no data)	(no data)		No
Pro Vélo TP8	French Dutch English	Outsiders	Moambe and mint tea	Multicultural	3h–4h	Brussels	Individuals or groups	In bars and restaurants

Tochten van hoop TP9	Dutch	Outsiders and insiders (partly uses guides from TP6)	Congo in Brussels	Colonial Exotic	2h30	(no data)	Associations, schools	Only with craft shop
Jeugd en vrede TP10	Dutch	Outsiders	Walk in Matonge	Exotic Multicultural	2h30	Flanders	Schools and young people (4–25 years old)	Yes
Polymnia TP11	Dutch French	Outsiders	Matonge	Exotic	2h30	(no data)	Seniors, enterprises, associations, schools, people with intellectual disabilities	Yes, contact with one shopkeeper and with one bartender
Vizit TP12	Dutch French English	Outsiders and insiders (from a sociocultural association)	Expedition Matonge; Matonge culinary Matonge for born to be champions	Colonial Exotic	2h00	Flanders	Enterprises, schools	Sometimes
VtbKultuur TP13	Dutch	Outsiders	Matonge: African traces Walking to Congo: A walk along the former colonial ministries and in a section of Matonge. Art@noen: A tour in Matonge, Brussels	Colonial Exotic	2h30	Flanders	Associations, individuals	No

Source: Adapted from Paolillo (2012)
[a]Translation by the authors

'there were problems with the concept [of guided tours] as whites come with the aim to see how blacks live', TP6 trained guides from the neighbourhood. TP6 also developed partnerships with five tour providers who now use the local guides in a section of their guided tours. Some tour providers have also included shopkeepers and hairdressers as actors in their tour who help visitors answer quizzes or meet some challenges (Paolillo, 2012). However, shopkeepers seem to lose interest in participating in these tours as they do not derive benefits from them (Diekmann & Cloquet, this volume).

Valorisation and Mediation of Matonge Through the Guided Tours

Most tours are walking tours that include a minimum of two hours walking through the area (see Table 2.2). Two organisations offer bike or bus tours; their tours do not focus solely on Matonge but include other ethnic quarters with the aim to show to visitors the cultural contribution the visited ethnic communities make to the capital city. While all 13 organisations offer tours in Dutch, only 6 have tours in French and 5 have tours in English. One tour is also offered in German. Most tour providers use the services of guides who are external to the quarter; seven also hire guides with African origins as part of their efforts to reduce the perceived negative impacts of tours on the hosts. A considerable number of tours are led by two guides: outsiders introduce visitors to the quarter, its colonial past and/or its 'exotic' features, while insiders lead visitors inside the neighbourhood and familiarise them with the specific goods and services found in the quarter.

'Exoticism' is the aspect which is most emphasised in the short descriptions of tours (see Figure 2.1). In those descriptions, Matonge is presented as a sample of Africa or Congo. TP2 explains that the 'African' feature is also Matonge's major draw for visitors:

> (...) schools imagine that they will visit an African quarter (...) there are guides who adapt their speech to what visitors want to hear. (TP2)

The analysis of the general image projected by the descriptions of all tours in each language shows some dissimilarity between overall discourses according to the language. While the general image projected by tours in Dutch is particularly marked by exoticism, the total number of tours in French and in English convey blurred images, as both emphasise almost equally the 'colonial', 'exotic' and 'multicultural' aspects. Only one tour, in Dutch, provides a discourse insisting on the 'fusion' features of Matonge:

> Together [the business owners, the inhabitants and the visitors] give a contemporary intercultural twist to the development of that part of Brussels, which since the end of the 19th century has been proud of its cosmopolite character (...) a quarter which for more than a century has become globalized in a unique way.[2] (TP2)

The concept of this tour is very different from that of other tours. Indeed, it encourages visitors to consider the quarter from different perspectives (different functions; changes in the configuration of the neighbourhood on weekdays or at the weekend). It presents Matonge as a testimony of Brussels' globalisation, and addresses topics such as multiculturalism, glocalisation and multilingualism.

Another distinctive characteristic of this tour is its representation of the spatial delimitations of the neighbourhood, which are broader than that of other tours. It includes in the surface area of the neighbourhood of Matonge places that other tours present as being part of other non-administrative quarters (e.g. Saint-Boniface). While both definitions of the spatial delimitations are correct, as it depends on whether Matonge is examined according to the mental representations of its users or the representations of the public authorities, the choice of a broader spatial conceptualisation of the quarter reinforces the aspect of fusion and globalisation. Indeed, as a result of the pressures exerted spatially by the European Union quarter, new inhabitants and businesses with diverse European origins have settled in the area. On the contrary, the representations that limit the spatial delimitations of Matonge to the African-oriented commercial belt – a few streets – emphasise the sense of visiting a 'little Africa'.

While the choice of points of interest depends on the focus of the tours, it is worth noting that some tour providers whose tours address the colonial past of the area choose to discuss the topic outside the African commercial belt (e.g. TP12). The aim is to avoid hurting shopkeepers and users, even if the guide's interpretation is not necessarily paternalistic and highlights how Belgium benefited from Congo's natural resources in colonial times (Paolillo, 2012). Despite this measure, Paolillo's notes on her experience during a tour refer to the unpleasant gaze that passers-by held upon the group while the latter was being introduced by a grocer to fruit and vegetables commonly found in African dishes (Paolillo, 2012). The gaze of the hosts can be understood as a sign of weariness, as suggested by TP2 in the following quotation:

> [In the past] groups used to stare through every shop windows; they spent a quarter of an hour and watched how hair was braided (...) [Nowadays,] there are still tour providers who work that way. (TP2)

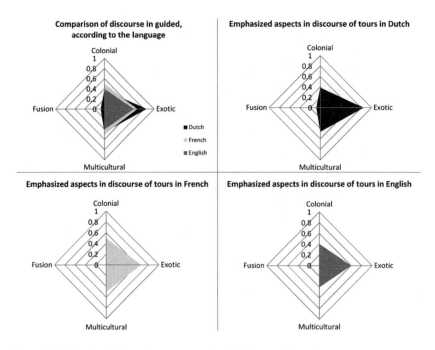

Figure 2.1 Principal discursive aspects of guided tours about Matonge

Several organisations have made efforts to foster encounters between visitors and guests. One tour pushes visitors to interact with all kinds of users, i.e. inhabitants, shopkeepers, cultural associations and customers, while others organise activities in shops, hairdressers, bars or restaurants (see Table 2.2). Those activities are appreciated by visitors (TP12) but do not seem to succeed in mediating positive and meaningful encounters between hosts and guests. While they create an environment favouring encounters, the latter remain short and goal oriented, i.e. to answer a quiz or meet a challenge. Moreover, establishing contact with hosts in such contexts seems to be easier for children than it is for adults (Paolillo, 2012). The encounters have also created frustration among shopkeepers and restaurant owners. Complaints mainly concern the fact that visitors do not consume in shops; a restaurant owner, interviewed in April 2013, also spoke about the disrespectful behaviour of certain visitors towards African culinary specialities (personal communication, April 2013). Cultural centres are aware of the problem, and are starting to think that guided tours might not be an appropriate mediatory mechanism in the neighbourhood: TP2 is thinking of ceasing the provision of guided tours (Paolillo, 2012) and TP6 has started to organise culinary, music and dance workshops.

Concluding Discussion

Considered an asset for tourism and business development, cosmopolitanism has gradually been integrated by gateway cities in their projected image. To this end, ethnic-tinted urban spaces have been valorised in the communication and tourism development strategy of cities. Brussels has followed the trend and started a few years ago to include its African commercial belt, Matonge, in its tourism promotion and development scheme. In this study, the authors have analysed how tourist valorisation and mediation in Matonge contribute to create a cosmopolitan experience of the city. As the Congolese community is one of the largest ethnic groups in Matonge, and the relationship between Congo and Belgium is marked by colonial history, the authors have adopted a postcolonial stance. Constituting a basis for multicultural fusion, Bhabha's concepts of 'hybridity' and 'third space' were considered to be one of the ultimate forms of cosmopolitanism. In the backdrop of that analytical framework, the study has examined guided tours, which are the main form of tourist valorisation in the quarter; it has focused on key elements of tourist valorisation and mediation of the experience offered in guided tours. The study results have shown that Matonge is most valorised for its 'exoticism'. Even if the tourist discourse is less paternalistic than it used to be, the current focus on 'exoticism' continues to create tensions between hosts, tour providers and visitors. The tensions result from the emphasis on the 'otherness' and the type of activities offered by tour providers in the quarter. The negative impact of gazing seems to affect both the hosts and the tourists. The study results invite us to discuss further theoretical and operational issues.

Leading the way, tour guides have a central function in tourism mediation. Their role is threefold, including the mediation of access, of information and of encounters (Yu et al., 2004). As intermediaries between hosts and guests, it is incumbent upon them to negotiate modalities of access to hosts, to determine the discursive content through which they present hosts and the visited spaces to visitors, as well as to create an environment favourable for positive and meaningful encounters between hosts and guests. In each of those tasks, the involvement of both hosts and tourists is needed if guides want to inscribe their activity in a sustainable tourism approach (Van der Duim et al., 2005). In Matonge, most guided tours have developed following a top-down process. Some tour providers have attempted to improve their tours after receiving complaints from hosts, but solutions implemented have so far failed to meet hosts' expectations.

Moreover, most shopkeepers who have been involved in tourism activities show no real interest in tourism development. In fact, they consider the current form more of a nuisance to their core business than an opportunity to promote their culture or their goods and services. The lack of interest of hosts in tourism development in the quarter can also be attributed to the fact that most tours still do not address the complexity of the host 'community' in their narratives and in the planning process. The host community is composed of a wide diversity of social, cultural and economic interest groups (e.g. Africans of diverse origins, non-African origins, different languages, genders, ages, socio-economic profiles and power positions in the quarter) having different representations and usages of the neighbourhood. Failing to understand the interests of and the power relations in and between the main interest groups, tour providers have not been able to stabilise the relationships between brokers and hosts nor between hosts and guests in the tourismscape (Van der Duim, 2005). Moreover, the top-down process and the focus on exoticism have reinforced hosts' feeling of being the object of a touristification in the hands of a hegemonic white power. Indeed, hosts' perception of being 'animals in a zoo' somehow recalls colonial times.

Tourist valorisation in Matonge has not physically transformed the quarter yet; markers are almost non-existent. Interpretation could thus adopt different perspectives and highlight different aspects of the multifaceted reality of the urban quarter. However, most guided tours in Matonge focus on exoticism, emphasising otherness rather than togetherness. While exoticism has received much attention in the literature (cf. Salazar, 2006, 2010), approaches based on multiculturalism and fusion have been less scrutinised. The case of Matonge tends to indicate that organisations which offer interpretations valorising 'togetherness' tend to be cultural centres or organisations with altruistic values (e.g. peace). There is a need for an in-depth analysis of those mediators and the profiles, motivations and expectations of the tourists participating in those tours.

In conclusion, the outcomes of the study highlight how complex cultural and social mediation can be in intercultural and multifunctional spaces. Most tour guides and providers design their tours to meet customer needs, and fail to include hosts in the planning process. As they are embedded in the tourism language, being part of its producers, they tend to follow the traditional logic of tourism discourse production based on exoticisation. Cultural centres seem to operate according to another logic: as they represent the hosts, they seem to be more sensitive to the impacts that guided tours might have upon the latter. They play a role in raising other tour providers/guides' awareness of impacts. None of the tour guides/providers has succeeded in creating a cosmopolitan experience that would offer visitors and hosts the ability to enjoy a you/me relationship.

Questions are raised regarding the suitability of guided tours for the creation of a tourism third space. The following considerations deserve further research.

- The limited time spent in the neighbourhood and at each point of interest seems to hinder interpersonal relationships between hosts and guests.
- The choice of points of interest might also impede visitors and hosts from interconnecting.
- While guided tours add a new usage to the local businesses, none of the tenants or their customers seem familiar or at ease with this usage. Visitors, for their part, are not used to the goods and services that are presented to them.

All of this might contribute to the strangeness of the situation and a general feeling of intrusion. Moreover, in ethnic tourism, visitors remain in their home country. Roles are inverted as compared to indigenous tourism. Power relations inside the tripartite system might thus be different. Power relations need to be examined further as they are at the heart of the 'third space' concept.

Notes

(1) The Congolese were in fact Belgian citizens until the independence of the Congo in 1960. However, before 1952, only a few Congolese were allowed by the colonial administration to travel into Belgium (Cornet, 2004).
(2) Translation by the authors.

3 The Potential for Roma Tourism in Hungary

Anita Zátori and Melanie Smith

Introduction

This chapter focuses on Roma or Gypsy (Gipsy) communities in Hungary, analysing the extent to which their culture has been or could be developed as interesting products or attractions for tourists. Durst (2010) notes that the use of the terms 'Gypsy' and 'Roma' often seem to be interchangeable, but that it has become more 'politically correct' to use the term 'Roma' even though the people themselves often prefer to be called Gypsies. Károlyi (2010: 158) says that the term Roma 'is a collective term used by the social majority that denotes very different groups who do not necessarily regard themselves as forming a single community'. The Roma vary widely in terms of their lifestyle, social characteristics and everyday practices.

Unfortunately, the status of Roma people in Europe, especially in central and eastern Europe has not been a happy one for many decades. Although the Jewish populations of Europe suffered immeasurably throughout history, Stewart (2010) states that:

> The institution of cistizenship brought emancipation for the Jews and – the horrors of 1930–45 notwithstanding – integration into modern European life; the same period has seen the gradual marginalisation, the criminalisation and immiseration of the great mass of Europe's Gypsies. (Stewart, 2010: 6)

This is a far cry from many of the recent lifestyle television shows that are currently popular in some countries in the world, such as 'My Big Fat Gypsy Wedding', which imply that Gypsy life is colourful, glamorous and fun. Hungary is no exception to this. Scission (2010) stated that in Hungary 'The eight hundred thousand Roma and between fifty and one hundred thousand Jews face a very troubling future'. This is partly due to the increasing popularity of the far right-wing political party. A European Union (EU) report (FRA, 2012) suggests that Hungary is not alone in this respect and that Roma continue to face discrimination and social exclusion across the EU. Kállai (2002: 8) is seemingly right to lament that 'It is intolerable that an entire people today lead their everyday lives in utter misery with no hope for the future – right in the centre of Europe'.

On the other hand, there are many aspects of Gypsy culture and lifestyle which are still rich and vibrant. This is especially true of the songs, dance and music. One only has to think of the musical and dance heritage of the Andalusian Gypsies in Spain, for example. It will be argued in this chapter that in lieu of political and economic support for Roma at European or national level, the role of cultural and tourism organisations in creating positive representations of Roma lifestyle and traditions can play an important role.

Background to the Study

Sometimes even Hungarians were strangers, sometimes strangers became the best Hungarians.
Babits, 1939

This chapter will consider the social, economic and political status of the Roma communities in Hungary and the potential for tourism development based on their culture(s) and traditions. The main focus will be on the capital city Budapest, but other areas of Hungary will also be considered as 90% of the Roma population lives outside the capital (Janky, 2004). The areas of Budapest which are inhabited by concentrations of Roma communities tend to be socially and economically deprived and many of these were traditionally considered to be 'no-go' areas for locals and tourists alike. However, some guided tours now take place within the more deprived quarters of the city. The authors include a case study of the socially responsible company Budapest Beyond, which is based on an in-depth interview with the founders who are also guides, and participant observation of one of their 'sociocultural' tours showing 'the hidden backyards of Gypsy families'. Interviews with the founder of Rockhoppers, a tour provider, and with a freelance guide Zoltán Nagy, were also carried out. They offer Gypsy-themed tours in Budapest and in the countryside. All of these tour providers involve the local Roma community in their tours, where visitors not only observe them, but also directly interact with the individuals and their communities.

Other facets of the 'alternative' tourist product are also considered, such as Roma festivals, music, arts, fashion and gastronomy. Additionally, an interview was undertaken with Katalin Bársony from the Romedia Foundation, which focuses on positive representation of Roma through media and film, and another one with Károly Gáspár, a Hungarian Gypsy jazz musician and novelist.

This stage of the research did not include analysing demand for tourism based on Roma culture nor did it include perceptions of existing or potential tourists to Hungary. However, some netnographic research has been included based on the researchers' observations of TripAdvisor comments using the search words 'Gypsy' and 'Gipsy' in the context of Hungary and Budapest (the word 'Roma' yielded few useful results as it tended to refer to the Italian capital instead).

Although this chapter aims primarily to focus on positive aspects of Roma culture(s), some of the more tragic aspects of past and present narratives (e.g. the Holocaust, hate crimes) are included, as it would be a misrepresentation to exclude them. As much of the Roma culture is intangible or non-material, this represents an additional challenge for tourism development and experience creation. It necessitates the direct involvement of communities in order to avoid issues of appropriation, the creation of fake authenticity and to maximise empowerment and ownership. Roma tourism is also new to Hungary and is being attempted at a time when the political circumstances and social environment are not very conducive to ethnic or minority tourism.

Hungarian Gypsies or Roma

Gypsies are a population about whom it has until recently remained acceptable to be unapologetically racist.
Stewart, 2010: 1

Szuhay (2002) clarifies the classification of Gypsies in Hungary: Hungarian Gypsies ('Romungro', often called 'musicians') who mostly only speak Hungarian; Vlach or Rom who speak the Gypsy language; and Romanian-speaking Boyash. Gypsies first appeared in Hungary in the 14th and 15th centuries and for some time they played a considerable role in Hungarian society as craftsmen and musicians. While Hungarian Gypsies were assimilated into society mainly in the 18th century, Vlach and Boyash only arrived in Hungary's present territory in the 19th and 20th centuries. Hungarian Gypsies represent more than 70% of the Roma population in Hungary and many of them live in cities or in the northern parts of Hungary. Vlach and Boyash live in big, multigenerational families, Vlach are typically traders, while Boyash mostly live in villages in south-west Hungary, and often work as craftsmen (Munk *et al.*, 2005).

A TripAdvisor search for the words 'Gipsy' and 'Gypsy' in Budapest resulted in 786 reviews and of these at least 70% refer to restaurants playing Gypsy music. Hungarian Gypsies are often presented as being musicians, even though a vast majority are not. Musicians have higher economic and perceived status in society, and they are also more assimilated (usually they do not speak the Roma language). They differentiate themselves from other Gypsy groups, who are mostly characterised by a lower degree of assimilation and are perceived as being lower status. Kemény (2002: 57) writes that 'music offered the sole avenue of social elevation' and by the end of the 18th century the Hungarian national movement valued Gypsy violinists. During the Budapest Beyond tour undertaken by the researchers, the chosen family visited was a Roma family of musicians (but it should be noted that this usually only refers to the men). This is not necessarily misrepresentative of a typical Gypsy lifestyle in Hungary, but it does mean that the experience of tourists is directed towards a relatively more affluent, less traditional group with a higher social status.

In the 18th century, Gypsies were forced to settle down as their traditional wayfarer lifestyle was banned. From that time onwards, there was more and more pressure on them to assimilate into Hungarian culture and forget their native language. However, Havas (2002a) suggests that Roma in Hungary were better integrated into society in the 19th century than during the decades following World War I, culminating tragically in the Nazi Holocaust in 1944. The Jewish Holocaust in Hungary is of course better documented than the Roma Holocaust, as stated by Vidra (2010: 197) 'the fate of the Roma was much less systematically recorded that that of the Jews'. In his poems about the Holocaust, the Hungarian poet József Choli Daróczi (1939: 63) writes how 'They took away the Gypsies, took them all to dig enormous ditches'. Requiem for Auschwitz (2012) stated that 'awareness of this "forgotten Holocaust" is essential in combating current anti-Gypsyism in Europe'. It should be noted that the Holocaust Memorial Centre in Budapest emphasises in sensitive detail what happened to the Gypsies from Hungary. Many of them fought back, but were sent to labour camps and ghettos, died of hunger or were similarly murdered in gas chambers or shot into mass graves. Unfortunately, unlike the Jews, Gypsies did not have a 'motherland' after the Holocaust which could provide them with financial and moral support (Kállai, 2002). During the Russian occupation of Budapest, many poor Jews and Roma people lived in the same districts (e.g. VIII), some were even half Jewish and half Roma by birth. Together they tried to fight oppression.

During communism, Gypsies were also integrated socially, although 'very slowly and not very successfully' (Vidra, 2010: 207). They still remained one of the poorest sectors of society. At this time, many Roma families moved into the old unrenovated apartments in District VIII in Budapest and also into the former Jewish ghetto (District VII) and District IX. After the 1990 political transition, Hungary developed a democratic structure for the political, social and cultural representation of traditional minorities. Sociopolitical programmes dealing with the Roma population extended to a large array of activities, such as education, cultural heritage and arts. However, the results of such voluntary policies to strengthen the rights and opportunities of the Roma population have not been so promising (Keresztély & Szabó, 2006).

Unfortunately, it is thought that the Roma people were the biggest losers after the post-1989 transition took place. This includes unemployment, a decline in health, lower life expectancy, exclusion from the schooling system, including an 'apartheid-like segregation' (Havas, 2002b; Pidd, 2012) and discrimination (Kállai, 2002; Kováts, 2002; Ministry of Foreign Affairs, 2004). The unemployment rate of the Roma is double that of non-Roma. The extensive work of János Ládanyi since the early 1990s is an excellent source of information documenting all of this and more, but is too detailed to quote here. Since the country joined the EU (2004), Roma people have been targeted by EU structural funds for specific programmes. Act LXXVII on the Rights of National and Ethnic Minorities gave them the right to self-govern on matters of culture and traditions, so a Roma parliament and Roma cultural and community centres were established, but arguably all of this had little impact on economic and political marginalisation.

Based on the 2011 census, Roma form 1.2% of the population of Budapest, which means 20,000 people; furthermore, 16% of the Roma population claims the Roma language as their native one. At the same time, other sources say that the population could be 10 times bigger (Keresztély & Szabó, 2006), at least 500,000–600,000 (Munk et al., 2005). Tárki (2012) showed in their research that Hungarian citizens generally thought there were far more Gypsies (and other ethnic minorities) living in Hungary than there actually are and many stated that there are 'too many'. Memories of the Holocaust, experiences of atrocities and ongoing discrimination mean that many Gypsies are 'mortally afraid of being recorded as such' so they try to camouflage themselves (Vajda, 2010: 153). In one research project, Ladanyi and Szelenyi (2001) showed that only 36.8% of Roma respondents in Hungary self-identified as Roma compared to 73.3% in Bulgaria. Many Roma live like any other Hungarians, working and educating their children. Differences among Roma ethnic groups also account for non-identification. The Hungarian Roma novelist and musician Gáspár (2013) argued in his interview with the researchers that Hungarian Gypsies have much more in common (e.g. costumes, language, culture) with Hungarians than with other Roma ethnic groups (Vlach, Boyash), and that is why the majority of them identify themselves as Hungarians rather than as Roma. It should be emphasised at this point that what is common in different Roma groups is their capacity for cultural change, which explains why certain elements of their culture – lifestyle, language, customs and beliefs – show such diversity today; meanwhile, the non-Roma population typically sees them as one ethnic group (Munk et al., 2005). Another reason for non-identification might be that they do not necessarily want a spotlight on their origin, 'ethnicity' or their difference. This may therefore pose a problem for developing forms of tourism which focus on Roma culture(s). Problems may also arise as there is not one uniform culture to promote, but many variations based on origins and family roots.

Pidd (2012), a *Guardian* journalist, describes how Roma in Hungary 'are the prime targets for right-wing hate and more general discrimination'. There have been many so-called 'hate crimes' in recent years. However, a relatively large number of the (petty) crimes in Hungary are committed by Roma people, which influences and biases the society's attitudes and behaviour, and feeds right-wing hate. It is not surprising that many Roma people turn to petty crime, as they have much lower education, employment and income levels than most other citizens and their opportunities are fewer partly because of racial bias. They can quite easily be distinguished physically from other Hungarians because of their darker skin and hair colour and sometimes their clothes too. Janky (2004) showed that 72% of Gypsy families live in a segregated living environment; only one fifth of Gypsy children attend secondary school; only 28% of Gypsy males and 15% of females aged 15–74 were employed in 2003; and 71% of Gypsy family income is within the lowest quintile of the Hungarian population. Harper *et al.* (2009) show that Roma neighbourhoods in Hungary (and elsewhere in central and eastern Europe) have unequal access to sewerage, indoor water, sanitation and green space.

Large Gypsy communities can be found in the north and north-east of Hungary in the counties of Szabolcs-Szatmár-Bereg and Borsod-Abaúj-Zemplén. Many of the villages are extremely poor. The majority of different Roma communities in central Budapest live in Districts VII, VIII and IX, and some live in almost slum conditions (Kemény, 2002). Some of these areas are not visited by tourists, but District VII includes the so-called Jewish quarter and District VIII features on Budapest Beyond's tours. The Topbudapest website states that:

> Before, the 8th district was considered the nightmare of tourists (and Hungarians as well). The area was said to be dangerous, slummy and strongly advised to avoid. Although the 8th district is continuously developing, the changes remained unnoticed and the strong negative stereotypes against the 8th district remained. We feel we happened to stop this bad automatic response with inventing and guiding the 'sociocultural' walking tours. (Topbudapest.org, 2012)

Roma Culture as an Intangible Tourist Attraction: Creating Experiences

Stewart (2010: 4) notes that it is easy to forget, even in academic research, that Roma are citizens of modern nation states and not 'paragons of a lost world'. Okely (2010: 38) similarly suggests that Gypsies have some-times been 'frozen in a mythical past' by researchers wishing to romanticise or exoticise cultures. This is also one of the pitfalls of tourism and the representation of indigenous or ethnic cultures. Unfortunately, media representation in Hungary of contemporary Gypsy life is rather negative (Bernáth & Messing, 2002), and public opinion is prejudiced and stereotypical. Any tourism promotion could therefore aim to focus on more positive aspects of Roma or Gypsy life and culture.

Okely (2010) notes that there is little material Gypsy culture. This clearly has implications for tourism development, as the product is based more on experiences of living culture than gazing on objects. Organisations like the non-governmental organisation (NGO) Romedia Foundation in Budapest uses culture, arts and events to try to combat anti-Roma prejudice and contribute to positive perceptions of Roma ethnic identity through films, videos, media and public events. In the researchers' interview with Katalin Bársony from the Romedia Foundation, the researchers asked her to describe Roma culture, which she summarised as language, myths and fairy tales, ballads, oral tradition (unwritten history) and the idea that 'we could survive even without written language for 700 years'. According to Bársony, it is important not to show too much poverty surrounding Roma culture when promoting tourism, as this can create a negative image. People must be involved and benefit, rather than creating a 'human zoo' situation. There can be positive promotion of negative heritage so that Roma also learn about their history and the past. This might include the Holocaust as mentioned earlier.

Creating experiences around intangible ethnic cultures is quite challenging in tourism. It is not uncommon that this is also attempted in difficult political circumstances. Although the consumer experience should be prioritised, sensitive handling of local communities is also essential, as they play a major role in the experience. Product development is more likely to be conceptualised by tour operators or guides, but the communities should clearly be consulted during this process. Products based on intangible resources and 'real' peoples' lives fit well the growing trend of the last decade of being focused not only on the physical attributes of destinations, but on experiences and fulfilment (King, 2002; Ritchie & Crouch, 2003). According to Lichrou et al. (2008), destinations should be viewed in a metaphorical sense, as a narrative and not as a product. Zátori (2012) adds that consumers should be personally and actively involved in experience co-creation through participation and interaction; that narratives and stories are more engaging than facts and script; and that flexibility and responsiveness to both consumers and communities are essential. The case study introduced later in this chapter confirms that this perspective is used by Beyond Budapest in their tour focusing on Roma.

Creating experiences based on community culture raises questions about the issues of 'staged authenticity'. Smith (2009) states that:

> Although the authenticity of the tourist experience is of some importance, it is more crucial to ensure that local communities feel comfortable with their role as performers and entertainers. This includes the degree to which they are prepared to allow the commodification of their culture for touristic purposes. (Smith, 2009: 217)

Ideally, the host and guest should co-create the experience via mediation from the tour operator or guide (if any). He or she acts as a kind of interface, ideally understanding well the needs of both. Local communities are keepers of stories, which might be the building blocks of the destination narrative or story. Fairy tales and ballads are one of the highlights and specialities of Roma culture. If individuals from the local community are involved, they meet and interact with the tourists in spontaneous or (willingly) staged circumstances, and they share their stories. The tourist experience will be influenced by their presentation and interpretation skills, local knowledge and passion for both their culture and the given location. While in the case of Jewish Budapest, a large number of built and tangible elements (e.g. synagogues, memorials, museums, community centres) represent popular tourist attractions of Budapest, Roma Budapest is a somewhat hidden dimension of the Hungarian capital.

Developing Roma Tourism: Opportunities and Challenges

The Athe Sam Festival creates the setting for Roma and non-Roma people to meet, for Vlach, the Boyash Roma people and Hungarian Gypsies to get together; for people to make friends, fall in love, plan joint initiatives. It brings new talents into the lime-light and makes us cry or laugh by highlighting the problems, values and the beauty of Roma life.
Athe Sam, 2013

It would be politically naive to suggest that this is an 'ideal' time to develop Roma tourism in Hungary or Budapest with the currently increasing prejudice. However, it could also be argued that developing international tourism could help to cast a spotlight on the problems that minority groups are facing, to support them and maybe even to increase understanding among the Hungarian population. An extremely small number of TripAdvisor comments refer to any negative aspects of Gypsies in Budapest (less than 1% of 786 comments). This implies that foreign tourists' experiences of Budapest are very rarely affected by any negative incidents caused by Gypsies. Many of the cultural and tourism initiatives cited here have the motivation of addressing prejudice and negative stereotyping. Of course, it would be preferable to do this through politics or education but this is not currently a very viable option.

Visual arts

An outdoor photography exhibition by Roma photographers and artists and featuring Roma communities in October 2012 was organised in Budapest as part of the Decade of Roma Inclusion 2005–2015. The aim was 'to enable us to overcome prejudice and to defy negative stereotypes and negative feelings'. Photos were shown of Roma and non-Roma living together and interacting. There were uplifting photos of 'local (Roma) heroes'. When one of the researchers visited this exhibition, she also met Dutch and Spanish tourists as well as local Hungarians. Other exhibitions pop-up on a regular basis in Budapest, either organised around a specific ethnic theme, or an exhibition of individual artists.

Festivals

The most popular of all is the Athe Sam Festival, a three- to four-day Roma multi-arts event which started six years ago. It includes music performances, exhibitions, literary events, artisan workshops, roundtable discussions, film screenings, theatre performances and dance houses. One of the features of the festival is the joint productions of Roma and non-Roma artists. The founders state that 'We hope to make a lasting contribution to the mitigation of the harmful prejudice towards the Roma community' (Athe Sam, 2012). Such an event may be attended by tourists who happen to be in Budapest and who find some information on it, but this is not easy as it is not widely promoted. In the future, there may be potential for this festival to become even more popular with visitors. For example, in 2010 the world-famous band leader of the Gypsy Kings performed.

Music

Music has a central role in many Gypsy families which is passed down from generation to generation. The first famous Hungarian bands in the 18th century were formed by Gypsy musicians – e.g. Panna Cinka, Janos Bihari – who created and played a genre, which is known today as 'Gypsy music' (in Hungarian: 'cigányzene'); however, later they played other genres as well, such as classical music, jazz, pop. Partly because of tradition, 'cigányzene' was always popular among Hungarians, and Gypsy violinists or bands could be found everywhere, in restaurants, in markets, in pubs, at events, etc. When Hungarians immigrated to the USA in the 19th century, several Gypsy musicians went with them, and they continued to play their traditional music overseas. It could be argued that the golden age of 'cigányzene' was in the 1970s.

There are some world-renowned contemporary Gypsy musicians such as Béla Szakcsi Lakatos a jazz musician and István Snétberger a guitarist who also founded the Snétberger Music Talent Centre in Hungary for Gypsy and talented Hungarian youngsters. However, since the 1990s, the popularity of Gypsy music has declined. This is the reason why the Gypsy culture of today – especially the music – might be seen as stereotyped or as offering staged authenticity. An online restaurant guide in Budapest states that:

> Please note that many tourists assume that a real Hungarian restaurant is unimaginable without a Hungarian Gypsy band, but most locals would call restaurants with live Gypsy music *touristy* and *fake Hungarian*.... The idea of Hungarians eating drinking and even singing along with Gypsy musicians, who are playing right by the table, into the very ears of the restaurant guests may have been well circulated in touristy videos and romantic films, but the reality is that most Magyars would definitely avoid 'Hungarian style restaurants', and would probably advise against eating out at such places. (Topbudapest.org, 2013)

As stated earlier, at least 70% of all TripAdvisor comments on Gipsies/Gypsies in Budapest refer to music mostly played in restaurants. The vast majority of these are positive, using words such as 'traditional', 'authentic', 'romantic', 'superb', 'wonderful', 'divine', 'sensational'. A relatively small number of reviews (only about 2%) contain negative descriptors, such as 'annoying', 'loud', 'obnoxious', 'intrusive', 'kitschy', 'touristy' and 'tacky'.

Organisers of the Athe Sam Festival share the view that Roma music should be more open to contemporary genres (Papp, 2008), which could help to revive its popularity, overcome perceptions of staged authenticity and reaffirm Roma culture as a dynamic living tradition.

Gypsy dance is also an extremely important part of the musical heritage and is deeply rooted in folk traditions in Hungary. Some tours into the countryside include the opportunities to join in Gypsy dances.

Fashion

Romani Design is a Roma fashion house, which was established by Erika Varga in 2009, and was the first of its kind in Hungary. It is a workplace where Roma and non-Roma work together. The aim of Romani Design is to design and produce typical Roma fashion pieces which contain traditional elements, colours and motifs. Their mission is to strengthen the identity, traditions and cultural values of the Roma community, and to mitigate the misunderstandings between Roma and non-Roma. They have both Roma and non-Roma customers, as well as foreign customers and tourists. They initially opened a shop in District VIII, but have recently moved to St. Stephen's Square, which is heavily visited by tourists. Consequently, these typical fashion products might reach a large number of tourists and make them aware of Roma culture in Budapest.

Gastronomy

Although many traditional Hungarian restaurants tend to feature Gypsy musicians, there is so far only one Roma restaurant called 'Romani Platni' ('Roma Stove') which opened in Budapest in 2012, and calls itself 'authentic'. The restaurant is unique by being the first of its kind; it is not a simple restaurant, but rather a community place. The *Malaysian Insider* (2012) described it as 'Part home restaurant, part social experiment', as it aims to open Hungarians to better understanding the ways of the Roma. Its founder (Malaysian Insider, 2012) states that 'food is as good a way as any to cultural understanding' and guests often talk to the women who cook the food. Such a venture may appeal to tourists with an interest in 'alternative' experiences. However, the dishes cooked here do not differ much from other Hungarian local dishes – it is more about the social experience than gastronomy.

Outside Budapest

There are one or two initiatives outside Budapest, but unfortunately few foreign tourists are likely to venture to remote and poverty-stricken parts of the country where many Roma people are resident. In 2009, there was a unique initiative by a group of activists to turn a poor Roma village called Bódvalenke into a tourist destination by inviting a group of Hungarian Roma painters to paint murals on the walls of houses in the village. In early 2011, Roma artists from across Europe were also invited to participate in the project. Unfortunately, although tourists may come, they are unlikely to stay long as there is little infrastructure, so the economic benefits for the village and local people are limited. Only two comments on TripAdvisor currently mention Bódvalenke with one tourist giving advice to another about how to get there (five hours by public transport from Budapest, so it cannot easily be visited).

Apart from Budapest Beyond, Zoltán Nagy (Rockhoppers), a tour guide, claims to offer an 'authentic Gypsy/Roma program for tourists in Hungary'. His aim is to offer guided tour programmes which cannot be found with another tour provider, and 'to show the incredibly interesting facet of Budapest and Hungary, not the mainstream sights with mainstream interpretations'. The tour includes a short walk in District

VIII and a trip to a village with a higher percentage of Roma population outside Budapest with eating, drinking and dancing. In the village, they visit a local pub where Roma people (especially men) used to come, they play music and sometimes they dance together. Since it is a small group or an individual tour, the interactions are more personal and direct. 'The local Gypsies are really happy these people are interested in them', states Nagy; however, there is only an occasional demand for this tour. An analysis of the small number of TripAdvisor comments from tourists who had been on this tour showed that their experiences were very positive. This included eating, drinking and dancing with local people in 'real Gypsy dances'. 'The Gypsy tour was fantastic!', 'I did not know that this authentic kind of Gypsy music still exists', 'It was the real, the authentic Gypsy music'. One stated that 'It was especially the Gypsy village that made us feel less like tourists or foreigners and more like guests', and another that 'We wined and dined and danced our hearts full connecting a bit to the Gypsy in us all'. Clearly, authentic cultural and gastronomic experiences and connecting with local Roma people are important to this segment of tourists.

Tours of Budapest Districts

The blocks of flats built mainly in the 19th century in District VIII in Budapest have a colourful history. They were built to give a home to Budapest's booming population in the 19th century under the Austro-Hungarian monarchy, including Jewish, Slovak, Croatian, Romanian and Gypsy craftsmen and wageworkers. The district was mainly populated by Hungarian 'musician' Gypsies and the poorest stratum of the Jewish population. It was severely damaged during the war (90% of the buildings were bombed). Although the bombed buildings were renovated, the residents' social situation declined, which attracted more low-status individuals. The apartment houses (many built in art nouveau, neo-romantic and neoclassical style) were in state ownership at this time, and their maintenance was heavily neglected. Over the past two decades, the district has kept its problematic image as something of a slum. New immigrants such as Chinese, Vietnamese, African, Arab and Albanian families have settled down in this area. Some view it as 'slummy' and scary, some romanticise it, but there is also a growing tendency among young, not so well situated, socially sensitive intellectuals to move into the area.

District VIII has a high concentration of Roma people in one part but is quite gentrified in others. After the change of regime and privatisation (1989 onwards), Roma stayed in buildings and flats which were in very poor condition. Regeneration processes started after 2000, which predominantly meant the destruction of these old structures and moving Gypsies away from the inner districts of the city. Some of these areas have been rebuilt as higher-status areas which can be attractive for tourists. Despite displacement and gentrification, one positive example of social rehabilitation can be quoted in the regeneration of Mathias Square in District VIII where local Roma residents and children were integrated into the renewal process.

District VIII has a vibe and sights which are certainly intriguing for some tourists, which is why it has become the focus of some guided tours and walks, such as Budapest Beyond.

Case Study of Budapest Beyond: A Socially Responsible Approach to 'Alternative' Tourism

Budapest Beyond sightseeing company organises a number of tours around Budapest, including a 'sociocultural walking tour' featuring District VIII and a Gypsy family visit. The researchers engaged in participant observation of this tour from July to September 2012. They also interviewed the company's founder, Gyorgy Baglyas, and one of the tour guides, Csaba Szikra, in June 2012. This company was chosen after consideration of others because they were the first to include tours of the Roma areas of the city, they adopt a unique and innovative approach and they have an obvious commitment to corporate social responsibility (CSR), arguably essential when dealing with sensitive ethnic and minority cultures and communities.

The founders of Budapest Beyond were asked about their motivations for establishing the company. One of the reasons was that they believe that people make a city, not the buildings, and that a small number of tourists are open to experiencing this. The slogan of the company is 'Are you looking for Hungarian reality? Don't simply be a tourist: experience!'. The idea of reality here is about the lives of Roma people today and for tourists to understand what is happening now and to be positively surprised. They believe in the crucial role of the tour guide who interprets the sights and culture in a positive or negative way. Ultimately, they hope to change things in a good way, aiming for respect and togetherness and a common fight against prejudice. The website refers to the 'real and happy face of Budapest' and the aim to 'inspire for openness, for optimism'. The main aim of the company and its founders is 'to make a positive change through tourism'. However, the founders state that although people like the aesthetics and exoticism of other cultures, they also try to show the reality and the dark side.

There is no state support for the company's activities. Most tourism organisations have a very negative view of District VIII and Roma generally (their opinion is that District VIII is dangerous for tourists). Instead, the company has support from the Bálint Ház (a Jewish cultural and community centre) as well as Teleki Tér Synagogue and Glázer Jakob Memorial Foundation (an NGO).

For Hungarians, these tours have an intercultural educational function, while for tourists they might mean a brand new kind of tour experience. Ninety percent of tour participants are educated and the age range is quite wide; 50% or more are foreign and usually Western European. There are very few Asian visitors. For Hungarian tourists, it is a chance to have a cultural education and many open-minded domestic visitors come from outside Budapest (i.e. the Hungarian countryside). Backpackers are not easy to attract, as they prefer to do other activities. Encouraging school groups has not always been very successful either (as mentioned earlier, schools in Hungary are often segregated). There are different groups in the summer and winter. Autumn is the high season for foreign tourists, but in spring there are more school groups and Hungarians.

Budapest Beyond describes their tours as 'personal', 'interactive' and 'creative'. Firstly, they are personal, because the tours are organised with small groups, which enables a higher degree of customisation. Secondly, they are very interactive. They encourage tour participants to ask questions and to interact. The guides use personal stories and histories and try to involve the tourists by applying different guiding techniques, e.g. interactive questions, pictures from the past, songs and quizzes. During the tour, direct interaction with communities takes place. Acquaintances and friends are involved as well as members of the same Roma family, who have been participants for many years. Moreover, people often come out of their houses spontaneously and want to talk about Roma culture, especially grandmothers! Thus, the possibility of the personal involvement of the tourist is maximised as well as the authenticity of the tourist experience. Customisation and personal involvement enable experience co-creation, which along with authenticity can result in a more memorable tourist experience. Thirdly, creativity is inherent in the tours thanks to the interesting and thought-provoking interpretations of the tour guides, and the attempt to evoke several human senses. The tours usually include a stop in a typical brasserie or coffee shop and listening to a song.

The locals they meet during the tour provide information such as personal stories and experiences – just like the tour guide. They demonstrate open-mindedness towards visitors, and are happy to talk about their neighbourhood, culture and everyday life. An idea was formulated recently to develop a tour where member(s) of the community take over the role of the tour guide. In this way, community involvement can be emphasised and the perceived authenticity of the tourist experience might be higher, too. The tour guide has a mediator role, and such a guide might facilitate a real insight. Beyond the important role of the tour guide, community support is even more crucial. It contributes to the formation of the community's positive identity, and it also might eliminate or reduce staged authenticity.

The tours are mainly promoted by word of mouth (90% of people seem to come because they were told that it is a great tour), sometimes by TripAdvisor, because of the (excellent) website of Budapest Beyond. At the beginning there was a lot of publicity from TV crews and journalists because of the novelty factor of tourism in District VIII, and TV companies are often still interested. Budapest Beyond is committed to CSR which they see as an inherent part of what they do and not simply a management and marketing tool. They want to show a good example, and emphasise that ethics is more important than profit.

Conclusions

This chapter shows that there are considerable political and social challenges for those who want to develop and promote Roma tourism in Hungary. However, it is also evident that there has perhaps never been a better time to highlight the problems and issues faced by minority groups in Hungary and to positively promote their culture(s) to tourists and local people alike. Roma tourism development is challenging, especially as there is little material culture. However, involving the Roma communities in creating tourist experiences based on their lives and traditions can be one way of deepening visitors' knowledge and experience of this relatively unknown ethnic culture. Those tourists who have already undertaken tours seem to value the opportunity to engage with local people in authentic contexts and it seems that local Roma people are happy that tourists are interested in their culture.

Although the Roma population constitutes a significant part of the poorest and most problematic central districts of Budapest – especially District VIII – some may argue that due to their traditional lifestyle (especially in the case of Vlach and Boyash Roma), tourism development in the countryside might be more successful, since their culture and lifestyle are better represented there. Bódválenke could become an excellent example of this with some infrastructural development and the establishment of small local businesses as perhaps within the framework of social entrepreneurship.

However, in Budapest the music, food and arts projects of Roma people are also increasingly being used to help overcome prejudice and negative stereotypes and, in time, may become more popular tourist attractions. Hungarian and Budapest tourism agencies should be careful not to overemphasise the 'dangers' of Gypsy communities and quarters, as at present, very few tourists report negative experiences of Gypsies (at least on TripAdvisor). International tourists also seem to enjoy the traditional Gypsy music in restaurants far more than their Hungarian counterparts and should not be discouraged from eating in restaurants with such music.

Although there is unlikely to be any formal support from government agencies in the near future, many cultural and tourism organisations are already active in supporting and promoting Roma culture. It is clear that Budapest Beyond and other alternative tour companies and guides are not only extremely innovative in their approach to representing and supporting Roma communities and cultures by making the guiding truly experiential, personal and engaging, but also provide examples of altruistic and socially responsible approaches. Perhaps with more examples like this in the future, Hungary may even move towards greater tolerance through its alternative tourism initiatives.

Part 2: Community Perceptions

Introduction

In tourism, host communities and residents play a significant role in the tourist experience. Tourism development shapes the destination and impacts on the host community and the residents. Impacts are broad ranging from economic benefits for some community members to increasing sociocultural impacts on the daily life of a community or its residents. The destinations under scrutiny in this book are either urban or rural spatially limited areas or clusters that are put on the tourism map. Tourism development is often instigated either by the community, residents (insiders) or by external tourism providers or public authorities (outsiders) who consider the destination as an attractive tourism asset in the context of diversification of tourism supply.

Who are the Host Communities?

A community is not a homogeneous group of people (Telfer & Sharpley, 2008: 117). Hosts are communities or groups of people that either live or use the space where tourism takes place. The hosts can be, but are not necessarily, residents of the visited place and therefore a distinction needs to be made between host communities and residents. Their interest and involvement in tourism development might not be the same. It is mainly the host community (not necessarily the resident) that shapes the place and contributes to making it appealing for tourism development. The promoted identity of the area is closely associated with the host community. It is the potential encounter with the host that attracts tourists. Residents can be impacted by simple tourism activity, negatively through pressure on the district and raised prices and positively through urban embellishment due to tourism development.

In the context of urban ethnic quarters, the host community members (i.e. those for whom the tourists come) are often not living in the area. For instance, in Little Italy in New York and Boston, only a few of the residents are Italian (Conforti, 1996). Indeed, most community members live in other areas and use the ethnic district as a commercial ethnic belt, to purchase culturally specific goods or to have social exchanges with other members of the community. They may also wish to maintain links with the community culture and identity, both socially and place wise.

With the disappearance of some ethnic districts, community members, often in collaboration with business owners and local entrepreneurs (including tourism providers), attempt to preserve the heritage of their ancestor migrants as the following example shows:

> The Little Italy Association (LIA) is the only district management corporation of its kind in any Little Italy neighborhood in the United States. LIA deals with a variety of livability issues that range from sidewalk cleanliness to new building design review; from community schools to no-leash dog run parks. The Association pledges to advocate on behalf of its members' best interests in the areas of public safety, beautification, promotion, and economic development while preserving the unique cultural resources that exist in the community.
>
> The LIA currently has 26 Board Members that is comprised of property owners, residents, business owners and community-at-large representatives. (http://www.littleitalysd.com/about/who-we-are/; accessed 14 February 2014)

The presence of the community then creates the atmosphere and identity of the place. The conceptualisation of place identity emphasises the physical characteristics of urban space and, together with the social meaning of space, can be seen as a social category. Thus, persons or groups can define themselves as belonging to this social category which is recognised by the members of other categories (Bernardo & Palma, 2005: 73). Palmer *et al.* (2013: 144) state that social identity suggests that an individual's sense of identification with a group encourages participation in a brand community. Identity theory helps to provide a conceptual framework establishing the link between identity, attitude and behaviour. The model also proposes that the resourced-based occupational identity, environmental identity and gender identity of the residents are the independent variables influencing attitudes towards the positive and negative impacts of tourism as well as support for the industry (Nunkoo & Gursoy, 2012: 244). This is also valid for non-resident community members of ethnic and other minorities' quarters, such as lesbian, gay, bisexual, transgender (LGBT) areas. The question, however, is whether and how these considerations can be adapted to slums, favelas or township communities that very likely do not 'shape' their places to create and identify with a brand. Indeed, here, most of the hosts are residents of the slum districts, favelas or township areas, but often leave the area for work.

In the light of these discussions, analysing host communities and how they deal with tourism is a challenging task. The active support of host communities can be crucial for successful tourism development (Gursoy & Rutherford, 2004), even if mutual beneficial transactions between tourists and residents in poverty tourism always run a risk of being exploitive. There is little opportunity to determine whether a given tourist is exploitive since tourists lack good access to the residents' perspectives (Whyte *et al.*, 2011: 338). Woosnam and Norman (Woosnam, 2012) developed the Emotional Solidarity Scale comprising the welcoming nature of residents towards tourists, such as feeling proud to have visitors in destinations, feeling community benefits from having visitors, emotional closeness and sympathetic understanding. The widely promoted idea is that tourism development should be supported by the hosts and that costs should not outweigh the benefits (Sharpley, 2014: 37). Yet, what happens if 'hosts' are not able to withdraw because they are the core attraction without having been involved or asked?

Research on Host Communities

Host communities have been an object of study almost since the beginning of tourism research. Along with numerous case studies, different theories have been adapted in order to develop conceptual models. While there is a very wide literature on residents' perceptions, there is surprisingly little on residents' perception when residents or community members are the core tourist attraction, as is the case of the communities considered in this book.

Residents' attitudes towards tourism have often been studied in the light of social exchange theory, defined by Nunkoo and Gursoy (2012: 244) as 'attitude toward the positive and negative impacts of tourism influence support for the industry, the ultimate dependent construct in the model'. Gursoy and Rutherford (2004: 496) state that 'its basic tenet is that locals are likely to participate in an exchange if they believe that they are likely to gain benefits without incurring unacceptable costs…. They are inclined to be involved in the exchange, and, thus endorse future development in their community'. This model indeed reduces tourism impacts on communities to a cost-benefit analysis, but the social exchange theory also suggests that residents are more likely to have a deeper identification with a destination brand and a more positive attitude towards tourists if the perceived benefits gained from involvement with tourism exceed the perceived costs (Palmer *et al.*, 2013: 144). Another criticism of research on host communities is linked to the fact that they are often based on case studies and that eventually only a few models exist to allow comparison. Yet, as quoted in Tosun (2002: 232), 'Dann, Nash and Pearce (1988) and Van Doorn (1989) have argued that it is not easy to derive theory from individual tourism impact case studies, since each individual case brings with it so many idiosyncratic peculiarities'.

Promoting distinctive communities as a tourism asset started in the late 1980s and early 1990s, when places like Harlem, Chinatowns, the favelas, etc. became popular tourist destinations. The development dynamics came either from inside or outside. Discussing the attitude of residents towards tourism is therefore not always a key issue in the sense that residents or community members are the main tourism attraction, but not necessarily the organisers (developers) nor the beneficiaries. In some contexts, when tourists are taken through an area by bus/coach or even on a walking tour, residents do not (whether they might want to or not) have the opportunity to exchange with the tourists – often for language reasons, but also because of the invisible barrier of social, cultural and economic distance. They are gazed at by the visitors and explained as objects of otherness by guides belonging only in some cases to the community (cf. Chapter 2 on Matonge).

As pointed out by Sharpley (2014) and Woosnam (2012), most research is related to the residents' perception of tourism and not their attitudes towards tourists. These may be rather different from those related to tourism development and are rarely addressed (Sharpley, 2014: 38). The perception and attitude towards the tourist are of particular importance in the context of tourism development in minorities' districts where otherness is promoted. How do the residents or community members deal with the gaze of the visitors; of being the object of the tourist attraction of the place? The encounter is clearly an unequal one. One might question even whether an encounter really exists. Is there an organised tourist space that integrates the host community? In most cases of slum tourism there is no actual contact between the visitors and the visited, just through an intermediary, the guide (Dahles, 2002; Diekmann & Hannam, 2012; Dyson, 2012). The encounter is consequently controlled and limited to the 'sharing of the place' (Sharpley, 2014: 38). The visited community thus only indirectly takes part in the tourism encounter, as mere extras of the tourist experience. In the case of ethnic quarters, the encounter depends largely on the involvement of the community and examples are wide ranging.

Tourism can indeed represent a source of income, employment and development. However, who benefits and how depends largely on the organisation of tourism at the destination. In some cases, it can be the government that benefits in terms of image, in other cases private entrepreneurs develop tourism businesses and sometimes the community as such can gain from tourism development. Klepsch (2010) has shown that in many slum tours all over the world, the beneficiaries are often private entrepreneurs that are not necessarily from the destination itself but professional national tour-operating companies. These new urban spaces offer multiple opportunities to the local community linking entrepreneurship with initiative: tour guiding, accommodation, gastronomy, souvenir shops and local entertainment (Rogerson, 2004: 251). However, while, for instance, there is an increased emergence of black-owned tour-operating companies in township tourism in South Africa, often tourism businesses are still white owned (Nemasetoni & Rogerson, 2005). Another example is in Cambodia's Tonle Sap Lake where commercial tour operators take visitors by boats through the floating villages to literally stare at poverty. Here, interaction is staged and benefits hardly go to the communities in need.

In contrast to the former, many ethnic districts, however, such as Harlem's Afro-American community have benefitted from the interest of the visitors to develop tourism-related businesses in Harlem, New York, contributing to the regeneration of the district. Hoffman defines the transformation from:

- A distinct 'ghetto' economy to increased integration into mainstream urban economy.
- Social/spatial isolation and exclusion to Social capital and contact.
- Negatively perceived culture to Revalorised culture.
- Political patronage to Political Player.
- Social policy to economic policy. (Hoffman, 2003: 105)

While economic and sociocultural impacts on host communities have been widely studied, they have not received much attention particularly when it comes to slum host communities (Freire-Medeiros, 2012). Very few studies have tried to explain why residents perceive tourism the way they do (Woosnam, 2012). Implicit in much of the research on residents is the idea that tourism is a disruption to community life leading to inherent conflicts between tourists and residents or residents and the social structure of the community (Woosnam, 2012: 315). The present literature on residents' attitudes does not address how residents feel towards tourism and how these feelings might influence their behaviour (Woosnam, 2012: 315).

Most of the research on the attitudes of residents has been undertaken in the developed and industrialised world with only a few studies in the developing world (Nunkoo & Gursoy, 2012: 244). Moreover, the majority of research focusing on pro-poor tourism and community-based tourism has been centred on rural tourism, and cities have been largely neglected in the discussion of those concepts (Mowforth et al., 2008). Common to all research is the idea that tourism changes the host community and residents. Reisinger (2014) for example analyses the changes in the light of Mezirow's transformation theory based on 11 phases and ending with building competence and self-confidence in new roles and relationships. Only some of the community destinations under scrutiny in this book may have reached that latest phase and are able to avoid exploitation.

What We Know about Minority (Migrant) Communities

The widely defended idea is that the economic impacts of tourism are mostly valued by the host community and that tourism contributes to income and the standard of living (Nunkoo & Gursoy, 2012). In the case of many segregated districts, the community forms a homogeneous group when tourist development is orchestrated by outsiders. In that case, the community does not benefit from the tourism development, but in some cases maybe indirectly through donations or the funding of a community centre as is the case in Dharavi in Mumbai.

While the visitors seek an authentic experience when visiting slums or ethnic quarters, they mostly only encounter a sanitised version or frontstage experience of the community. For example, communities dress up for visitors and perform selected or modified expressions of their culture (see Chapter 9). Alternatively, tour operators might pretend that a slum dwelling is a genuine family home when it is not (e.g. in Chapter 6). Lin (2011: 257) notes that guided tours give access to the 'internal operation of an ethnic community'. However, this process generates both positive and negative effects, including accelerating economic development and broader social changes, but with some cultural compromises:

> The conversion of the 'back regions' of ethnic neighbourhoods and business enclaves into 'staged front regions' of ethnic tourism involves a valorization of authentic ethnic traditions. At the same time, some of the authenticity of ethnic culture is degraded and denurtured, through the commercial aspects of ethnic tourism and the creation of kitsch. (Lin, 2011)

It is widely recognised that understanding the perception of the visited community is essential to sustainable tourism development. In the context of the ethical debate that surrounds particularly slum tourism, this almost absence of conceptual research seems somewhat surprising. Freire-Meideros (2012: 176) suggests that this scarcity of research is due to two groups of factors:

(1) Operational factors linked to the large area of investigation if wishing to analyse all directly and indirectly involved persons.
(2) Socio-epistemological factors including the obvious distance between the researcher and the local residents related to social class, lifestyle and language.

Moreover, up to now, a lot of research in slum tourism has been undertaken by Western researchers in developing countries involving from the start intercultural challenges and very likely a postcolonial positionality on both sides making an exchange between community members and researchers a difficult task, not only for obvious linguistic reasons. However, some research exists showing that tours of impoverished areas which are commonly criticised for being unethical are actually perceived as being of interest to the residents in these areas. People are often neither particularly positive nor negative towards tourism (Conway, 2008; Freire-Meideros, 2013; Kieti & Magio, 2013) but the visits provide recognition of residents who are often stigmatised (Freire-Meideros, 2012, 2013; Mekawy, 2012) and are often considered as a possibility for counterpresentation (Freire-Meideros, 2013).

However, in many cases, the local community, the object of the tourist gaze, does not benefit economically from tourism. Indeed, in many places, tours are organised by private tour operators and entrepreneurs that do not redistribute benefits to the community. Moreover, tourists generally buy little (or nothing) during their visit and often tour operators have their preferred sellers and artists. Depending on the type of tour, tour guides discourage tourists from getting off the bus or out of the car (Freire-Medeiros, 2009a; Mowforth & Munt, 2008; Rogerson, 2004). Yet, examples exist where local people are involved in multiple ways in the tourism industry: accommodation, guiding, craft, art and many more. While obviously a whole community cannot participate in and benefit actively from tourism, small-scale, unregulated, labour-intensive and sometimes even illegal tourism enterprises are an important feature and contribute to the diversification of the economy in developing countries (Gladstone, 2005: 32).

Sustainable tourism development is generally linked to active participation and community involvement. Particularly in developing and emerging countries, this aspect is promoted by international agencies such as the International Monetary Fund (IMF) and the World Bank (Cejas, 2006: 224). As we have already seen above, tour operators are thus interested in the cultural value of the tours, which changes the negative images and stereotypes of slums. Yet, the tour operators also want to invest in the economic value of the tours by increasing visitor numbers (Zeiderman, 2006: 12). In terms of community benefits, two statements can be made with regard to this analysis: there is evidence that those companies solely or mainly focusing on slum tours may be more concerned with community benefits due to the fact that the main objective of the tour operator is different. That does not mean that diversified tour operators which do not mainly focus on slum tourism cannot also be concerned with community benefits. Participation and involvement in community projects and social improvement projects are perceived as an important feature of slum tourism and are important to slum tour-operating businesses. However, the size and the number of slum settlements make it almost impossible to perceive improvements as significant benefits. Nonetheless, participation and upgrading can help progress the overall situation of the local community as well as their living conditions little by little and thus benefit not only some individuals but the community as a whole (Conway, 2008). Nevertheless, scholars concerned with community-based and pro-poor tourism concepts criticise that:

- Existing power structures remain unchallenged (Gibson, 2009: 531) and the tourism industry in developing countries remains largely dominated by Western approaches – pro-poor tourism projects shift responsibility for poverty onto the poor while they merely recognise the principal actors (Gibson, 2009: 531).
- Meaningful community participation, relationship building and ethical decision-making are missing (Duffy & Smith, 2003; Scheyvens, 2002; Wright et al., 2007).
- Effects of poverty relief may be moderate (Blake et al., 2008: 112) and benefits from tourism expansion do not benefit the poorest, except when the government channels earnings directly to the lowest-income group.
- Communal management options in the tourism industry have been acknowledged as complex and time consuming and appear very difficult to achieve (Klepsch, 2010: 94–95; Murphy & Roe, 2004: 121–122).

What is Missing in Research?

As previously mentioned, there are relatively few studies analysing in depth the impact of tourism on host communities or residents in the ethnic and minority groups discussed in this book. One difficulty lies in the fact that these tourist assets are based to a large extent on the simple presence of residents and that often they are not involved in the tourism development. Analysing residents' attitudes towards tourism (and tourists) should also include the situation of the local economy, the existing degree of tourism development of the zone and tourist density (Vargas-Sanchez et al., 2011: 462) as well as sociocultural and identity aspects. Hughes (2006, 2010) suggests that few studies have examined host attitudes towards certain types of tourists who visit an area. For example, gay tourists may be attractive in economic terms but locals may dislike and disapprove of their lifestyles. Ethnic tourists may also be subjected to similar prejudices because of their apparent differences from the majority society, especially if they are confused with local immigrants. A central question is related to identity matters. Indeed, many of the communities discussed in this book have been displaced in some way, they are migrants for different kinds of reasons and their present community has been constructed in a new context and may or may not bear a resemblance to the same communities 'back home'. For example, in the African district of Matonge in Brussels (Belgium), various nationalities (and cultures) from central Africa identify with the quarter as it provides them with specific goods not readily available in other parts of the country. People come to the slums from different areas of a country, people arrive from the countryside all over a country. While they often settle in the slum areas with migrants from their home region, they do not necessarily have a common background.

Conclusion

It is clear that more research is needed not only on the impacts of tourism on ethnic and minority communities' lives, but also on their attitudes to tourists, the nature and extent of encounters and interactions, and the mutual gaze generally (Maoz, 2006). The following chapters go some way to filling some of these gaps in the research. Yvette Reisinger and Omar Moufakkir consider the host gaze in a number of different cultural contexts, arguing that mutual respect and a better understanding of each other's cultures is essential to improving relationships and enhancing experiences on both sides. Joshua Schmidt shows how different communities living within the same space perceive existing and new developments, including tourism. It is often assumed that communities living in tourism destinations share the same feelings and emotions as each other, but they are highly variable depending on social, cultural economic, temporal and other factors. Anya Diekmann and Nimit Chowdary consider how slum tourism to some of the poorest communities in the world is perceived by their inhabitants. Slum tourism is commonly thought to be intrusive and voyeuristic, but this chapter shows that such assumptions may be too simplistic and that host communities can feel more positive about tourism development and visitation than one might expect from the apparently limited economic or financial benefits.

4 Reflections on Ethnic and Minority Communities as a Tool for Improving Intercultural Change in Tourism

Yvette Reisinger and Omar Moufakkir

Introduction

Academic literature argues that contact with other cultures offers the opportunity for developing mutual appreciation, understanding, respect and liking, developing positive attitudes and reducing ethnic prejudices, stereotyping and racial tension (see Reisinger, 2009; Reisinger & Turner, 2003). Contact with other cultures improves communication skills (Cushner & Karim, 2004; Ledwith & Seymour, 2001; Milstein, 2005), increases independence and enhances tolerance and cross-cultural skills (Bock, 1970; Cushner & Karim, 2004; Gudykunst, 1998; Noy, 2003; O'Reilly, 2006; Tucker, 2005), develops a culturally relativist mindset (Ryan & Hellmundt, 2005) and allows individuals to become more mature, well-rounded and culturally enriched and sensitive (Van Hoof & Verbeteen, 2005). It is argued that contact with foreign cultures encourages cultural learning that leads to a reduction in world conflict (Gudykunst, 1998; Huntington, 1993) and improves world relations (Noy, 2003; O'Reilly, 2006). According to Brown (2013), contact with other cultures leads to the development of an international perspective; it not only transforms individuals into global citizens with cultural knowledge, tolerance and understanding, but the acquisition of culture-specific skills also equips them to operate in an increasingly globalised multicultural business environment.

Today, the most significant manifestations of an increasingly globalised multicultural environment are immigration and the growing number of ethnic groups in host countries. The populations of many developed countries worldwide are currently becoming more ethnically diverse than in the past due in part to individuals choosing to immigrate to these countries. The Unites States has the largest foreign-born population in the world, which is home to nearly 40 million foreign residents or more than 13% of the total population (US Census Bureau, 2010). The biggest portion of newcomers comes from Latin America (53%), especially Mexico, followed by Asia (28%) and Europe (12%). In 2010, ethnic minorities represented one third of the US population and are expected to become the majority by 2025. In particular, Hispanics and Asians are predicted to become one of the largest minority groups in the United States in the next 20 years (US Census Bureau, 2012). In Canada, the foreign-born population represents 10% of the total population and it is expected that by 2030 nearly 25% of people living in Canada will have been born elsewhere. The biggest portion of newcomers to Canada comes from Asia and Latin America (World Bank, 2011). In Australia, a country that depends on immigration, almost 26% of the population has been born overseas, mainly in Asia, and this percentage is predicted to increase (Australian Bureau of Statistics, 2013) (see Table 4.1). In Europe, foreign citizens account for 6.6% of the EU27 population, including 2.5% living in another member state and 4.1% are non-EU citizens (Eurostat, 2012). Large minority groups, especially of Islamic background, constitute sizeable communities in European countries including Germany, the Netherlands, Austria, Belgium, Switzerland, Spain and the UK (NationMaster, 2012) (see Table 4.2).

The increased immigration and the number of ethnic groups represent enormous opportunities for growth and development in host destinations. It is argued that a high number of residents being born overseas increases outbound tourism (as the immigrant to the host country returns to their home country for short visits) and inbound tourism (as the proportion of visitors coming to the host country for the purpose of 'visiting friends and relatives' [VFR] increases). Also, the new residents of the host country promote their new country as a destination when travelling back to their home country. In addition, they offer accommodation to their

Table 4.1 Number of immigrants and as a percentage of state population

Country	Population	Immigrants as a percentage of country population
Australia	23,000,000	26.0
Canada	34,500,000	19.0
Europe,	740,000	7.1
including EU27	500,000	6.6
New Zealand	4,410,000	15.5
United States	315,000,000	13.5

Sources: Australian Bureau of Statistics (2013); US Census Bureau (2012); World Bank (2011)

Table 4.2 Number of immigrants in Europe and as a percentage of state population

Country	No. of immigrants	Their percentage of state population
Germany	10,144,000	12.31
France	6,471,000	10.18
UK	5,408,000	8.98
Spain	4,790,000	10.79
Italy	2,519,000	4.28
Switzerland	1,660,000	22.89
Netherlands	1,638,000	10.05
Austria	1,234,000	14.90
Sweden	1,117,000	12.30
Greece	974,000	8.66
Portugal	764,000	7.20
Belgium	719,000	6.90
Denmark	389,000	7.16
Norway	3,44,000	7.37
Luxembourg	147,000	37.42
Finland	156,000	2.96

Source: NationMaster (2012)

friends and relatives, which can considerably lower the cost of holidaying in the host country. They form business links with partners in the country of their birth and hence promote business tourism (Seetaram, 2008). The results of the study by Seetaram (2008) strongly support the hypothesis that when the number of residents born from a different country rises, the number of arrivals from that country increases although the effect is felt with a two-year lag. The results also point out that the effect of immigration on tourism demand in Australia is relatively higher than that of growth in trade flows and population growth (Seetaram, 2008).

The increased immigration and the growing number of ethnic groups make their host countries increasingly more ethnically diverse. As a result, cultural differences within host countries are increasing, whereas they are decreasing among countries (Reisinger & Crotts, 2010). This implies that the number of distinct subcultures within host nations is growing and they culturally differ from their hosts' dominant culture. Consequently, with an increasing ethnic diversity in host societies, it is important to consider the significance of this diversity to international tourism. According to UNWTO (2010), cultural diversity contributes to the social and economic development of destination countries, their cultural enrichment and the enhancement of the tourism product. Cultural minority groups provide labour for the travel, tourism and hospitality sectors (the supply side of tourism) and are also important sources of guests (the demand side of tourism).

Ethnic and minority groups as a tourist attraction

It is a given fact that tourists choose a vacation destination for its uniqueness, attractions, facilities, peace and stability. However, the importance of ethnic diversity in promoting tourism is ranked among the first in importance. What makes a given destination more alluring is its culture, especially the customs and traditions of the people inhabiting it. Different people of the world have their own distinct cultures and way of living that set them apart from others. So, what could be an ordinary part of daily life for someone might be a mysterious and awesome sight for someone else. People instinctively desire to discover what is different and strange. The need for a sense of newness stimulates their eagerness for developing relationships and acquaintances. And that keeps tourism alive (Ghebrihiwet, 2009).

International tourism depends on the encouragement of diversity of cultures, languages and traditions. Under ideal circumstances, ethnic and minority groups can be tourist attractions if their cultural diversity is celebrated and strengthened. Cultural diversity is a blessing that enables the fostering of mutual respect and coexistence. This subsequently secures harmony, stability and peace in any given society.

Case study

Eritrea (meaning 'red land') is a country in the Horn of Africa, bordered by Sudan to the west, Ethiopia to the south and Djibouti to the south-east. Its north-eastern and eastern parts have an extensive coastline along the Red Sea, a population of 6 million and an area of 485,000 square miles – about the size of Pennsylvania, US. Eritrea is gifted with fascinating landscapes and locations that serve as tourist destinations, including marine resources, historical and archaeological sites and many buildings of colonial legacies, including Turkish and Italian colonisers, that are located mostly in Massawa, Asmara, Keren and other cities of the country. Efficient transportation, first-class hotels, and tourist and travel agencies also contribute significantly to the flourishing tourism sector in Eritrea. However, a crucial aspect of tourism in Eritrea is its cultural diversity, which Eritrea is specially endowed with. Eritrea is a multi-ethnic country, home of nine recognised, different ethnic groups speaking three official languages (Tigrinya, Arabic and English), mostly Afro-Asiatic languages. The adornment and clothing of the different ethnic groups, their hairstyles, their houses embellished with creative handicrafts, their customs' and traditions are so remarkably beautiful that they leave a lasting memory imprinted in one's mind. Harmony and mutual respect for one another are exhibited by all members of the different ethnic groups and they are exemplary. The shared experience of a harmonious coexistence constantly enriches and strengthens the Eritrean people's common values and unity. In fact, unity in diversity is the basic social fibre of the Eritrean people's culture (Ghebrihiwet, 2009).

Ethnic and minority groups as a source of conflict

Despite the fact that minority groups help build up the cultural capital of the host country, making that country a more culturally interesting tourism destination (Seetaram, 2008), there are also some negative aspects to the growing number of ethnic groups that in many instances include social tension, violence and hate. It is often reported that cultural diversity in most parts of the world serves as a cause for division. Many countries today are constantly involved in conflicts of racial intolerance, political disorder and division along religious lines, which adversely affect their progress. As such, ethnic and minority groups are also viewed as a problem rather than a tourist attraction.

Host gaze upon ethnic and minority groups

The explosion in world migration has certain consequences for public opinion about immigration, perceptions of ethnic and minority groups and their importance to host countries. Most recently, attention has been drawn to the growing tensions between natives and minority groups who are perceived as an economic threat and an unwanted cultural invasion of natives' customs and traditions, and a problem for national security and welfare (Alonso & da Fonseca, 2011). For example, there are about 350,000 people of Moroccan origin living in the Netherlands, representing 19% of the total Dutch immigrant minority groups (Statistics Netherlands, 2005).

Their reputation in Dutch society is overwhelmingly negative. The Dutch see the Moroccans living in the Netherlands as criminals, causing trouble, danger and disturbances on the streets, mistreating gays and women and carrying out robberies and muggings (Blass, 2009). The Dutch fear Muslim violence, foreign values and losing their own values. The Dutch people believe they are losing their country to minority groups that they can no longer control. According to the leader of one of the Dutch political parties, the Netherlands is losing its cultural authenticity to a culture of backwardness and violence, to the Moroccans who go through life scoffing and spitting and beating up innocent people, making the streets unsafe, threatening and abusing locals, but who, however, happily accept Dutch benefits, homes and doctors but not Dutch standards and values (Wilders, 2008). This raises the immigration-integration drama between natives and minorities. Shadid (2005) argues that the ongoing media reporting and the way the media is portraying Moroccans have a direct and indirect influence on the negative image of this particular group. The Dutch media is reporting about the Moroccans as one homogeneous group (Fennema, 2001). Homogenisation leads to stereotyping and thus to stigmatisation.

Such public opinion and media content no longer go unnoticed in tourism studies, especially that a number of developing countries represent major tourist destinations for international tourists from developed countries. Ethnic and minority groups influence destination perceptions as well as the tourism product and service culture from different perspectives: first, as a tourist attraction through their cultural differences; second, as national tourists; third, as international tourists; fourth, as diaspora tourists; and fifth as host communities, whether in their country of origin or in their country of residence.

Case study

By examining perceptions of Morocco as a tourism destination by potential Dutch tourists and how these affect the destination's image and travel propensity, Moufakkir (2008) shows that the Dutch have a negative perception not only of the Moroccan community living in the Netherlands but also of Morocco as a country. The negative perceptions of the Moroccan living in Morocco are even more negative than the perceptions of the Moroccans living in the Netherlands. However, Dutch tourists positively perceive Morocco as a tourism destination. Unfortunately, although they seem to have knowledge of and appreciation for Morocco as a touristic place, they seem to lack knowledge of and have negative perceptions of the Moroccan people. Only a minority of respondents wanted to learn more about the Moroccan culture, while the majority remained indifferent. According to Fridgen (1991), people hold negative stereotypes about other people when they lack knowledge about each other. Also, respondents who have never visited Morocco were not inclined to visit Morocco in the future because of their perceptions about (a) the Moroccans living in Morocco, (b) the Moroccans living in the Netherlands and (c) Moroccan women.

Negative perceptions seem to have a big impact on travel intentions and visitations. If members of a native group hold negative perceptions about an ethnic minority group at home, they are less likely to visit the country of origin of that ethnic group for tourism purposes (Moufakkir, 2008). According to Rosello (2001), people who perceive their own homeland as threatened by dangerous foreigners do not want to encounter these foreigners elsewhere. In the light of the increasing number of immigrants and minority groups in host countries, particular attention should be paid to this notion, especially when cultural differences are important elements of shaping tourists' and hosts' mutual perceptions. A clear understanding of tourist perceptions is crucial for developing a sustainable tourism industry and for developing successful positioning strategies (Reich, 1999; Sonmez & Sirakaya, 2002). The decision to travel comes from a perception. Negative perceptions and misconceptions affect the propensity to travel. Perceptions help to understand the target market and play a major role in determining the most effective position of the destination in the marketplace (Reich, 1999).

Reisinger *et al.* (2012) identify negative Turkish hosts' gaze upon Russian tourists. Arrogance, a high consumption of alcohol, being loud, disrespectful of locals and tourists, unwilling to socialise with other tourists and unwilling or refusing to speak any other language but Russian are identified as typically Russian. There are no clear positive characteristics, such as 'friendly' or 'well-behaved' mentioned by Turkish hosts. Similarly, Chan (2006) finds the Vietnamese perceptions of the Chinese very negative. The Chinese are viewed as 'making a lot more requests, complaints and troubles than others', 'littering the hotel rooms and smoking on beds' (Chan, 2006: 195). Reference is made to unsocial Chinese behaviour. The above examples of the perceptions that host communities have about the selected ethnic groups imply the potential for growing social tensions between both groups and a lack of acceptance of culturally different groups by locals. It is clear that some ethnic groups are not wanted due to their strongly manifested different 'traditions' and/or 'different lifestyles'. The following case study shows how a host community resists the influences of international tourists on their ways of life.

Case study

The Kuna host community of Panama resists massive tourism and makes efforts to counteract the loss of their traditional ways of life. According to Savener (2013), Kuna men and women do not initiate communication with tourists, treating them mostly with ambivalent indifference or mild disinterest. Kuna who do not want to be bothered with tourists seek solace in distant villages that lack tourist lodging. Kuna mothers often pull toddlers inside, close windows and doors to prevent peering and protect themselves from the curious faces of tourists. Although many of these tourists come to learn about the Kuna, what they learn is limited to myopic observations of traditional dress, the landscape of clustered palm-thatched cane houses and a few personally constructed museums on various islands. Kuna men discourage Kuna women from interacting with foreigners. The Kuna do not allow tourists to participate in community rituals or celebrations, although some are occasionally permitted to watch. They clearly forbid tourist cameras at communal chicha preparations – an elaborate and athletic process involving jumping on logs to press sugar cane juices and boiling the frothy juice over an active fire – a process overseen by dozens of Kuna men and women. The Kuna have little patience for irritations, demands or orders. Tourists who enjoy the freedom of unplanned travel may encounter some difficulties in Kuna Yala as their demands are not always met. Those tourists who expect a certain level of hospitality experienced in other destinations may be upset. When their dissatisfaction escalates and they complain and/or raise voices, Kuna men do not take offence; they just go away. They even laugh and joke about tourists. Savener (2013) notes that Kuna Yala is a vector of power inversion for the tourist experience. The Kuna remind tourists that Kuna Yala is not their home; tourists are not necessarily welcome. The tourist is a visitor and the power balance created by mass tourism is inverted. The Kuna challenge the expectations of tourists. They resist cultural diffusion due to their voluntary spatial isolation and their unique manner of communicating only *in ways that serve them.*

The perceived incompatibility of cultural groups and their values creates a negative effect. This argument is supported by an extensive literature (see Reisinger, 2009; Reisinger & Turner, 2003) showing that the greater the dissimilarity among the groups, the less likely they are to agree with each other's views and beliefs, the less likely they are to interact with each other, and the more likely they are to be in conflict. The tendency of individuals to disassociate from dissimilar others of different values or religious beliefs makes communication and relationships more difficult. Perceived cultural incompatibility increases uncertainty, anxiety and social distance. Those who are perceived as culturally dissimilar are also perceived less positively, whereas those who are perceived as similar are usually perceived more positively. This supports Blau's (1977) argument suggesting that the rate of human interaction, especially across different cultures, between people with different characteristics decreases as the population increases in heterogeneity.

Does Contact with Ethnic and Minority Groups Improve Intercultural Change?

The literature disagrees with the commonly accepted claim that the presence of an ethnic community can foster cultural awareness and tolerance in the host society. Academic literature argues that contact with cultural 'others' may develop negative attitudes, stereotypes and prejudices and increase tension, hostility, suspicion and often violent attacks. Cultural gaps among groups can generate clashes of values, conflict and disharmonies that lead to tension, misunderstanding, exclusion from mutual activities, feelings of inferiority, resentment and rejection, difficulty in forming relationships, communication problems, irritation and stress, problems of adjustment, ethnocentrism and even threat (see the literature in Reisinger, 2009; Reisinger & Turner, 2003).

Alongside an appreciation of the cultural diversity of ethnic and minority groups and the acknowledged advantages of contact with cultural 'others' there is also a simultaneous tendency of various cultural groups to isolate and gravitate towards the same culture members (Brown, 2013). One of the reasons for cultural gravitation and segregation is shared cultural heritage. By belonging to the same group, members of ethnic groups have a comforting sense of shared origins, and believe that they are distinctive from other groups in some way (Arora, 2005). Social interaction among same nationality members is influenced by the ease of communication, emotional and instrumental support that is a powerfully reassuring antidote to the stressors involved in cultural transition or adjustment, on behalf of either minority groups or locals. Cultural isolation or segregation is often motivated by the need to find safety in numbers that strengthens the group identification (Brown, 2013).

Some members of the local community are portrayed by minority groups as unfriendly and at times threatening. One of the most commonly cited obstacles to interaction with locals is the unapproachability of local people. For example, British exclusivity and disinterest are often perceived as powerful deterrents that provoke strong reactions among minority members (Brown, 2013). In the model of intergroup conflict (Branscombe & Wann, 1994), the tendency to group together features as a common reaction to perceived external attacks or a fear of discrimination. Correctly or not, sometimes perceived racism lies behind the lack of contact with locals. Considerable evidence exists that race can influence the way that individuals evaluate people (Tadajewski, 2012) e.g. who should have access to goods and services (e.g. Clark, 1996; Crockett & Wallendorf, 2004; Rugh & Massey, 2010; Wolff, 2006) or how people should be treated (e.g. Booms & Ward, 1969; Harris et al., 2005; Mallinson & Brewster, 2005). It is also very unlikely that a person who is perceived as a racist or who has developed a phobia against some minority groups would travel to the homeland of that group to experience its tourism products (Moufakkir, 2008).

The above raises a question about the benefits and importance of ethnic and minority groups and their cultural diversity to the development of intercultural communication and understanding, the reduction of stereotypes and prejudice, or broadening one's cultural horizons. The above perceived benefits may be hard to obtain.

Social inclusion and integration

There are concerns about the social inclusion, integration and cultural harmonisation of minority groups because of their different cultural and religious backgrounds and associated lifestyles as well as questionable economic and social benefits derived from immigration and ethnic diversity (Moufakkir, 2008). More recently, politicians have acknowledged the failed integration of ethnic minorities in their host countries that may also have a negative effect on tourism. However, some argue that minority groups try to improve their integration into the host community; they usually accept the fact that their life opportunities and those of their children depend on their participation in the mainstream culture and institutions operating in the language of that culture. They do not necessarily need to constantly distinguish themselves from the majority and recreate their identity. However, this notion may not hold. Some ethnic groups may be resistant to change and disapprove of many of their host's cultural norms and values. As such, this requires considering the unique needs and values of minority groups. This also requires an understanding of them and how quickly the minority groups abandon aspects of their native culture and become fully assimilated into their adopted host culture. Given that acculturation often involves the interaction of multiple cultural legacies, the process can be characterised at times as a process of assimilation while at other times as a great need to maintain a traditional culture. Some individuals assimilate on certain levels, but at the same time hold onto other culture traits.

Case study

By examining the acculturation process of foreign-born residents of the US, Reisinger and Crotts (2012) identify the degree to which acculturation takes place and its effect on individuals. A sample of Korean-born residents of the US is surveyed regarding their socio-demographic and cultural characteristics and lifestyle preferences and compared to their host country members. The study results show that acculturation of Korean-born residents occurs, as measured by language preferences and cultural measures, but only to a limited extent. Time, age, marital status, spouse's country of birth and preferred country of residence have only modest influence on acculturation. Most foreign-born Korean residents of the US maintain a strong preference for their native culture. Marrying a US-born individual influences their acculturation, whereas marrying a Korean-born spouse limits acculturation. Those Korean-born individuals residing in the US who frequent Korean-American businesses are more Korean than American in their thoughts, values and behaviours regardless of their length of residence. Even though their desire may be to remain in the host culture, most maintain a strong preference for their native language, food, social environments and values derived from their cultural legacy. It is clear that acculturation does occur, but only to a limited extent, especially during the lifespan of the first-generation residents. The percentage of one's life lived in the US has only a modest influence on acculturation.

Ultimate integration of minority groups into the mainstream society may not be possible because of large differences between the host and guest original cultures. Gladwell (2008) offers a unique perspective on the enduring impact of cultural legacy on one's beliefs, attitudes and behaviours. 'Each of us has his or her own distinct personality. But overlaid on top of that are tendencies and assumptions and reflexes handed down to us by the history of the community we grew up in, and those differences can be extraordinarily specific' (Gladwell, 2008: 175). It is obvious that strongly enrooted cultural values preclude individuals from being fully integrated in the host society. Firmly established cultural values may not allow minority groups to properly blend into and function in the host country. Naturally, a high degree of variability always exists: some easily assimilate into the dominant culture and others resist such assimilation, while still others pick and choose the selected aspects to adopt. Grabowski (2013) notes that some members of minority groups have difficulties with articulating their ethnicity and nationality, and may feel that they are different people depending on the social situation.

Excluded communities

Millions of people from all corners of the world leave their motherland for other destinations for economic, political or other reasons, in search of a better or a different life. Immigrants bring their bags of culture with them wherever they go. The intensity of the interaction between the mainstream culture and the minority culture becomes stronger as immigrants spend more time in the host country. While ethnic minority groups contribute to the livelihood of the mainstream culture in so many ways, including the economy and cultural enrichment, ethnic minorities, in some contexts, can be seen as troublemakers and culture polluters (Stephenson & Hughes, 2005). An important societal sphere that ethnic groups are excluded from in many communities is leisure and tourism participation. Leisure and tourism participation are important integration facilitators. In many leisure and tourism contexts, participation in some leisure and tourism venues is smaller for ethnic minorities, especially visible ethnic minorities, compared to that of native residents. Stephenson and Hughes (2005) note that the perception of discrimination also acts as 'a barrier to leisure and tourism enjoyment.

When people immigrate to a new country, they inevitably encounter many challenges, including adjusting to new customs, languages, social/political systems and social norms. Tsai and Coleman (1999: 243) report that 'Throughout the process of leisure engagement, people are exposed to various constraints which can affect their leisure preferences, inhibit their desire to undertake new activities, reduce their enjoyment in leisure, and limit their full involvement in leisure'. Jackson (1993) identifies six categories of leisure constraint: social isolation, accessibility, personal reasons, cost, time and facility. These sets of constraints are related to three broad dimensions: intrapersonal, (e.g. personality, past experience, self-efficacy), interpersonal (e.g. authority figures, peers, family, strangers) and structural (e.g. facilities, gender, money, ethnicity, institutions, time, distance, transport, awareness of promotion, competitive choice) (Clarke & Critcher, 1985; Crawford et al., 1991; Kelly, 1987; McDonald & Murphy, 2008; Raymore, 2002). Marginality and ethnicity theories explain constraints to participation (see Moufakkir, 2011). More recently, discrimination theory was added to the minorities' constraints portfolio. Discriminatory attitudes make certain minority groups less motivated to engage in tourism and leisure activities while in the 'host' country (Moufakkir, 2011; Stephenson, 2004; Stephenson & Hughes, 2005).

Case studies

Stephenson and Hughes (2005) identify several factors restricting Afro-Caribbean groups in the UK from visiting certain places in the UK and enjoying the benefits of participation in leisure. For example, Afro-Caribbean minority groups are found to be reluctant to visit the British countryside because it is not accessible to them for the following reasons: access to the countryside or to other 'non-indigenous' places by minorities may not only constitute a threat of criminality, but more importantly it may represent a threat of what may also be termed 'pollution of authenticity of culture'. While perceptions of 'unwelcomeness' may lead to negotiation of existing constraints, they may also limit access to desired participation. In the tourism context, minorities prefer to visit places that are perceived to be secure. Philipp (1993) attributes the lack of participation in leisure to hostility or racism.

Similarly, the September 11 terrorists' attacks in the US made international travel difficult for people of Arab and Muslim origins. Racial observations 'carry greater poignancy since the 11th September 2001 attacks in America, which seriously aggravated the difficulties experienced by ethnic minority travelers. Due to "terrorist concerns", Asian and Muslim travelers have been subjected to hostile treatment from immigration officials, aviation authorities and other passengers' (Stephenson & Hughes, 2005: 152). Home-grown terrorist attacks like the ones in London and Madrid made participation in international and domestic tourism even more cumbersome for visible ethnic minorities.

In a study about tourism behaviour and the constraints of 'immigrants' of Turkish origin who live in Germany, Moufakkir (2011) reports that the respondents are interested in both domestic and international travel, with a bigger preference for travel outside Germany. Respondents who are born in Turkey are less likely to feel comfortable travelling inside

Germany than those who are born in Germany. They are also less inclined to visit rural places in Germany. The findings relate to the process of acculturation and to the perception of discrimination. The feeling of belonging to mainstream culture or otherwise has an effect on tourism behaviour.

Conclusion

The growing number of ethnic and minority groups in host populations no doubt increases the need for taking ethnic values into account. There are countries that have long been considered to be racial melting pots (e.g. Australia, Canada, US) for their abilities to absorb immigrants into a single national identity where immigrants impact their hosts and hosts impact the immigrants. Since information technology makes it easier today for ethnic minorities to maintain their linguistic and cultural ties to the land of their birth, these countries may no longer be called melting pots; they are better described as salad bowls. This calls for particular attention to be paid to ethnic diversity in host countries and the effects that this diversity has on tourism.

The value of ethnic and minority groups has become a controversial topic in many countries. Debates revolve around the increasing numbers of minority groups, the rise of nationalism and identity crisis. This calls for extensive tourism research. Tourism academics should explore further the assumption of ethnic diversity as being a tourist attraction versus a source of conflict, perceptions of minority groups and their effect on destination selection and intentions to visit, and the impact of ethnic and minority groups on social integration and tourism consumption.

The paradox is that while in many contexts the ethnicity that is portrayed in ethnic food and cuisine and ethnic dance, arts and culture is highly valued, appreciated and consumed, the ethnicity that relates to immigration remains a concern for public policy, politics and public opinion. Tourism studies have yet to seriously engage in the discussion about the effect of ethnic minorities on travel propensity, intention to visit and destination choice. Such reflections can provide us with tools for improving intercultural change in tourism and between cultures.

5 Shifting Perceptions: Negotiating Place and Space in the Israeli Desert Frontier Town of Mitzpe Ramon

Joshua Schmidt

All experience is construed experience
Geertz, 1973: 405

Introduction

This chapter examines how subjective feelings affect personal aware-ness by considering a case in which the same environment holds multi-ple interpretations for its diverse inhabitants. As its theoretical basis, the chapter uses Tuan's (1977) seminal distinction between 'space' – associated with mobility, openness and independence – and 'place' – equated with security, stability and safety. According to Tuan, these concepts, fashioned from a composite of factors including a person's ethnic, economic, social and spiritual background, frame how individuals make sense of the com-munity, neighbourhood, town or nation in which they reside. The chapter, therefore, applies these complementary terms in its discussion of Mitzpe Ramon, a small but ethnically diverse town situated in the remote Israeli Negev desert, to analyse the dissimilar ways in which the different local communities variously perceive their shared environment.

Mitzpe Ramon (pop. 5000) is inhabited by communities of different sociocultural origin and orientation. Having few common experiential denominators, these diverse communities coexist in parallel socio-economic realities and largely abide by a casual 'live and let live' interaction. Overall, the town's local residents divide into two basic categories: those who came to Mitzpe Ramon due to government settlement policies and those whose move to this peripheral location was a personal choice. Arriving during dif-ferent periods and under disparate circumstances and conditions, the vary-ing reasons connected with their appearance in Mitzpe Ramon continue to frame these communities' idiosyncratic attitudes and practices and distinguish among them.

Mitzpe is unique in that it is situated alongside *Makhtesh Ramon* (Ramon Crater), a world-renowned erosion cirque. An internationally recognised term, the *makhtesh* consists of geomorphological anticlines which expose layers of the earth's crust that are normally covered in rubble and vegetation. Affording a rare glimpse into 200,000 millennia of the earth's geological processes, the massive (40×8 km) Ramon Crater forms the basis for Israel's largest national park (Mazor, 1992).

As the town's hallmark, the *makhtesh* is variously conceptualised by Mitzpe's different resident communities. Until recently, the dominant point of view belonged to the town's veteran community – Jews from Arab countries in North Africa and the Middle East who in Hebrew are collectively known as *Eidot Ha'mizrax* (lit. Eastern-Oriental communities) or *Mizraxim* ('Orientals'; *Mizraxi* in singular). Since members of this group were settled in Mitzpe Ramon by the government, who furnished them with housing and employment, they likewise assumed their handlers' initial perceptions of the *makhtesh* as a source of raw materials to be mined and shipped north for use in the construction industries. Yet, recently arriving environmentally conscious newcomers are altering this perspective so that the current dominant opinion is that the chief asset of the *makhtesh* is its natural beauty, which should be preserved and appreciated through sustainable ecotourism.

Based on extensive ethnographic research of Mitzpe Ramon and its multi-ethnic communities, this chapter compares and contrasts the degrees to which veteran and newcomer groups are involved in Mitzpe's transformation from a peripheral mining town to a popular ecotourism destination. Using the *makhtesh* as a point of reference, the chapter relates how newly arriving residents are developing its natural bounty in directions that earlier inhabitants had either ignored and/or were without the financial support and sociopolitical inclination to pursue. The next sections therefore provide a brief contextual history of Mitzpe Ramon and then portray the ways in which each of these groups – long-standing, working-class *mizraxi* residents and secular and Orthodox middle-class newcomers – varyingly relate to Mitzpe Ramon and the adjoining Ramon environment.

Regarding methodology, the following depictions blend theoretical data with empirically grounded anthropological fieldwork. Data were collected both from online and offline historical and archival sources, administrative, academic and popular texts, photographs, documentary films and other official and personal media. This information was corroborated with insights supported by participant-observation research methodologies. Informants included an array of long-term (35 years or more) and short-term local residents. In addition, structured and semi-structured interviews were conducted with community leaders, government workers, institutional administrators, local business and culture entrepreneurs, educators, merchants, wage labourers, the unemployed and the retired. These were combined with countless informal conversations with people of all ages and walks of life from each of the three communities as well as with residents from the town's other communities, former residents and visitors. Overall, findings from the ethnographic fieldwork enable a clearer, first-hand understanding of how these groups relate to themselves, to each another and to their consigned or chosen place of residence.

Brief History of Mitzpe Ramon: Reluctant Pioneers Resent a Peripheral Town

'Just a 10 Minute ride from Tel-Aviv'
Deceptive response of bus driver to his North African immigrant passengers who, en route to Mitzpe Ramon, inquired about the whereabouts of their destination; Amar, Ben-Gigi, Vaknin, Ohana, Biton, p.c., 2012

Mitzpe Ramon began in 1951 as a military outpost named *Camp Independence*. The camp provided a base for security personnel, a handful of geologists and crews of workers who were constructing the highway from Beer-Sheva to Eilat, Israel's southernmost city. In 1956, after the road was completed and the workers sent home, the camp was relocated. In its stead, a few members from a nearby kibbutz assembled a small group of aspiring settlers and attempted to establish an 'urban economic cooperative' on the crater's edge. However, the burdensome bureaucracy and complicated logistics of recruiting new partners and providing them with steady employment, goods and services soon hindered this initiative. By the summer of 1958, with only a few of the original recruits remaining, the cooperative folded and its debts were transferred to its government underwriters (Elishav, n/d; Greenberg, 1994).

Later that year, the National Council for Immigration and Absorption was charged with the town's management. The council sought to convert Mitzpe to a 'development town', adding it to a roster of 32 other outlying urban settlements erected in the late 1950s and early 1960s to accommodate the more than 100,000 Jewish immigrants who had emigrated to Israel from former colonial holdings in Africa and Asia (Shapira, 2012). Due to their large numbers, these *mizraxi* immigrants were often sent to development towns 'straight off the boat' or else directly from government transit camps in the centre of the country where they were temporarily housed after their arrival.

The immigrants included a combination of people from rural and urban backgrounds, but in both instances they had mostly lived a traditionalised, patrimonial existence and were generally religiously inclined in their communal observance of age-old Jewish rites and rituals. The country's

Western-minded leadership and the Ashkenazi-dominated hegemonic religious authorities classified them as culturally inferior to their own European backgrounds and upbringings and denigrated the immigrants' Middle-Eastern mannerisms and practices and typically treated *mizraxim* as second-class citizens. Assigned to the intellectual, institutional and physical peripheries of the Israeli Jewish social order, the mainstream Ashkenazi and native-born Israeli public stigmatised the *mizraxi* residents of development towns whom they deemed poor, backward and out of touch with modernity.

In the following decades, lagging growth and lack of opportune employment triggered a reverse wave of emigration and a resultant process of 'negative selection' (Ben-Zadok, 1993: 103) in development towns in general, and in Mitzpe Ramon in particular. Residents who had marketable skills and/or family connections elsewhere in Israel migrated north, leaving behind community members who were either disconnected from, or perhaps disinterested in, the trappings of the Westernised, achievement-based lifestyle found in central Israel. As a result, the 'reluctant pioneers' (Weingrod, 1966) who remained in Mitzpe managed to endure but lacked the know-how and support to propel themselves or the town forward in concrete economic terms. To get by, members of this community worked as municipal-funded labourers or performed government-sponsored factory work, or else they were employed in the mining industries or in support of these businesses as kitchen staff, drivers, guards and similar tasks. Others found jobs in construction and maintenance or ran the few basic service shops about town. Moreover, a proportionately high number subsisted on social welfare in the form of unemployment, disability or retirement benefits.

While over the years the central government repeatedly attempted to improve local conditions, its efforts, often executed from afar, were persistently mishandled. Devoid of concrete native input, these development schemes typically trivialised local sensibilities, ignored the indigenous environment and lacked consistent, reliable national and local organisational follow-through. Thus, decades of inefficient mal-administration and institutional disregard ironically turned Mitzpe Ramon into a neglected government-dependent township that, in fact, never fully developed (Rapport, 1998). Despite two particular demographic alterations – namely, the influx of army personnel into the Ramon area after the 1979 Camp David peace accord with Egypt, and the arrival of nearly a thousand (from over a million) immigrants from countries in the former Soviet Union – for all intents and purposes, Mitzpe Ramon basically remained in its peripheral state well into the 1990s, when groups of newcomer residents began recasting the town in its current version.

It should be noted that the attitude of the veteran *mizraxi* community – who refer to themselves as *Mitzpa'im*, implying the town's long-standing inhabitants – towards the *makhtesh* is very much tainted by its members' original encounters with this locality. Having been sent to Mitzpe Ramon by unsympathetic government agents, in effect this group preserved its original government handlers' opinion of Mitzpe Ramon as a peripheral and insignificant location and of the rich *makhtesh* geology as an expendable economic resource. Thus, for many *Mitzpa'im* the town's natural environment stirs resentment rather than appeal. The vastness of the crater signifies the divide between the town and the rest of the country, its hyperarid landscape embodies this community's marginality and its distance is blamed for their deficient socio-economic advancement.

Recognising the barren local environment as inhospitable, this community's relationship to the crater is characterised by a mixture of avoidance and disregard. With no positive historic, psychic or folkloric role to play within their personal and marginalised immigrant narrative, the crater remains superfluous to this community's outlook and identity. As a consequence, most *Mitzpa'im* are uninvolved with the recent transformation of the *makhtesh* from a consumable mineral reserve to a consecrated biosphere, a shift which they interpret as an extension of Israel's continued adherence to a Western-dominated world view and attendant public agenda. This bitter sentiment was conveyed to me by a long-standing resident who, some 50 years ago at the age of 35, moved with his wife and children from a village in Morocco's Atlas Mountains directly to Mitzpe Ramon. When asked what he thought about living next to the world-famous *makhtesh*, he retorted without a moment's hesitation: 'I worked in the mines and was in the *makhtesh* every day for years. So what?! What EXACTLY did that get me??'. This unfavourable perspective is in direct contradiction to the stance assumed by the recently arriving communities of secular and religious newcomers whose confident middle-class stature facilitates their ability to frame the remote and undeveloped Ramon environment in a more affirmative light.

Secular Middle-Class Newcomers: Privileged Pioneers Occupy the Periphery

'Wherever you look, you'll see yourself'
Graffiti on Mt. Camel lookout point, Mitzpe Ramon

In the past two decades secular, middle-class newcomers have been moving from the centre of Israel to Mitzpe Ramon. As opposed to the veteran *mizraxi* community, this group sanctifies the Ramon Crater environment and draws spiritual inspiration from its primordial desert scenery. Members of this community are linked predominantly through their romantic interpretations of the rural outback and their assumed adoption of an 'idyllic' lifestyle (Mingay, 1989). Embracing the serenity found in

Mitzpe Ramon's outlying desert setting, they regard themselves as fortunate to conduct their lives outside the stresses of late-modern urbanity in general and the unending Arab-Israeli conflict in particular. Neither particularly group oriented nor ideologically motivated, their appearance in Mitzpe Ramon is a *reaction* rather than a *challenge* to mainstream conventions. Self-absorbed, their move to Mitzpe is not intended as a critique or an exit from mainstream society, so much as a veering off to pursue personal dreams away from the intensity and time-consuming processes inherent to city life. 'I live here for the silence', is the common reply offered when questioned about their motivations for moving to Mitzpe.

In a state of heightened fluidity that characterises the contemporary 'liquid modern world' (Bauman, 2011), the size of this community continuously fluctuates, ranging anywhere from several hundred to over a thousand. Some are permanent residents, others temporary and others, prompted by transient economic and domestic arrangements, move back and forth between Mitzpe Ramon and various communities both in Israel and abroad. Accordingly, when questioned about their communal allegiances, these newcomers will often deny belonging to this community, as such a standing would ostensibly inhibit their coveted sense of individualism.

While independent-minded environmentalists have always maintained a minor local presence, it is only recently that their ranks have swelled and more formal communal associations have been forged. Resourceful, confident and well informed, members of this community are mostly employed in a bourgeoning desert-themed cottage service industry that is primarily based on private funding and DIY labour. Steeped in a holistic aesthetic ambiance, enterprising newcomers are utilising available spaces around town to erect funky shops (restaurants, coffee-houses, craft centres, second-hand apparel), boutique factories (bakery, soap, candles, marble, woodworking), quaint desert farms (wineries, creameries, ranches) and similar small business ventures (artisan workshops, art, dance, film, yoga studios, a 'silent' bow and arrow range, a jazz club, a natural healing centre).

This community also provides hospitality services to tourists such as 'green' bed and breakfasts, off-the-grid camping huts, home catering, alternative medicine, herbal remedy treatments, backcountry tour guiding, stargazing and adventure sports such as jeep tours, rappelling and horseback and bike riding. Others work for the government environmental administrative authorities and are, therefore, are positioned as the *de facto* caretakers of the local natural environment. Since this community's livelihood is primarily derived from marketing the natural beauty of the *makhtesh*, its members go to great lengths to maintain and preserve the crater environment in its relatively untouched present state. As such, secular newcomers are popularly known about town as 'the greens' (*hayerukim*), a tongue-in-cheek appellation referring to their preoccupation with conservationalism.

It should be emphasised that despite their profound entrepreneurial contributions to the local economy, many members of the secular newcomer community seem uncommitted to Mitzpe Ramon per se. Rather, drawn to Mitzpe Ramon by the powerful transcendental qualities of the *makhtesh*, Mitzpe offers this group access to the nearby wilderness but not necessarily a place of permanent residence. Affiliates, therefore, take little notice of and have few personal interactions with veteran residents. Instead, they seek out each other for company and largely depend on like-minded holidaymakers for their livelihood. In a sense, the diverse communities in Mitzpe Ramon exist in intercommunal harmony mainly because they conduct their lives in separate socio-economic spheres. 'As far as I am concerned Mitzpe Ramon contains 25 people and the *makhtesh*' confided a newcomer artist when asked about his local social networks.

Globally aware and frequently from privileged backgrounds, these newcomers have formed a contextual appreciation of Mitzpe Ramon that differs greatly from the way that many long-term residents imagine the town. The conversion of the town's hangar-rowed 'industrial area' into the touristic 'Spice Routes Quarter' is a telling example. Implemented by the local municipality as part of its strategy to consolidate newcomer investment, this alteration – essentially renaming/rebranding the neighbourhood with the installation of benches, shade-patches and stylish street lights – has so far proven successful, and today the industrial area/Spice Routes Quarter is abuzz with nascent newcomer sociality and commerce. Yet, while consumer-oriented newcomers and their tourist clients duly refer to this neighbourhood by its new designation and purpose, *Mitzpa'im* largely still relate to this area by its old name and function.

Indeed, the flurry of recent local activity has allowed the newcomer community to fashion for themselves a 'scene' in Mitzpe Ramon and, in the process, convert the town into one of Israel's premier ecotourism destinations. Yet, veteran *Mitzpa'im* are generally unaware of the attitudes and activities of the newcomer community and, for the most part, are excluded from the town's recent strides forward. When questioned about their opinions of the current development in Mitzpe, informants repeatedly bemoan the emergence of local class distinctions, recollecting an earlier, pre-newcomer period when 'everyone knew everyone and we were all one town and no one locked their doors' (Ben-Gigi; Ben-Sa'id; Ohana; Shitrit; Shushan; Vaknin, pc, 2013). Sceptical from years of government attempts to superficially dictate local improvement, *Mitzpa'im* invoke an exclusive, if not chosen, past in order to offset their exclusionary present.

National Religious Settlers: Devout Pioneers Sustain the Margins

'Settling the Negev with Love'
Email signature on *Dati Leumi* Mitzpe Ramon list-serve

While Mitzpe Ramon has mostly been inhabited by a range of demographic groups, throughout the years the town was overlooked by the country's Orthodox populations. This changed in the winter of 2000 when a group of *dati leumi* (National Religious; *dati'im leumi'im* in plural) educators moved to Mitzpe Ramon to institute the *Midbara K'Eden* ('Eden in the Desert', Isaiah 51:3) *Yeshiva* (Torah seminary). The roughly 300 students who attend *Midbara K'Eden* divide their five to eight years at the seminary between theoretical Torah studies and compulsory military service, generally in combat units. While the students come and go, the stable core of this community are the educators and their families who have established themselves as permanent residents in Mitzpe Ramon.

The *Midbara K'Eden* community is part of a national socio-ideological network of *'gar'inim toranim'* or 'Torah clusters' (lit. 'Kernels of Torah'; *gar'in torani* in singular) whose primary aim is to settle Israel and spread Torah through personal example (Reichner, 2013). *Gar'in* members are part of a late-modern subset of Orthodox Judaism known as *Xardalim*, the abbreviation of *'Xaredi-Leumi'* or 'Devout Nationalists' who are known for maintaining elevated standards of religious devotion. As an extension of the Israeli religious Zionist settler movement, this community is predominantly formed from middle-class *Ashkenazim* (Jews of European descent), many with Anglo-Saxon backgrounds. Fusing ultra-religious zealousness with national-Zionist fervour, their sociopolitical viewpoint is underlined by a dutiful observance of the 613 *mitzvot* (biblically commanded moral precepts) which are performed as a religious obligation.

Officially named *V'alitem Ba'negev* after a biblical passage meaning 'and you ascended in the Negev' (Deuteronomy 13:17), the *gar'in* translates this phrase as *Negev Rising* and focuses on promoting the 'education, welfare and settlement of the Negev in general and the socio-cultural-spiritual advancement of the citizens of Mitzpe Ramon in particular' (https:www.keremramon.org). Thus, this community comprehends its settlement in the peripheral Negev desert – which covers roughly 60% of Israel's landmass but holds only 8% of its total inhabitants (Central Bureau of Statistics, 2012) – as the fulfilment of a divine national imperative. At the same time, an additional point of attraction is that Mitzpe's physical–cultural detachment from the rest of the country lends the town a semi-monastic quality, and so permits the fervently religious *gar'in* to remain apart from what they consider to be the decadency of contemporary media-saturated global culture.

Since its arrival, this young and spirited community has grown exponentially. The oldest members are in their early fifties, while the median
adult age is around 30. The *gar'in* encompasses some 200 families, each
with an average of 4 children – although, abiding by the decree to 'be fruit-
ful and multiply', 8 and 10 children families are quite common. Organised,
focused and highly motivated, this community is quasi-self-sufficient having established internal educational, economic, political, cultural, housing,
socio-commercial and media-information networks. As a result, the majority of its members are employed in community-related jobs, particularly in
teaching, administration and social welfare services.

The daily activities of the *dati-leumi* community are steeped in col-
lectivist-oriented Zionism, which implies that its members spend large
portions of their time together. Yet, unlike the secular newcomers, the
Midbara K'Eden community makes a conscientious effort to be in regular
contact with other local residents. That is, since their behaviour is community directed rather than individually motivated, by extension, they focus
on improving the town and the condition of its inhabitants as a whole
rather than advancing private causes and achieving personal communion
with nature. To this aim, members of this community regularly donate a
portion of their income to sustain the *gar'in*'s extensive local charity network and volunteer in various social welfare outreach programmes. These
deeds, however, are not overtly personal and normally occur within the
course of the fulfilment of *mitzvot* – religious acts and commandments.

It should also be noted that the relationship between the *dati'im* and
the town's long-time *mizraxi* residents is partly facilitated by the traditional mindset of the *Mitzpa'i* community. In fact, until recently, religious
observance in Mitzpe Ramon was the domain of the elder *mizraxim* who, at
first, were somewhat opposed to the arrival of the Ashkenazi newcomers,
perhaps in part overwhelmed by their assertive religiosity. Yet, because the
gar'in endeavours to be an inclusive group, it consciously chose to honour,
rather than challenge or ignore, the town's long-standing official (*Mizraxi*)
head rabbi. This standpoint has enabled the *gar'in* to temper *Mitzpa'i*
antagonism by establishing common ground with local residents based on a
mutual respect for shared religious observance.

Although both the *dati* and the secular newcomer communities
arrived in Mitzpe on their own accord, their motivations for moving there
are quite different. While secular newcomers seek personal betterment
through self-fulfilment, the *dati'im* aspire to nation building through
divine collectivism. This distinction impacts upon their relationship
towards the development of the town, its residents and the local environment. Hence, the activities of the secular community adhere to a conventional commercial model (investment–labour–revenue), while the *dati'im*
view personal profit as secondary to the Torah-construed value inherent
in their settlement venture. Accordingly, the for-profit undertakings of

the *gar'in* are limited in scope and lack a certain financial emphasis since, in effect, they are extensions of various religious commandments. Thus, for example, the *gar'in* runs an apartment-hotel guesthouse ('hospitality to strangers') which operates at cost or with a very low profit margin. Moreover, *Kerem Ramon*, the *gar'in* owned and operated vineyard planted on the outskirts of town ('settling the land'), 'donates 50% of its net profits to be used by the local community for education and welfare programs' (keremramon.org, 2012).

Environmentally, the *Midbara K'Eden* community considers the *makhtesh* to be a wonder of nature created by an almighty deity. Thus, members feel a sense of awe and honour to be living in its immediate vicinity. Yet, while the *makhtesh* is certainly a source of inspiration for this community – who hike and otherwise recreate within its confines – the *dati'im* generally do not attach additional spiritual interpretations to their interactions with the natural environment. This conduct is in contrast to secular Israelis, particularly younger ones, who due to the decline in the import of organised religion, are seeking alternative spiritual outlets (Tavori, 2007). Thus, rather than embellishing the *makhtesh* with New Age eco-spiritual significance, *gar'in* members contextualise its exceptional natural resources within their broader, God-driven, socio-theological imperative.

Shifting Perceptions: Space Versus Place Among the Communities of Mitzpe Ramon

Space is the Place
Title of 1974 film by avant-garde musician Sun Ra

To summarise, situated alongside the wondrous *Makhtesh Ramon* in a remote part of the southern Negev desert, the town of Mitzpe Ramon is inhabited by communities of diverse sociocultural origin and orientation who were either sent there by government agents or arrived on their own accord. Mitzpe's peripheral status is variously interpreted by its distinct local communities. On the one hand, isolated from the rest of the country and sociopolitically marginalised by/from the national hegemonic agenda, those residents who were unilaterally directed to this outlying location have historically experienced limited socio-economic development. In response to their peripheral position within Israeli society, *Mitzpa'im*, Mitzpe Ramon's mostly Moroccan veteran community, maintain many of their former customs and cultural attitudes while professing scant regard for the surrounding natural environment which they associate with their marginalised standing. On the other hand, in the last two decades, secular and Orthodox middle-class newcomers are moving to Mitzpe Ramon out of personal preference. Even as they have formed two parallel communities, they both celebrate the autonomy granted by the town's detached setting and perceive the gap between Mitzpe and the centre of the country as a 'fringe benefit' of life on the periphery. Likewise, they are equally enchanted by the *makhtesh*, even though its exceptional natural environment fulfils different purposes for each community.

Returning to the discussion of Tuan's distinctions between space and place with regard to the *makhtesh*, the three communities discussed in this chapter – working-class *mizraxi* veteran immigrants, secular eco-spiritual privileged newcomers and devout National Religious settlers – are readily identifiable according to their idiosyncratic relationships with the Ramon ecosphere. By and large, the *mizraxi* community views Mitzpe Ramon as a far-flung *place* that provides permanence and shelter from the hitherto unfamiliar and frequently pejorative socio-economic realities of Western-oriented Israeli society. In contrast, the secular newcomers view the town as a sacred *space* of refuge that provides them with cultural and financial autonomy, if not a permanent *place* of residence. Meanwhile, the Orthodox settlers view Mitzpe as a divinely adorned *space* waiting to be converted into an eternal *place* of settlement and Torah-mandated sociality.

'Mitzpe's for dreamers', the former *Mizraxi* mayor, Flora Shushan, matter-of-factly quipped to a visiting dignitary on a cold and wet winter day (31 January 2013). In fact, her claim is reinforced by the Israeli historian Yael Zerubavel (2008: 211) who notes that, in the context of the contemporary middle-class Israeli narrative of personal gratification, the desert functions as a *'counter-space'* – a remote location from which to draw inspiration and revelation. Indeed, for each of the two newcomer communities, Mitzpe Ramon acts as a kind of perpetual 'backspace' (Goffman, 1963) by affording them the latitude with which to construct their identities in accordance with their particular interests and priorities. Although the veteran *mizraxi* community provides a limited example of Shushan's claim, the secular and *dati* newcomers recognise the undeveloped prospects and latent potential imbued in Mitzpe's emptiness. For this reason, whereas once the *makhtesh* was a disregarded site of ecologically destructive industrial activity, today it is a haven for ecotourism and spiritual fulfilment.

Certainly, in the past, Israelis treated the desert as an empty space fit to be 'conquered' (settled) and 'greened' (urbanised) for the benefit of the nation. Currently, the emphasis has shifted to deriving socio-economic revenue from preserving and maintaining its barren nature. This change of perspective was partly enabled by the country's increased prosperity and the bourgeoning of a cosmopolitan middle-class sector who have impressed upon the Israeli agenda the importance of environmentalism and eco-consciousness (cf. Ben-Porat *et al.*, 2008; Feige, 2009; Ram, 2000). As a result, the peripheral desert has gained a more favourable position within the public imagination. Hence, particularly among the well-placed secular newcomers, the so-called 'yellowing' of the desert is frequently stimulated by entrepreneurial opportunities for the 'greening' of pockets (Efrati, 2012; Reichel & Uriely, 2003). At the same time, the ever-pragmatic *dati* community views the desert as a ripe location for advancing their ideo-political platform. Meanwhile, many *Mitzpa'im* continue to resent the desert as the source of their ignominy and thus find it difficult to appreciate the changes occurring in their town (Table 5.1).

The above ethnographic examination compares and contrasts the diverse *Weltanschauung* of three of the six core Mitzpe Ramon communities. Further inquiry into perceptions which the other resident communities – indigenous Bedouin tribespeople, immigrant *'Rusim'* from countries in the former Soviet Union and American-born African Hebrew Israelites of Jerusalem – have towards Mitzpe/*Makhtesh Ramon* will yield additional knowledge and insight into the socio-historical factors that shape how these different communities formulate their particular attitudes towards their place of residence. This chapter, therefore, makes a modest contribution to improving our understanding of the multilayered dynamics and the often uneven relationships that parallel communities maintain with regard to their shared environment.

Table 5.1 Attitudes and practices of three core Mitzpe Ramon communities

Community	Conditions of arrival	Ethnic bearing/ language	Belief system	Socio-economic standing	Employment	Relationship to Mitzpe Ramon	Point of interaction with/perception of makhtesh
Mizraxim/ mitzpa'im veteran immigrants	Directed by government	*Mizraxi* Moroccan, Hebrew, Moroccan, Arabic	Traditional, observant, patrimonial	Immigrant working class	Government employee, wage labour, welfare, pensioner	Ambivalent	Industry/mining, disinterest
Secular, globalised newcomers	Voluntary, personal choice	Ashkenazi, Anglo-European Hebrew, English	Secular, cosmopolitan, New Age	Privileged middle class	Tourism, alternative medicine, nature conservation	Self-interest	Eco-entrepreneurial, spiritual
Orthodox, national religious settlers	Divinely mandated	Ashkenazi, Anglo-European Hebrew (modern, scriptural)	Devout national religious zionist	Principled middle class	Education, counselling, caregiving	Ideological	Devotional, sacred

6   Slum Dwellers' Perceptions of Tourism in Dharavi, Mumbai

Anya Diekmann and Nimit Chowdhary

No it (visits) isn't a trouble
Pental Bhai

Introduction

In many countries in the world, particularly in the developing or emerging ones, urban megapolis development goes hand in hand with the development of slums. They consist of rundown areas of a city characterised by substandard housing and squalor and lack tenure security. They generally appear as uncontrolled settlements in abandoned areas or empty grounds in a city. Slums are managed by 'slumlords' and are rarely, if at all, controlled by authorities.

The inhabitants of slums are often rural migrants and among the poorest in society. Along with the urban decay, high rates of poverty and unemployment constitute the life of a slum. Moreover, slums have high rates of disease due to insufficient sanitary conditions, malnutrition and lack of basic health care. They often have little or no power or water supply and lack sewage systems.

In these living conditions, their inhabitants are generally excluded from the tourism landscape. However, since the 1990s, they constitute a growing pull factor for Western tourists allegedly aiming to understand the reality. Multiple terms are used to describe tours through impoverished areas, which are promoted by tour operators as 'authentic', 'off the beaten track' and including 'interactive features' (Rolfes, 2010:432), highlighting the opportunity of exchange with locals. Other scholars and journalists, however, describe the phenomenon as voyeurism using terms ranging from poverty tourism and poorism, slum tourism, sick tours, negative sightseeing and social tours to reality tourism or even revolutionary tourism.

The underlying debate is whether this form of tourism is ethical or not. Some defend the idea that it may contribute to fighting poverty, but others are convinced that it is purely voyeuristic. For instance, while the tour operators in Mumbai slums are convinced that they are improving the image of the slums and its residents through the tours, Sudgen (2013) in an online article on the rights and wrongs of slum tours quotes Jackind Arputham, the president of Slum Dwellers International (a community group based in Mumbai): 'These tours are very derogatory for the people of Dharavi. The majority of those living in the slum question why white people come to visit them "like monkeys" in a zoo' (http://blogs.wsj.com/indiarealtime/2013/05/03/the-rights-and-wrongs-of-slum-tourism/).

However, while research has increased over the last years (Frenzel & Koens, 2012), particularly in destinations such as the favelas of Rio, the townships in South Africa and Dharavi a slum in the city of Mumbai, surprisingly very little research looks into the perceptions of the host communities (Freire-Meideros, 2012, 2013; Kieti & Magio, 2013). As mentioned in the Introduction to this book, reasons are varied but sociocultural and linguistic obstacles of the currently mainly Western researchers play a significant role. The decision whether slum tourism is ethical or not depends largely on the perception of the host community independent of the often discussed motivations of the visitors. This chapter aims therefore at analysing slum tourism from the host community's perspective in India, where organised slum tours only date back to 2006 when 'Reality Tours' started offering walking tours through a quarter of Dharavi, the biggest slum in Mumbai. With the increasing demand for slum tours and the film *Slumdog Millionaire* located in Dharavi, multiple companies have developed, particularly in the last two years, offering slum tours to mainly Western tourists. In the centre of the current research are thus the people that live and work in the slums and receive daily groups of visitors.

Slum Tourism Research

Since the early 1990s, slums have re-become 'tourist attractions'. Indeed, Koven (2004) shows that in Victorian London during the 1890s, 'slumming' was already a popular activity for the English upper classes. By visiting the urban poor in London's metropolitan slums, first-hand experience was gained in order to be in a position to speak about social problems. Districts such as Whitechapel and Shoreditch were even represented in the important Baedeker travel guide (Koven, 2004: 1). In the US, in cities like New York and Chicago, the wealthy middle class visited poor migrant areas in the city to escape the social constraints of their own class and experience the unknown culture (Heap, 2009). With World War II, slumming became less important. In the 1990s, however, the phenomenon shifted from Western countries to the developing world, starting with the development of the favelas in Brazil as a tourist destination, nowadays the third most popular tourist attraction in Rio de Janeiro.

Researchers took an interest in slum tourism about 10 years later, with a particular focus on Brazil's favelas and South Africa's townships (Freire-Medeiros, 2007, 2012; Koens, 2012; Rogerson, 2004; Williams, 2008). In

India, where organised slum tourism is rather recent, little research exists. In general, studies mainly concentrated on the visitor and his or her motivation to visit such a place and the organisation of the visits. Until now, very little research has been focused on the perceptions of the host community, nor on the economic or sociocultural impacts on the visited people. Reasons are multiple, but in the case of India, this is very likely linked to the cultural and linguistic context. Researchers are mainly from Western countries and slum tourism is not very popular with the Indian government. With very few Indian visitors in the slums, the topic has not yet attracted the attention of many Indian researchers.

However, understanding slum tourism in its entirety, why and how it is organised, who comes and why and how it is experienced by the host community appears to be of great importance when considering the ethical debate and governmental opposition to this kind of tourism. The host community is diverse in its composition and numerous people are met during the two to three hours walk through a slum. The hosts are residents, workers, factory owners, schoolchildren, teachers, shop owners, sellers, etc.

What do they think about the visitors? Do they perceive the tours as an intrusion or do they actually enjoy them? How far are they involved in the preparation and do they consent? Do they see any benefits, social or economic? Does the tourist (public) interest help to improve the living conditions in the area? And so forth.

While many researchers connect slum tours to volunteer tourism, for instance that both types of tourism share common motivations: those of seeing the real country and being at the centre of it, in Dharavi this comparison does not really withstand the way the visits are organised. Indeed, the visitor has almost no contact with the population and no collaborative initiatives are proposed. However, many of the new companies organising slum tours base their promotion on the fact that all the guides have a close link to Dharavi, either they have grown up there or family members have a factory there.

Slum tours

Before analysing the perception of the host community, it is useful to look into the profile of the visitors and explain briefly the organisation of tours in Dharavi, Mumbai, one of the largest slums in India (Diekmann & Hannam, 2012; Rolfes, 2011). Indeed, there are approximately 1 million people living in the slum that is located next to the well-off area of Bandra. According to an online article in 2012:

> 11,000 joined a Reality Tour, which generated 7.2 million rupees (£80,300). Eighty per cent of this was donated to its sister non-government organisation, Reality Gives. This yearly donation has provided English classes

to 142 young adults, trained 17 local women to become teachers, supported a kindergarten, provided English classes in a local school and paid for cricket equipment and art lessons. (http://metro.co.uk/2012/11/07/virgin-holidays-responsible-tourism-awards-2012-614996/)

The area of Dharavi shown to the visitors includes all sorts of economic activities, but mainly recycling factories, schools, kindergartens and some housing. The shown district lies next to Mahim railway station, where the actual tour begins. The groups meet the guide either in Colaba (tourist part) and together they take the train to Dharavi or they meet him directly at the Mahim railway station in Dharavi. Each tour follows a strict script and visits to factories, schools, kindergartens and a private house are meticulously prepared. It is the owner of the place who negotiates with the tour organiser. According to the organisers of the tours, Reality Tours, they take a non-intrusive approach. For example, groups are small with a maximum of six people only. More importantly, there is a no camera policy. All companies operating in the area provide visitors with some 'dos' and 'don'ts'. However, these may not be strictly adhered to. Observing other groups, visitors with Reality Tours also tend not to follow the instructions given to them.

Some of the newer companies clearly dwell on the film *Slumdog Millionaire* and on the participative and ethical approach of their tours. Companies like 'Slumgods' or 'Bethelocal Tours and Travels' or 'Magic Mumbai' seem to have taken on the successful formula of Reality Tours that aims to show a different picture of slums to well-off visitors from the West.

It should be underlined that the government and other authorities have taken offence to slum tourism as presenting the country in a bad light. Tourism authorities have been said to instruct the companies in Mumbai to stop selling slum tours. An enthusiastic sales pitch in this case refers to a slum tour as a 'tour of real India', which has not gone down well with others outside the slums and is also considered wrong as this is just a facet of life in India, which comes in a variety of shades. In India, many middle- and upper-class (elite and educated) Indians in the bigger cities, such as Delhi and Mumbai, are not aware of the existence of slum tours. When asked about their feelings about such tours, the reaction is often shock and they deny that such a thing exists. It is not the image that the middle and upper classes want to put forward to visitors. Also, some of those familiar with the existence of the tours are not in favour of such tours.

Who are the visitors?

The visitors come mainly from Europe and other Western countries, as can be seen in Figure 6.1. Indeed, Indian visitors are in the minority in Dharavi.

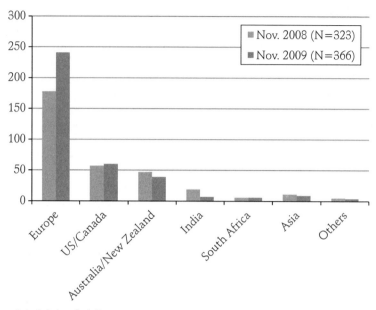

Figure 6.1 Origin of visitors
Source: Reality Tours

Visiting a slum is widely considered as gaining an insight into the *real* India and the commodification of poverty is not often a concern for the visitors. In 2009, most of the visitors discovered the existence of slum tours in Western guidebooks as an opportunity to leave the beaten track. Other important sources are friends and by word of mouth. This shows that people who visit Dharavi think that it is an interesting tourist site. Interviews with visitors showed that their concern was rather self-centred, about how they would be perceived as Western tourists and how they would feel in the slums.

Who are the hosts?

The hosts are the workers and residents of Dharavi, people who often arrive from the countryside in order to improve their living conditions. The part shown to the visitors consists of concrete – often constructions with several floors that house factories and living space alike. The area is provided with water and electricity for a limited time each day. Sanitary provision does exist, but it is rather insufficient and the sewage system is lacking. In an article, one of the Reality Tour guides is cited as saying 'this is a five star slum' (Sudgen, 2013).

Reality Tours suggest two visits both focusing on the industries within the slum. The aim according to the owner Chris Way is 'to show the spirit of the place and the sense of community and how much the people work here'. When reading the appreciations of the visitors, this goal is clearly achieved.

Although verbal communication is difficult (the host community does not speak any English), communication exists based on signs, handshakes and smiles. Considering the contents of the visit (the factories), agreements have been made with the bosses to allow people to see the working place of the hosts, but then that is the case in most visited sites.

Analysing around 800 questionnaires submitted by Reality Tours after the tours, which the authors have been allowed to use anonymously for the research, and having realised interviews with visitors (Diekmann & Hannam, 2012; Hannam & Diekmann, 2011), the friendly welcome by the host community has been highlighted. According to Reality Tours, no negative experience has been recorded (information dates from 2010). One reason might certainly be the small groups with a maximum of six people and the good relationship between the guides and the slum residents and workers. In 2010, according to a guide for Reality Tours, guides venturing in the district who were not from Reality Tours were directly noticed by the local community and pointed out to the 'official guides'. One of the authors was present during such an exchange in 2010, when a community member told the author's guide about another unknown guide. Although she could not understand their conversation, it was obviously a very important matter for the respondent.

With the appearance of new commercial companies showing people round Dharavi, the situation has largely changed. It is also important to note that when Reality Tours were the only operator in Dharavi, tourists met only a few other tourists. Now it is rare if tourists do not meet other groups of guided tours and the small spaces have become increasingly crowded. It is worth mentioning that although Dharavi covers a very broad area, the tours all take place in the same district, maybe to use the successful formula of Reality Tours. The researcher notes in January 2014:

> Last time during this two and a half hour tour, we (my group) came across only two other groups all handled by Reality Tours. But this time there were around nine or ten groups (only two were organized by Reality Tours, while others by competitors). At times so many groups almost jammed the narrow alleys of the slum and the tour leader had to often take to alternative routes to keep the time. Despite these many visitors rushing though the alleys and creating a kind of chaos, it was not really noticed by the hosts. They appeared to be largely unconcerned. The children however seemed amused by this commotion.

Methodology

The research is based on an intercultural exchange between the two authors from two cultural backgrounds. Getting in touch with the host community is a rather difficult task when one is not familiar with the different languages used in Dharavi. Being an outsider, the researcher has to familiarise himself with the location and meet members of the host community. For the present research, the Indian researcher visited Dharavi and participated in various guided tours in 2012 and in January 2014. During his visits, he had informal discussions with residents and workers in order to understand their perception of organised tours in their working and living environment. Moreover, the cultural background of the Indian researcher allowed him to grasp information and behaviours that would be difficult for a Western researcher to understand due to language and cultural patterns. For example, the Indian researcher realised immediately that the guide was not – as pretended – from the area because his expressions highlighted a different background from those of the visited quarter in the slums. As explained by Diekmann and Hannam (2012), the guide is the only link between the visitor and the host community. Being (normally) the only one in the group of six visitors who is able to communicate with the residents or workers in the slums, what he will translate for the visitors is entirely his decision. The guide is the one who sets the limits to the exchange between visitors and hosts. Another example from 2012 is the house shown to the tour participants. The guide declared that its inhabitants had left for the day; however, on closer observation, the Indian author noticed that the house was unoccupied, but some of its contents were being displayed for tourists only. Although the guide explained that they had an arrangement with the residents to visit the place, it seemed very likely that the house belonged to the company and that the experience was staged. During his visit in January 2014, the researcher notes:

> They (the guide of Reality Tours) took us to the same house but the story was different. They have now converted it into a small gallery. There was a programme of teaching photography to children in the slum. Photographs of slum children taken by slum children were offered from that place for a price. This reinforced our original belief, that the tours are not a hundred percent real. Given the competition (this time there were many groups of international tourists who were being handled by other operators), staging of experience is gradually becoming part of the script.

The informal discussions with residents and workers in the visited district followed some pre-established guidelines relating to the potential benefits of the tours for the host community, the relationship and contact with the various tour organisers and the perspectives that the tours might provide in terms of poverty alleviation.

The Commodification of Poverty – Host Perceptions

No, they (visitors) do not disturb us
Babu Lal, factory worker

One of the aims of the research was to understand how the residents and workers feel about being gazed at. Indeed, during the tours, groups of visitors enter all sorts of factories, schools and shops to get a glimpse of the *real* life of the slum dwellers. This act seems shocking to many Western critics and appears as a confirmation of the commodification of poverty as the visitor crosses the line of privacy. Yet, from a cultural perspective there is a different perception of what privacy means and how it is lived. India, like most Eastern cultures, is indeed a collective society, with limited individualism. Further, the spatial arrangement in the community is such that individual homes are too small and are therefore restricted to limited use by females in the family, more so at night; for keeping valuables; and very importantly to extend an idea of 'having a home'. For all practical purposes the household spills over to the common area with members of the community freely living and interacting in public space. The idea of privacy is therefore very limited. Life takes place in common areas with 'others' being part of the routine. Visitors as part of this 'other' are therefore not considered intrusive or obstructive or as violating any kind of privacy.

Since hosts and visitors exist in the common space with little inhibitions or any kind of idea of one violating others' privacy, it is an interesting experience for visitors, especially for those from the West. In general, for them it is an opportunity to glimpse into the lives of the hosts, whereas the hosts are not offended by the presence of the visitors. On the contrary, some of the residents declared feeling some kind of excitement at being noticed and being with people who are visibly different from them. In fact, for many among the host community, it is exciting to meet the foreign visitors. Indian visitors go unnoticed.

Reality Tours may have some code of conduct in place but it seems to be diluting under the pressure of competition. While Reality Tours still pursue a no camera policy, other tour operators might not follow this. Part of this is explained by the fact that the hosts are neutral to being photographed in general, provided it is not very close or intrusive. In many cases, some children and adults are actually excited at being photographed. But it needs to be interpreted carefully. For them it is just a photograph. They might not concur with the visitors' idea of capturing their deprivation and poor living conditions. Visitors might like to capture the moment where they saw people living in misery and awful conditions, whereas the hosts are just presenting themselves (not their life or misery) for a photograph.

Very similar to the results of the survey of slum residents in Kibera in Kenya (Kieti & Magio, 2013), the host community is just neutral to the whole concept of tourism in their living and working environment. Good if it is there, better if it is not there. If some are making a living, it is good for them. They do not feel demeaned or embarrassed by such visits. On the contrary, they receive the visitors well and with good humour. Respondents consider that for tourists, it is just one of the variety of experiences that they are seeking in India/Mumbai.

The idea of observing others' misery and poverty is too 'academic' in the eyes of the host community. In the discussion, the respondents did not perceive it as 'their poverty is being noticed (and it is demeaning or embarrassing or offensive)'. For them, they are being noticed because the foreigners are excited to see their different way of living. They do not relate *Slumdog Millionaire* to something that captured the attention of the world about their living conditions, they see it as adding awareness (that visitors came to know about them). It has made them 'kind of heroes' and that people are coming from far and wide to see them… it is a good feeling.

But there are also several residents who do not know (nor do they have time to ponder over) why foreigners are visiting slums. If asked and pressed to give an answer, many said that foreigners come to see how they live and work (this does not mean their poverty, deprivation, etc). Overall, they are neutral '…must be coming to see something (not sure what exactly)'.

At the time of encounter there is a short-lived, momentary excitement of interacting with 'white' people. The inquisitiveness of visitors about the host life in turn amuses the hosts who are willing to show what the visitors want to see. It is important to note that during this encounter, the hosts are not quite able to understand what the visitors would like to see (and know); nevertheless, they are forthcoming to tackle the desire of visitors and 'whatever' they are willing to see.

While most replies showed indifference, for some factory workers, given their difficult/adverse working conditions, they got time to look up and relax whenever there were visitors. It appeared to be a welcome break from the monotony of the job.

Yet, on the question of whether they feel intruded on, offended or disturbed by these visits, which have actually increased as compared to 2012, the respondents mentioned that given the density of the place and the collectivistic culture, individuals' public space has actually shrunk. This in consideration that the lives of residents already spill over into the public areas of the community.

The company that pioneered the idea of slum tours in Dharavi, Reality Tours, adheres to the no-camera policy. This policy aims to be non-intrusive in respect to the visited community, and to allow people to experience the visit through their own eyes and not the protective lens of their camera. Interviews with visitors highlighted that this type of policy shows that the organisers are thoughtful people organising sustainable and respectful tours. This perception contributes to lowering the degree of discomfort experienced by most visitors when starting the tour (Diekmann & Hannam, 2012). However, since the arrival of new tour organisers, some companies have sprung up that are not so particular about this policy. Discussion and observation showed that the community in general does not appear to be bothered by the use of cameras. Photography is not part of their concerns. They are rather neutral about this technology and they do not appear to be bothered by it.

Consent

Selinger and Outterson (2009) highlight the importance of the consent of the locals. The impression of most visitors is that of a very friendly welcome by the host community. Enquiring on the consent of the host community, residents and workers have demonstrated interest in interacting with tourists. This is largely because of the interactions at individual level between the owners and guides of the company (Reality Tours). Otherwise, there is no give and take between the company and the host community. In fact, hosts say they are happy and feel elated in interacting with the guest. It is, however, worth mentioning that tourism in general in India like in many other developing countries, where tourism development is still in its nascent stages, is not with the consent of the host community (in the sense that often there is no buy-in by the host community and the correlate that tourism will return economic benefit is often weak). Tourism is an enterprise's effort to which the community is often neutral. Moreover, after the release of the film *Slumdog Millionaire*, the slums have got attention and the respondents are not averse to this idea. Rather it is welcome.

However, once the negative impacts of tourism become visible, there is often a backlash (as the community is not educated about the benefits of tourism). Therefore, the tourism organising companies must keep the impacts of their activities to a limit. Reality Tours in that sense has some good tour guides who have maintained good relationships with the host community – children, households, factory owners, employees. Initially, Reality Tours had a policy that tourists may not buy anything from the locals during the tour (the underlying belief being that such a purchase may be out of pity and to give something back to the deprived hosts). However, over time, the factory owners (leather factory) set up a small display-cum-sales counter where the visitors can purchase leather products. While factory owners respect the tour operator's right to earn, perhaps Reality Tours on a reciprocal basis has been forced to respect the factory owners' right to an opportunity to sell.

Impacts

If someone is making money, how does that affect us?
Pyarelal

Everyone has a right to earn a bread
Anwar Ali

The tours of the different suppliers cost between $11 and $50 depending on the length, means of transport and meeting point. To our knowledge, only Reality Tours gives 80% to its charity Reality Gives. The charity runs a kindergarten and community centre in the Dharavi area with English and computer lessons. Moreover, Reality Gives provides English language support at a local government school, and supports projects run by other non-governmental organisations (NGOs) in the Dharavi area.

Discussing the benefits with some residents and workers, it appears that they do not necessarily understand the economics of these tours and the suggested benefits that they might return. Yet, respondents have quite a positive disposition towards Reality Tours, who give back to the community through their welfare interventions. One point raised, however, is that this could happen without slum tours. The company could continue to offer other products (other than slum tours) and still contribute to the community. Therefore, the arguments that 'because of the slum tours the community benefits' are a bit too far-fetched.

Another observation that came up between 2012 and 2014 was the development of the visit to the leather factory. In 2012, visitors would stop there and spend some time trying to learn/see the process. They could inquire but were not sold anything. In 2014, the leather factory came up with a display, where some of their products were offered for sale. It is interesting to note that the items for sale were priced to be sold to foreigners (slightly less than what was available in the market, as against the low price of production at which they are sold to the routine distribution network). To sum up, the community was readying itself for a tourism marketplace. The researcher noted another event showing the possible extent of participation of the shop tenants:

> One of the stops on the circuit was a paint box refurbishing shop. The local guide was telling that they (local shopkeepers) buy the old paint boxes at a price, refurbish it and sell back at a higher price. Until this point the shopkeeper allowed the guests to be inside the shop/workshop and allowed the local guide to deliver his commentary at the site (which meant that the work at the shop had to be halted for those few minutes). The owner suddenly got upset with the guide and the reason for his annoyance was that he (the guide) was telling the wrong prices of procurement and selling. The shopkeeper scolded the guide for that

but then took some time to explain to guests that he has nothing against the guests or the visit but it was wrong on the part of the guide to quote the wrong prices. On being asked if such visits disturbed their work he said 'No. Everyone has a right to earn their bread. I have no problem if he earns by bringing visitors...but he should not giving the wrong information'. (Shop owner)

The tourist (public) interest, however, does not help to improve the living/working conditions. The economic benefit to the individual supplier is too little to be generalised as a benefit to the community. Moreover, the deplorable conditions (unhygienic and miserable) of the slum is the unique selling characteristic of the slum tour for the tour operators. Indeed, over the 18-month period between the last two visits, while the number of visitors had increased significantly, the quality of life had perhaps deteriorated. It was more pungent, dirtier and crowded and partly because of visitors.

The tour was also rushed through and superficial. This time there was less interaction with the community not at the will/desire of the community but by design of the tour party movement. It was more playing to the audience.

Contact with the organisers

When asked whether the different residents and visited factory workers had been informed or consulted before the visits, the reply was a clear no – no consent had been asked. The factory owners agree with the tour operators to have people visiting their shops and factories. The workers only get to know the tour guides through their repeat visits. In that sense there is no staging of the visits as the workers do not take any offence to such visits and they are also fine with the idea of slum tours and that some money goes back to the community through the community centre as previously mentioned. A number of residents declared that 'they (Reality Tours) are good people and are doing a good job (contributing to the society through their school and the NGO)'.

Advising the host community on how to deal with tourists seems just too great an effort. Whatever is learnt is through socialising and experience. For example, children are excited to say 'hello' to passing visitors. They are excited and will run past the visitors/their group and shout 'hello'. However, workers in the factories visited have learnt to continue to work as if they are not bothered or disturbed by the visit. Their supervisor may occasionally come forward to talk to the tourists and offer explanations if any are desired.

Factories are not considered private places and visits are permitted following agreement with the factory owner (who often does not live in the slum). The situation with houses is different. They are personal spaces and very small. In the first years of the slum tours, no private house was part of the tour, accentuating the philosophy of Reality Tours of respectful and non-intrusive tourism. However, as previously mentioned, around three years before the writing of this chapter, an allegedly private house had been integrated in the tour. The guides explained that the house was owned by workers who were away at work. They also claimed that they had arranged with the residents to permit a visit. A second look (but not perceptible to tourists) revealed that it was very likely that the house was owned by the company and that the experience was a staged one. The residents are indeed not too thrilled by the idea of having visitors in their house, for houses are too small to allow access to a group of five or six. Moreover, such a visit is not a natural visit and it is at this level that the hosts become conscious of being formally visited. Indians would typically make up their house in anticipation of a visitor (even local). To remain alert and updated throughout the day is asking far too much. And if this is done then it has to be staged, which will take the experience away from reality. So, there appears to be an equilibrium 'watch, but don't come in'.

The reasons for integrating an allegedly genuinely occupied house are not known to the authors, but it might be due to the increasing demand of visitors to see how people live and the increasing competition of the slum tour market. In previous years also there were stops to allow a glimpse of a family. The speed of the experience was such that visitors could interact with the hosts. During the 2014 visits, it was more rushed through. Perhaps the excitement among the host community has died out and they are neutral to visits and it is only good if they are looked at but not talked to.

Conclusion

When the researchers started visiting Dharavi in 2008 only Reality Tours provided slum tours to a small number of people (around 300/month). They had a strict policy on the dos and don'ts to ensure respectful visits on the one hand and, on the other hand, they did not want local residents to participate in the tourism market through selling products. The argument was that they redistribute the benefits to the local community. The situation has largely changed in a few years because new commercial operators have arrived on the market greatly increasing the number of visitors to a point that at some moments the already confined public spaces become overcrowded with tourists. This relatively new occurrence leads to a decrease in communities' appreciation of the visitors and in the long run might induce negative views on slum tours as expressed by Jackind Arputham (as previously mentioned).

At present, there seems to be no particular opposition to and annoyance with the tourism activity, but there is no particular enthusiasm either. The first excitement and interest when the tours started have faded away because now too many visitors come with too many different groups. The quantity of people also makes the experience an even more staged one for both sides, as personal encounters between hosts and visitors have become rare. The combination of the commercialisation of the tours and the number of visitors may eventually lead to a less-welcoming encounter and push the poverty commodification level to an extreme without bringing relevant benefits to the community. The development of slum tourism in Dharavi is at a critical turning point and stakeholders and the host community need to act in order to preserve a balanced relationship.

If companies are to continue to lead tours through the slums, they should take on board the members of the host community and buy-in their acceptance. With growing numbers of tourists and tour companies, a code of conduct should be put in place.

More research is needed, but the discussion with residents and workers allowed the researchers to develop the following recommendations for the future of slum tours:

(1) Tours should be limited or organised in different parts of the slum so as not to crowd the same routes. More creativity is required in developing alternate routes and experiences.

(2) Tour companies should contribute directly and visibly to the development of the locals. They must make efforts to inform the community along the itinerary to improve every day life. The routes are getting crowded and messier. There is a feeling that the tour companies want the slum to be the way it is. They are competing and aggressively selling the deplorable conditions of slums without concern for the hosts and the community is not complaining, at least explicitly.

(3) Tours should be designed and conducted without being obtrusive and intrusive. This is becoming like any other popular tourist destination. Because people will not complain (as they think that because they themselves are spilling over the place that does not belong to them, they have no right to stop others) does not mean that all is fine.

(4) Tour companies must come together to take on board the community leaders, explain the intentions of the tours to the community, seek formal permission and come up with a code of conduct that is self-imposed and with strict adherence to the same.

(5) Instead of showing visibly appalling things, the focus should be more on explaining life in slums. This means that the physically appalling things should be improved with the concurrence of the community and made better for the benefit of the community.

Part 3: Visitor Experiences

Introduction

Since the beginning of tourism research, numerous researchers have focused on the visitor. Being aware of the motivations and decision choices as well as the expectations and experiences of tourists not only helps tourism management but they also relate to human behaviour and sociological and psychological processes (Smith, 2001) and for that reason attract the significant attention of researchers. The challenge for visitor research is the diversity of individuals travelling, as highlighted by many authors. Also, travel motivations and behaviour can vary from one trip to another and even change during one trip. In the context of this book, however, it is interesting to look into some attempts at the categorisation of visitors, for they may reflect the type of visitor – at least partially – who visits the communities in question. Indeed, by looking at different communities and cultures as tourism assets, the visitor plays a substantial role in understanding the fascination of 'otherness' and the 'exotic'.

However, before doing so, it is important to recall briefly the process that led to the valorisation of ethnic and minority communities in cities all over the world. The process of touristification of these districts reflects the need for diversification of the tourism supply in a competitive and developing urban tourism context. The globalised middle classes anticipate a broader offer and the former visiting of monuments and sites is replaced (or joined) by the aspiration to experience the atmosphere of a city or to consume new spaces. Indeed, the travelling middle classes have 'played a central role in establishing the relationships between consumerism and tourism' (Mullins, 1999: 253).

The Changing Face of Urban Tourism

Ashworth and Page (2011: 9) support the idea that the consumption of urban tourism experiences is a fashion activity and, like all consumption of culture, part of contemporary lifestyles. Urban tourism thus becomes a lifestyle accessory as particular cities are 'in' or 'passé'. For Smith (2001: 54) the offer is constantly adjusted as tourist motivations change. This statement is equally valid for 'destinations' inside the city. Next to historical buildings, museums and other traditional tourist assets, new and creative cultural districts have become fashionable. As pointed out by Richards (2011: 1227), creative tourism is considered as being an extension of cultural tourism, for it broadens the notion of culture with the aim of generating distinction for social groups, economic classes and places. This 'creative' turn (Andersson & Thomsen, 2008) linked to tourism in terms of helping economic growth contributed to the development of distinctive cultural quarters leading to a different level of commodification of ethnicity, poverty, etc. In ethnic quarters it can generate a revival of neglected arts. For instance, Harlem is notable as it had lost most of its music traditions and bars due to economic and social deprivation. However, through tourism development and the need to be creative, many professional gospel choirs have become the basis of new productive activity (Hoffman, 2003: 294). In Chapter 3, Zátori and Smith also show how the music of the Gypsy community contributes to the tourism experience through festivals and performances in tourist spots. The diversification process of cosmopolitan cities has been an inspiration to numerous urban tourist destinations. The development of ethnic tourism attractions and the integration of minority quarters in tourism promotions have played a significant part in the diversification of the offer. The aim is not only to internally regenerate impoverished districts, but also to show the world how open and tolerant the city is – in fact, many cities used this policy to redevelop their image. For instance, Brussels having formerly a reputation of being a boring and dull destination due to an all overshadowing European bureaucracy, successfully changed its image to a cosmopolitan and highly multicultural and creative city through the shaping of new events and 'destinations' within the city.

As ethnic and minority quarters have been successful elsewhere as a tourism asset, cities tend to duplicate and follow fashion. The paradox is that on the one hand the quarters are unique for the cityscape, but on the other hand they fail to differentiate from other competing cities (Ashworth & Page, 2011).

> The local is explored and exploited in search of the unique global competitive advantage by a tourism industry that is itself with a strong tendency towards risk-averse replication of products and their delivery. (Ashworth & Page, 2011: 13)

This duplication can also be observed at local level. For instance, the slum/favela tours that were originally organised by non-governmental organisations (NGOs) or religious charities have seen their model of visiting the slums/favelas being copied by private entrepreneurs. Through this mechanism, the favelas have become the third largest tourist attraction in Rio de Janeiro and recent developments in Dharavi (see Chapter 6) suggest a similar development in the coming years.

Motivations of Visitors

Since the beginning of tourism research, scholars have attempted to fit tourists into categories. The approach for developing tourist theory and models was either descriptive, psychological or quantitative (Smith, 2001). Plog's model, published for the first time in 1973 (and later in 1991), divided visitors according to psychographic types. Among others, he described 'the allocentrics as the travel doers, ready to try new products and exercising more intellectual curiosity about the tourism experience' (Smith, 2001: 57). He then replaced the allocentrics with venturers and linked the popularity of a site. Increasing numbers wear out the physical and social environment of the site and the venturers are replaced by centrics and near-dependables (Plog, 1998). In this context, we might also cite Cohen's (1972) drifters and explorers because all these categories can contribute to understanding the types of tourists who visit ethnic, minority and slum quarters. Not so long ago (depending on the destination) visits to a slum had an 'explorer' connotation. This was linked to the imaginaries of dangerous, unhealthy, decayed urban areas scarcely visited by the middle classes. The challenge and fear to cross the comfort zone intensified as the tourist experience took place in other cultural and developing environments. Today, there is a growing interest in visits to the poorest areas of cities, preferably not in one's own society, but in developing countries. The category of allocentrics as people with allegedly greater curiosity than the 'mainstream' tourist is probably still representative of many visitors to impoverished areas. However, this perception is about to change in most slum destinations as visitor numbers increase and visits become more and more staged and systemised to accommodate as many visitors as possible.

As for ethnic and other urban minority quarters, the categories only reflect a small number of visitors. Indeed, as pointed out below, visitors to urban ethnic and minority quarters are extremely diverse. That may be one reason why relatively little research has been published on visitors to these districts.

The above-mentioned development of diversified tourism products is only possible as long as visitors continue to come. This is indeed the case for slum tourism, which is 'enjoying' a steadily growing demand in the past few years with new 'destinations' developing all over the world. Linked to an also steadily increasing mobility and a wish for new cultural consumption, slums represent an opportunity not only to visit the 'real' side of a country, but also to cultivate postcolonial romanticism of the 'all odds fighting hero' in the slum, drawn from films and novels. The visitors' perception of the slum nowadays in developing and emerging countries is not far away from the perception of the bourgeoisie back in earlier centuries. In his *Pensées*, originally published in 1670, Blaise Pascale (2010) already stated that the higher and middle-class ladies visited out of charity for the poor in order to make themselves feel better. In the 19th century, it was a pastime of the upper classes to go and visit poor areas in big cities (Koven, 2004). Charles Dickens himself went several times to visit the places that became famous in his novels. Heap (2009) who examines the history of slumming quotes the cultural historian Alan Mayne:

> the practise of slumming, firmly embedded in bourgeois ideology, actively created in the very balance of pleasure and danger that, in alternate guises of benevolent reform and bemusement seeking, it both pretended to rectify and exploited. Indeed, the practice of slumming was responsible not only for helping to naturalise the middle-class conception of the slum that permeated the popular imagination of turn-of-the-century America but, to a significant extent, for its very creation. (Heap, 2009: 23)

In fact, tourists visiting slums in Asia and Africa in the 21st century are from the same sociocultural background as the visitors a hundred years earlier. Dürr and Jaffe (2012: 118) describe the slum tourist encounter as premised on pre-existing national, class and racial inequalities. The tourists are mainly Western middle-class men and women who wish to get a glimpse of 'unspoilt' poverty corresponding to the 'romantic' image (Von Egmond, 2007) that inspires people to go there. A visitor interviewed in 2010 in Dharavi in Mumbai expressed his feelings:

> I expected to be depressed after the tour, I also expected confirmation that Dharavi was seething with criminal activity, organized crime, poverty and hopelessness. I based some of these expectations on descriptions of Dharavi I got from novels and movies. (Diekmann & Hannam, 2012: 1327)

The motivations for the visit are of a psychological nature as they concern the experience and background of the individual visitor to come and see places like Dharavi. According to Crompton's (1979) different reasons, only 'the Exploration and evaluation of self' might be hinting at the motivations to visit a slum, adding thus to the above allocentric vision of the tourist. Mowforth and Munt (2008: 270) argue that the urban and rural poor are being viewed by the West in a certain noble, sympathetic and even romantic way. The values of the slum as something chaotic in the order of the city show the exotic 'in-betweenness' and determine the physical and psychological itinerary which will be toured (Cejas, 2006: 225). Ultimately, the tours are about Western tourists' performative engagement with an uncanny space – a notion that combines the familiar with the strange – where things that are hidden and secret become visible to the tourists' gaze (Diekmann & Hannam, 2012: 1331).

Rolfes (2011: 74) states that tour organisers do not promote poverty, but they wish to change the image of the slums and promote authenticity and reality. But authenticity is subject to discussion. McIntosh and Prentice (1999) declare:

> As such, in Western societies, what is and is not authentic is largely the consequence of replicated interpretation which although contested by professionals, are commodified for mass consumption. (McIntosh & Prentice, 1999: 590)

Indeed, most tour operators in slums, favelas and townships insist on the local dynamics and economics of the area. Yet, the insight that the visitor gets is staged and commodified. As highlighted by several authors (see Diekmann & Hannam, 2012; Dyson, 2012) and in other sections and chapters of this book, visits to the slums follow a prepared script, reducing the encounter between the visitor and the host to smiles and body language of appreciation or ignorance. The guides constitute the only real interlocutor for the visitors. However, the absence of direct exchanges is not felt as lowering the quality of the experience. As highlighted in Chapter 6, indeed visitors having followed a guided tour of the slums with Reality Tours show a great level of satisfaction, some talking about the 'best' experience on their trip through India. This is also due to the fact that the tour is only paid for at the end, giving the impression of making a contribution to the community rather than a simple entrance fee. However, while tourism certainly contributes to the growing visibility of slums and slum dwellers, visitors certainly do not mend economic growth or improve living conditions in the disadvantaged areas (Freire-Medeiros, 2009b).

Using Harlem as an example, Hoffman (2003: 288) has highlighted how far visitors can contribute to the development of ethnic and minority quarters in cities. Considered as a 'ghetto economy' back in the 1980s, the demand by foreign visitors stimulated tourism to Harlem rising from 2,000 to 800,000 visitors yearly including an increasing number of domestic visitors. Like back in the early 20th century, visitors' representations of Harlem were connected to Black America, its music and entertainment traditions.

Ashworth and Page (2011: 7) draw attention to the fact that there is only a little research on how visitors actually use cities. In the literature it is often assumed that tourists use the diversified offer; however, there is little research as to whether tourists visit 'off the beaten track' attractions on their first trip or whether they are already familiar with the destination and wish to deepen their experience through an 'adventure' into urban ethnic and minority areas. Also, the means of connecting to the destination and preparing the trip have not been studied extensively, particularly as far as ethnic districts are concerned. For instance, various guidebooks highlight the African district of Brussels, but field research shows that the visitor numbers have not increased (Diekmann & Maulet, 2009). In other destinations, the source of information is mainly from guidebooks, particularly when public agencies do not wish to promote a specific kind of tourism, e.g. slum tourism. The economic benefits (or their absence) from visitors have been highlighted in in the Community Perceptions part of this book, but it should be underlined that it is often not the majority culture, middle-class visitor that brings benefits, but the community or internal visitors (i.e. those who do not live in the area but who visit regularly) seeking specific goods and services. Most ethnic urban and minority districts are promoted as an 'exotic' asset to foreign and mainly middle-class visitors. By promoting an urban ethnic quarter as 'exotic', the aim is clearly not to attract visitors from the promoted ethnic community itself (i.e. those who already know the culture well or are from the same background). This might also include diasporic tourists from the 'homeland'. One explanation might be that as community members, they shift from being tourists themselves to becoming part of the 'otherness' underpinning the ethnicity of the place.

Although the geographical extension of friendship and kinship networks connected to migration generates tourism flows (Williams & Hall, 2010), there is a lack of research on these community or internal visitors. This might be because community members who are visiting friends and relatives (VFR) tourists are not considered in or they may escape official tourism statistics. This is problematic when trying to analyse the contribution of VFR in economic and sociocultural research (Asiedu, 2008; Backer, 2008; Shani & Uriely, 2012) even though some economic benefit stays with the community or at least the suppliers delivering to the community. Internal tourists come for the provision of specific goods and services and not necessarily the place itself. In other ethnic quarters, nostalgic reasons of a past period can attract community members. America's Little Italies are cherished by an Italian community of which many members have never even visited Italy, but who wish to preserve the spaces where their ancestors settled when they first arrived in the States sometimes three or four generations ago (Conforti, 1996). It is not very important for the community that Little Italy does not have much in common with the 'real' Italy. American Chinese citizens do not expect their Chinatowns to be representative of a Chinese town either, but they do enjoy the social encounters and possibilities to purchase specific goods.

Managing Visitors in Ethnic and Minority Quarters

The difficulty in urban ethnic and minority quarters lies in the rampant gentrification that threatens the social ethnic structures. As highlighted earlier in this volume, Chinatowns in Boston, New York and Philadelphia are already gentrified neighbourhoods. Additionally, tourists, particularly the foreign and middle classes, long for standardised products – even inauthentic if necessary – to satisfy their needs. An example would be the tourists visiting Matonge's restaurants with groups on guided tours, but wishing not to eat there for sanitary reasons. In the long run, restaurant owners are convinced that more and more ethnic restaurants have to close down because their private and public space is invaded by tourists, but not 'consumed'. This is becoming a recurrent theme in cultural and ethnic tourism, where many visitors might claim that they prefer authentic cultural experiences but do not wish to experience any level of discomfort or a perceived lack of hygiene or safety. This can lead to the over-sanitising of ethnic quarters, facadism in order to aestheticise and a degree of standardisation. The small-scale retail and service establishments are replaced by international brands and chains benefitting the urban ethnic environment. The success of Harlem as an ethnic destination and the following gentrification also attracted global investments of national and international chains partly replacing the original commercial structure (Hoffman, 2003). In that perspective, ethnic culture will be commodified and gentrified to address the demands and needs of the visitors and eventually new residents. This is a paradox, for the community culture constitutes the pull factor for visiting the area, particularly for community tourists. While some visitors may seek new destinations, others like the centric and dependables will follow because the public space has gained a standardisation level which is easy to consume.

But in the end, it is the diversity of the visitors, their individual motivations, perceptions and expectations that makes tourism management a difficult task for the host communities. Interestingly, at least in the earliest days of tourism development, the local people may be relatively enthusiastic about visitors. Some are surprised and even pleased at the interest in their lives and cultures, which are otherwise marginalised or even hidden by governments and mainstream society. One difficulty identified in some research, especially in slums and favelas, is that the local communities do not really know why visitors are there or what kind of experiences they may be looking for. Unfortunately, the other side of this coin is the feeling that ethnic and minority communities are in a kind of human zoo and gazed on with intrusive curiosity. This is a phenomenon that is not just common to ethnic minorities but to gay groups as well. However, visitors may be unaware of this and many of them would no doubt be somewhat dismayed to realise that their presence had upset or offended the local population, the subject of their curious gaze.

It seems that some visitors' motivations are based on curiosity alone, but for others it may be something of an education. Some may also want to feel that they are making a contribution to the local economies or the lives of the inhabitants. It is a source of great wonder to many visitors that communities can live in conditions of great poverty yet still radiate a certain amount of joy of living. This might encourage visitors to feel grateful for their relatively more comfortable lives and to question the most important values in life. However, in many ethnic and gay quarters, visitors may be simply there for entertainment purposes, to visit restaurants and bars and the occasional cultural event or festival.

Of course, the experiences of visitors tend to be heavily mediated and governments and tour operators will often carefully select what they want visitors to see. The experiences may be sanitised in some way or aestheticised. Communities themselves may even choose to perform their culture in a certain way, embellishing it or 'improving' it. This raises the inevitable question about authenticity but as mentioned earlier, this concept is both subjective and relative not only to communities themselves but also to visitors. Guided tours seem to be the most common way of presenting ethnic cultures, but the scope of these is inevitably limited. There are surprisingly few attempts at more creative activities in ethnic quarters such as workshops of dance, gastronomy or music making, but these are undoubtedly difficult to arrange and require a certain amount of pre-planning and booking.

Typologies of Visitors

It is important to distinguish between types of visitors as mentioned earlier, as there is a significant difference between local residents (e.g. from another part of the city); local community (i.e. who visit regularly to consume goods and services but do not live in the area); domestic tourists who may or may not be familiar with the culture of different immigrant groups; international tourists for whom certain ethnic experiences will be new; and diasporic tourists who know the culture but not the context. The latter may enjoy the chance to meet friends and relatives and to consume ethnic products and services, whereas those unfamiliar with the culture may be looking for education or simply an exotic experience. Such visitors can coexist in relative harmony, although tour operators or city agencies might need to think about multiple interpretation(s) in the form of guided tours or heritage walks. In extreme cases, the quarters may also attract unwanted visitors such as those who want to engage in racist or homophobic behaviour, but luckily this is relatively rare and is less common for tourists than for local residents.

The following table provides a summary of typical visitor or tourist types in ethnic quarters and slums.

A typology of ethnic quarter and slum visitors and tourists

Visited location	Typical visitors/tourists	Likely motivations
Ethnic quarters (e.g. Chinatowns, Banglatowns, Little Italies)	• International tourists from outside the country with no connection to the community • Diasporic tourists • Domestic tourists • Residents from other parts of the city/region • 'Community' members not resident in the area	• Attracted by the exoticism and entertainment value of the ethnic quarter • VFR; connecting to community • Exciting experience not available elsewhere in the country • Entertainment, shopping, food, festivals • Employment or consumption of cultural goods and services
Jewish quarters	• Holocaust memorial 'pilgrims' • Jewish cultural tourists (secular and religious) • Non-Jewish cultural tourists	• Commemoration, remembrance • Celebrating Jewish national holidays and festivals; VFR • Education about Jewish culture and religion
Gay quarters	• Lesbian, gay, bisexual, transgender (LGBT) tourists • LGBT visitors from the local area • Heterosexual visitors (mainly women)	• Meeting the local LGBT 'community'; entertainment • Socialising in a 'safe' space or sanctuary; meeting other members of the local LGBT 'community' • Entertainment in a 'safe' space away from the heterosexual male gaze
Slums, favelas, townships	• International (and a lesser number of domestic) tourists	• Fascination with poverty, curiosity, charity, reassessment of life's values

This table shows the diversity of visitors to ethnic and minority quarters without taking into consideration other factors like age and nationality. On the other hand, one could assume that most of these tourists are closer to Plog's allocentric or venturer typologies, middle class, they are looking for new and (co)-creative experiences on the fringes of cities or tourism destinations. They are likely to be open-minded, tolerant and liberal with a tendency towards more bohemian, artistic or even hedonistic lifestyles (especially some LGBT tourists). The development of ethnic and minority quarters as mainstream tourist attractions might become a welcome development for many communities, residents or hosts, but care must be taken not to compromise too much the sense of 'sanctuary', safety and authenticity or the very cultures that the visitors come to see may be eroded and will alienate all visitors, including local and diasporic ones.

Conclusion

Although there has been much more research on the perceptions and experiences of visitors to ethnic and minority quarters than on those of hosts, the complexity of visitor types, motivations and attitudes necessitates deeper analysis and further research. Ethnic, minority and slum tourism do not attract overwhelmingly large numbers of visitors, nor do they create huge economic benefits. On the other hand, the nature of the visitor experience can be quite unpredictable because of cultural differences. Bianca Freire-Medeiros and Márcio Grijó Vilarouca's chapter in this section looks at the difference between international and domestic tourists in the case of favelas, noting the different perceptions and expectations. Interestingly, international tourists' opinions about the nature of the favelas and the potential benefits of tourism can be more negative than those of domestic tourists. Many tourists claim to want authenticity in their experiences, but in actual fact they rather crave a sanitised, aestheticised version of ethnic or slum living that does not involve too much discomfort. Thus in Brazil, the government did its best to 'prettify' some of the favelas in time for the football World Cup in 2014. Jock Collins' research about Chinatowns also shows that visitors ideally wanted to experience more authentic Chinese culture and character, but commented on the dirt, lack of sanitation and the smell of the areas they visited. In Nelson Graburn's chapter about ethnic tourism in China, visitor experiences are often deliberately embellished to 'improve' them! Overall, these chapters show that there are many visitor stereotypes of the ethnic or immigrant other and their lives prior to visitation, but that living areas like favelas are extremely diverse and visitors also differ greatly in their responses and perceptions.

7 Would You Be a Favela Tourist? Confronting Expectations and Moral Concerns Among Brazilian and Foreign Potential Tourists

Bianca Freire-Medeiros and
Márcio Grijó Vilarouca

Introduction

Since the 1990s, selected and idealised aspects of poverty which are associated with specific territories – favelas, townships, slums – have been turned into a tourist commodity in various megacities of the Global South. Guided tours of diverse modalities abound, providing less or more interaction with residents, using different means of transportation (on foot, van, jeep, coach, bicycles or motorcycles), showcasing the area during the day or at night. Promoted on websites and recommended by reputable guidebooks, these incursions into territories of supposed dirt, danger and despair have an established monetary value agreed upon by promoters and consumers (for several case studies, see Frenzel *et al.*, 2012).

Such touristic valorisation of poverty – or 'touristic poverty', as one of us has phrased it in previous opportunities (Freire-Medeiros, 2009a, 2013) – is thus completely incorporated into the logic of the neo-liberal model of market-based economic and social organisation. Carefully planned and creatively packaged, that modality of tourism offers a peculiar juxtaposition of amusement and fear, leisure and guilt, emotional expression and exploitation. In so doing, we believe, it brings new insights into the politics of contemporary Western moralities and allows for an examination of how the tourist's behaviour and feelings connect to the macro-level patterns of

transnational arrangements which situate poverty, violence and segregation on specific 'orders of worth' – to use Boltanski and Thévenot's expression – within global tourism hierarchies.

Promising to sell emotions elicited by the first-hand contemplation of
'*the* poor' in their 'habitat', poverty tours are characterised as morally controversial, to say the least: unsurprisingly, media accounts which are bur-
dened with value-laden assumptions proliferate in the main international
newspapers, not to mention radio and TV shows.[1] It seems correct to suggest that potential tourists are not oblivious to these ethical debates and
judgements around what has been largely identified as an 'extraordinary
form of tourism' (Rolfes, 2010). While research on the actual slum/town-
ship/favela tourist has burgeoned in the last few years (Freire-Medeiros,
2009a; Menezes, 2007; Rolfes, 2010; Rolfes *et al.*, 2009), there have been
no such studies of the potential tourists nor of how such moralising views
shape tourism practices and encounters. This chapter may be taken, therefore, as a preliminary step in understanding the opinions, expectations and
moral concerns of potential favela tourists.

According to Boltanski and Thévenot's (1991, 2006) model, justifications fall into seven logics that correspond to seven different 'common
worlds': the *civic* world, the *opinion* world, the *market* world, the *industrial*
world, the *domestic* world, the *inspired* world and the *green* world. Although
reducing the debate around favela tourism to seven logics could be seen
as a drastic simplification, this framework is indeed useful here insofar as
it avoids having to presuppose inductively new principles of justice and
allows for interesting comparative studies. With this in mind, we address
justifications and moralities in a way that is dissociated from normative
perspectives, with the aim of answering three main questions regarding
favela tourism in particular and of provoking some reflection on poverty
tourism in general: (a) to what image of the favela – stereotypes and myths
– as well as principles of worth do potential tourists depart from and appeal
to when confronted with the possibility of engaging in a favela tour?; (b) if
'justification', as proposed by Boltanski and Thévenot (1991, 2006; see
also Lafaye & Thévenot, 1993; Lamont & Thévenot, 2000; Thévenot *et al.*,
2000), is a process of interpretation whereby different actors mobilise pre-
existing, socially accepted logic, what preconceptions and moral concerns
inform the idea of a 'touristic favela' and potentially influence the promotion of empirical favelas as regular tourist destinations?; (c) what does the
variable 'nationality' reveal in terms of triggering modes of justifications
for being for or against consuming favelas as tourist destinations? Inspired
by the new mobilities paradigm (Elliot & Urry, 2010; Sheller & Urry, 2006;
Urry, 2007) and its focus on technological mediation in the construction
of tourist destinations, the next section provides a brief overview of the
invention and consolidation of a Rio de Janeiro favela as a tourist attraction. In the third section, we describe the methodological approach and

briefly present the broader research project with which this chapter establishes a dialogue. In the fourth section, we discuss our research background and some of our empirical findings, paying particular attention to how international and domestic tourists provide justifications for their opinions and positions. We conclude with some reflections on the power of moralising views in shaping favela tourism as well as the ways in which such tourism practice functions as a means of reproduction or modification of established 'principles of worth' concerning the favela.

Turning Favelas into a Tourist Destination: A Brief Overview

Before standing for almost every poor and segregated area in urban Brazil which develops and operates largely outside the formal control of the state, the term 'favela' denoted a specific urban form: the agglomerations of substandard housing that emerged in Rio de Janeiro in the early 20th century. Throughout history, conventional wisdom has placed favelas in an ambiguous semantic logic which associates them not only with solidarity and joy ('cradle of samba, carnival and capoeira') but also with poverty, moral degradation and violent criminality ('cradle of marginality').[2]

Nowadays, more than 20% of Rio de Janeiro's population is comprised of favela residents: about 1.3 million people living in 1020 communities which are increasingly diverse both in social and economic terms.[3] This empirical diversity, nevertheless, is subsumed by encompassing narratives which produce what one of us calls the *travelling favela*: a space of imagination and a mobile entity that is travelled to while travelling around the world (see Freire-Medeiros, 2013, especially chapter 3). A trademark and a touristic destination, it is at one and the same time an effect and the condition of the possibility of flows of capital (legal and illegal), bodies (ordinary visitors and worldwide celebrities, from pop stars to US President Obama), cameras (filming and photographing), ideas (from within and outside academia) and images (midiatic and for private consumption). Part of global narratives which resignify poverty as an object of consumption, it is commodified many times in unpredictable configurations, adding market value to fancy restaurants and clubs – the Favela Chic chain being the obvious example – pieces of design furniture and smart cars. If travel guides, movies, fictional accounts, photologues, souvenirs, etc. are part and parcel of the travelling favela, so are academic books, articles, theses and dissertations.

The curiosity towards the favela is far from a novelty (Jaguaribe & Hetherington, 2006; Williams, 2008) and should be understood from a cultural-historical perspective as part of the so-called 'slumming' phenomenon (see Heap, 2009; Koven, 2004; Mayne, 1993; Ross, 2007). However, it was only in the early 1990s – parallel to the development of township tourism in post-apartheid South Africa – that a proper favela tourism market blossomed.

There is no documentation supporting an effective date in which favela tours would have begun, but their myth of origin is the 1992 Earth Summit (Rio Conference on Environment and Sustainable Development), when journalists and political activists went on a tour to Rocinha. Relating the origin of the favela as a tourist attraction to the 1992 Earth Summit is in some ways ironic if one remembers that, throughout the event, government authorities invested specific efforts towards isolating favelas from foreign eyes, even enlisting the army's aid to do so. Twenty years later and despite the lack of public support, around eight commercial favela tour companies and 20 informal guides do business in Rocinha, advertised in the tourist market as 'the largest favela in South America'.

Since 2010, not only has the number of travel agencies offering favela tours in different localities grown, but so has the number of groups that each season are taken on tours to these various localities. Meanwhile, the position of the three levels of government has shifted from an initial posture of opposition followed by indifference to open support in the present day. There is a general agreement on behalf of the public power around the idea that favela tourism is capable of promoting social and economic development. This significant shift should be seen as part of a broader neo-liberal ideology which places Rio de Janeiro as a competitor within the 'world-cities market' and that includes increased investments in strategic planning that are aimed at presenting the city as a non-violent and friendly site for the 2014 FIFA World Cup and the 2016 Olympic Games.

Spearheading the current public security programme in Rio de Janeiro state is the so-called Unidades de Polícia Pacificadora (Police Pacification Unit or UPP in the Portuguese acronym). In theory, it draws on the ideal of community policing, but in the UPP version, the 'community' is necessarily a favela and it must be permanently occupied.[4] The arbitrary intervention finds legitimacy in a decades-old discourse, propagated both by the government and different sectors of the civil society, which affirms that the city is undergoing a civil war. The official discourse claims that the UPP is capable of offering a long-needed level of patrimonial and juridical security for the capital to establish itself and profit on those territories.

Within this context, in 2010 a joint venture between the Ministry of Tourism and the State Government of Rio de Janeiro named 'Rio Top Tour: Rio de Janeiro from a new perspective' was released having as its overt goal to stimulate sustainable tourism in the favelas. In some of the 'pacified' favelas, selected residents are currently taking courses in order to become local tourist guides and others are benefiting from a new credit line for the renovation of kiosks and handcraft coops for tourism catering.

Going back to Boltanski and Thévenot's model (1991, 2006), one could say that we are presently facing a process of *market qualification* for the touristic favela supported not only by the state but also by civil society at large, including some historical leadership from within the favelas themselves (see Machado da Silva, 2012). The worthiness of a specific favela as a tourist attraction is thus measured based on the efficiency of the services it can provide for the tourists, its residents' performance as hosts and its capacity to ensure what is expected from a generic favela, i.e. poverty, some level of disorder and joy. According to this logic, tourists are also qualified in terms of their market worth: they are seen as customers who may contribute through their presence and various purchases – ticket, souvenirs, beverages and food, etc. – to the social and economic development of a specific favela. Let us now examine how potential tourists react to such assumptions and logics of worth.

Methodology

The chapter establishes a dialogue with previous reflections on the subject of converting Rio de Janeiro favelas into tourist destinations (Freire-Medeiros, 2007, 2009; Menezes, 2009) and is based on a more recent demand for consulting from the tourism ministry. In this larger project, we sought to understand the tourist activity in Rio de Janeiro favelas through a research design that combined quantitative and qualitative methods to produce diagnoses of current tourist experiences as well as of the tourist potential of other sites. To summarise, the various research stages consisted of:

(1) A case study in the Santa Marta favela, which consisted of a survey of 400 foreign tourists visiting the favela between March and May 2011 that sought to identify the tourists' and tour agents' profiles, tourists' impressions of the visit and how they evaluated not only the tourist equipment present in the favela but also their own experiences in the reality tour. In addition, we carried out 40 in-depth interviews with the main actors directly or indirectly involved with tourist activity at the site, among whom were inhabitants and local leaderships, local merchants, UPP staff, local tour guides and operators of receptive tourism.
(2) The second stage, which is the object of this chapter, was based on a survey with 900 interviews of 'potential tourists' carried out in the Galeão International Airport of Rio de Janeiro.
(3) The third stage required formulating a diagnosis, through ethnographic fieldwork, of the tourist potential of four favelas (Providência, Chapéu Mangueira e Babilônia, Cantagalo and Pavão e Pavãozinho) to produce a strategic plan to stimulate tourist activity in pacified favelas.

The empirical data come from an on-site survey carried out in the Tom Jobim International Airport's boarding area in Rio de Janeiro between 31 March and 16 April 2011.[5] The survey yielded 900 face-to-face interviews based on a non-probabilistic sample and was conducted in Portuguese, English, French and Spanish. Due to the lack of systematic information on the subject – the origin and nationality of the tourists who visit Rio de Janeiro city and the study population's socio-demographic profile – the sample was segmented to divide it equally between national and foreign tourists and, to a lesser degree, by gender. The purpose was not so much to take nationality as a set of supposed common cultural traits, but as a reference in a scale of proximity and levels of exoticisation (Urry, 1990).

The questionnaire consisted of 37 questions, subdivided into four parts: (1) identification of the tourist's socio-economic and demographic profile; (2) characterisation of type of tourism (reason for the trip, accommodation, means of transportation, duration of stay, etc.); (3) expectations and perceptions of tourist activity in favelas; and (4) interest in taking a tour of a favela, and justifications and evaluation of the potential for consumption of the favela as a tourist product.

From a methodological standpoint, in researching the potential tourist, our intention was much more to try to capture the image that participants had of the favela than to measure the 'real interest' in the visit. This is due in part to our findings in previous exploratory work in Rocinha and Santa Marta that the vast majority of visitors to the favelas were foreign tourists. Thus, we were less concerned with establishing that around 80% of Brazilian tourists had been to the city and had not effectively visited any favelas, and much more interested in establishing whether or not there was an understanding of the object as something prohibitive, whether morally or due to a perception of risk.

Research Background and Findings

As previously mentioned, our sample was equally divided between foreign and national tourists (non-residents of Rio de Janeiro) so as to confront the opinions and expectations of two groups that ideally had different levels of acquaintance with empirical favelas. Most national tourists who were approached at the airport were permanent residents of the north-east (29.2%) and south-east (28.2%) regions of Brazil. We likewise found that only 20.5% of Brazilians were travelling to the city for the first time. Inversely, the percentage of foreigners who had their first tourist experience in Rio de Janeiro was a considerable 79.5%. The sample of foreign tourists was mostly composed of informants from the American continent: 34.2% resided in Latin America and the Caribbean and 28.8% resided in North and Central America. The rest of the sample was composed of European tourists (30.6%) and visitors from Asia, Africa and Oceania (6.4%).

We asked the informants about the existence of poor and segregated areas in their city or country of residence. The existence of such territories was acknowledged by 88.9% of Brazilians and 75.4% of foreigners. However, when answering whether or not they had visited these areas, the result was very revealing. In the case of the Brazilians, 47.4% had visited a favela or poor area, while only 24.3% of foreigners stated that they had done the same in their countries. The reader should take into consideration that the respondents were not identifying themselves here as favela tourists, but as people who, for various reasons, had the opportunity to enter a territory that they consider to be poor and segregated. With regard to the foreigners, among the most significant results is the fact that 45.1% of residents of Latin America and the Caribbean answered that they had visited a territory with those characteristics versus 28.0% of foreigners residing in North and Central America and 14.6% of those residing in Europe.

Taking into consideration that the vast majority of favela tourists are from a foreign country to Brazil, our hypotheses was that Brazilians would be more acquainted with empirical favelas and the idea of favela tourism, but less favourable to this practice than international tourists. In a dialogue with the theory of justification, we attempt to unfold and contrast the logics of evaluation of these two main groups, as follows.

We presented to the participants a balanced list of positive and negative words, inspired by academic literature on slum tourism (Rolfes, 2009; Rolfes *et al.*, 2007), and we asked them to choose four options that most accurately represent their expectations regarding a generic favela. In Table 7.1, we classified in order of importance the first attribute chosen by the tourists to express their expectations.

Therefore, taking only this first mention into account, we observed a generic consensus, both among Brazilian and foreign tourists that

Table 7.1 What do you expect to see in the favela?

Brazilians			International
Precarious dwelling	18.1%	1	Poverty
Poverty	16.1%	2	Precarious dwelling
Drug trafficking	12.9%	3	Drug trafficking
Filth	8.3%	4	Tradition
Samba	7.8%	5	Samba
Solidarity	7.6%	6	Mess/disorder
Happiness	6.7%	7	Violence
Mess/disorder	5.1%	8	Happiness
Tradition	3.3%	9	Solidarity

associates favelas primordially with negative perceptions such as poverty, precarious housing and drug trafficking. In the case of national tourists, another negative characteristic followed, 'filth', while for the foreigners a positive concept finally emerged, that of 'tradition'. On the other hand, among Brazilians, there is a more diffuse, albeit negative, perception of the favela, while among foreigners the construction is centred predominantly in the idea of poverty.

As an alternative way of analysing this generic and imagined 'first definition' of what a favela is, we verified that 35.3% of Brazilian tourists made their choices within a supposedly positive semantic range (solidarity, joy, samba, etc.) while among foreigners that percentage was only 20.5%.

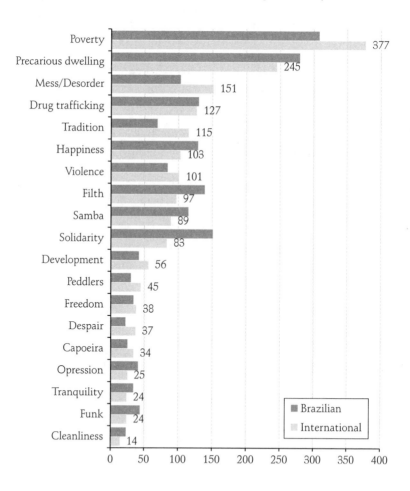

Figure 7.1 Brazilian and international tourists: Favela semantic definitions

In Figure 7.1, we present the sum of all four attributes chosen by the tourists to represent favelas. Therefore, the following data indicate the number of times each attribute was 'mentioned'. Thus, as we had previously seen, poverty and precarious housing are the most cited elements, representative of the travellers' expectations regarding favelas and that always appear far ahead of other possible attributes.

Solidarity, filth and drug trafficking, in the case of the Brazilians, and disorder, drug trafficking and tradition, in the case of the foreigners, are the subsequent most-mentioned words. Joy came next in both samples. However, Brazilians, to a larger extent, tend to give a more positive character to interpersonal sociability, not only with regard to joy, but also in characterising the favela as a space of solidarity. Foreigners, in their turn, differ from Brazilians in giving greater weight to the attribute 'tradition'. At the same time, on the negative side, patterns also diverge in the possible association of poverty and precarious housing either with filth or disorder. Another point we wish to highlight is that samba overrides funk and capoeira as alleged cultural marks of favelas. Generally speaking, however, we can point to a pattern of responses that exposes some degree of regularity/communality that crosses borders – in the construction of the generic favela.

On another occasion (Freire-Medeiros *et al.*, 2012), we interviewed 400 foreign tourists during an actual visiting tour of the Santa Marta favela and identified that the words most used to define the favela were, in order of importance: (1) poverty, (2) development, (3) solidarity, (4) joy, (5) tradition, (6) filth, (7) precarious housing and (8) disorder.[6] Thus, if on the one hand poverty remains as the first definition of the favela, corresponding to the dominant expectations, on the other, it is followed by more positive perceptions, being accompanied by the notion of 'development'. Poverty is therefore resignified through the 'poverty with development' binomial, and mostly followed by positive evaluations of sociability – solidarity and joy – that do not point to a situation of what one could call 'a Hobbesian state'.

Thus, even if, in the informants' view, some morally controversial aspects of favela tourism remain relevant, presence and proximity would act as a counterweight to predominantly negative media narratives. The empirical contrast is revealing. The foreign tourists interviewed at the airport, when asked to indicate what they expected to see in the favela, overwhelmingly chose negative attributes (67.5%) while those who experienced a visit to the Santa Marta favela inversely defined it with a choice of positive attributes (59.4%).

Brazilian and foreign tourists were asked to state the degree to which they agreed with certain statements regarding the tourist activity's impact on favelas. Sentences with positive and negative arguments were cited, to which informants were asked to react based on the following scale:

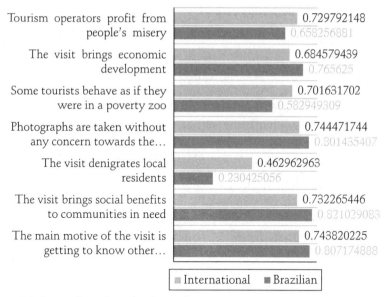

Figure 7.2 Perceptions about favela tourism

strongly agrees, somewhat agrees, does not agree or disagree, somewhat disagrees and strongly disagrees. To simplify, Figure 7.2 only presents the sum of agreement percentages (strongly and somewhat).

Based on Figure 7.2, we can observe that there is a relatively similar pattern of responses among the two tourist profiles. Two of the answers that drew a high degree of agreement among informants identified that 'people's main motive is getting to know other lifestyles' and that 'the visit brings social benefits to the favela'. However, that view must be mitigated by the negative though minority view by some of the foreign tourists that 'the visit denigrates the inhabitants'. This result accompanies, in a way, the results presented in Figure 7.2, which show that Brazilians show a higher tendency to point to positive aspects as defining of the favela.

With regard to the economic dimension, Brazilians are more optimistic: a larger percentage of them agree that tourism brings economic benefits and they tend to be less critical of tourism agencies' operations than foreign tourists are. Though these opinions may seem divergent, the fact is that a tourist may consider that tourism may benefit the favela through indirect effects on the community. Obviously, these data are not conclusive, but are marked by an ambiguity inherent to a morally controversial economic activity.

After asking tourists about their perceptions regarding the tourist activity, we directly asked whether or not they were interested in effectively visiting a favela. Most responded affirmatively, a percentage that was surprisingly higher among Brazilians (58.2%) than among foreigners (51.4%). The difference between these groups is not large at all; however, it counters what happens in practice, given the near complete predominance of foreign tourists observed in the empirical ground – but not officially measured, it is important to notice – in this type of tourism. But perhaps what is even more intriguing here is how both groups seem to depart from a common grammar (Boltanski & Thévenot, 2006) within which they make sense of the favela, its residents and supposed tourism practices that shape the touristic favela.

Final Remarks

Favela tourism is approached by many critics with eminently normative and reductionist arguments. More often than not, they depart from and idealise a singular, ideal type of tour and visitor: the image of a voyeur touring a poverty zoo. Nevertheless, on empirical grounds, what one sees is a rich profile of types of tourists, types of tours and means of visiting a favela. This chapter attempted to overcome this narrow view by dealing with some aspects of the moral complexity which results from a peculiar form of tourism, that which defines itself as a real encounter between hosts and guests with extremely different economic backgrounds. Our objective was to account for the way that potential visitors, both Brazilian and foreigners, place value on favelas as tourist destinations.

If potential tourists, when compared to actual tourists, seem less convinced that tourism activities in the favela would bring economic development to the community (Freire-Medeiros *et al.*, 2012), they are as confident that it may provide a more nuanced view of life in the favela. Thus, along with the logics of the *market* world which would justify favela tourism based on a purely economic orientation related to an improvement of the material well-being of favela residents, potential tourists present justifications which fall into logics that relate directly to the *opinion* world.

But from which *worlds* do the potential tourists depart to justify their positions within the controversy of favela tourism? Both foreigners and Brazilians, as our research findings suggest, mobilise higher-order principles based on some long-standing dogmas about poverty and its territories that tourism practices help to propagate. In the specific case of the favela, it is worth recalling here sociologist Licia Valladares's (2005: 151) writings on what she identifies as the 'three dogmas', which have been stemming from scientific research of the favela and which are maintained by different groups for various reasons. Those are: (a) its particularity, i.e. the emphasis of difference to other city areas; (b) its unity, i.e. the treatment as a homogeneous phenomenon by using 'favela' in the singular; and (c) the characterisation as the urban space of poverty per se. These three dogmas are problematic because they lead researchers (and by extension, policy-makers) to overlook the diversity within and across the favelas, as well as continuities with other parts of the city. As we attempted to demonstrate, favela tourism feeds on these dogmas at the same time that it gives them a renewed incentive.

Notes

(1) See 'Slum Tours: Real or Real Tacky?' (*National Geographic Traveler*, March 2009); 'Slum Visits: Tourism or Voyeurism?' (*New York Times*, March 2008); 'Slum Tourism: Good or Bad?' (Foreign Policy, February 2007); 'Next Stop, Squalor: Is poverty tourism 'poorism,' they call it exploration or exploitation?' (*Smithsonian Magazine*, December 2007); 'Slum Tours: A Day Trip Too Far?' (*The Guardian*, May 2006). In 2009, the Indian National Public Radio aired a show titled '"Poverty Porn": Education or Exploitation?', and asked: 'Are poverty tours really the moral equivalent of paedophiliac tourism in Southeast Asia?'. In the same year, Radio Canada aired 'Le tourisme de misère, amoral ou non?'.

(2) In October 2007, Sérgio Cabral Filho, governor of Rio de Janeiro state, suggested that legalising abortion might contain violence in Rio de Janeiro insofar as favelas were actual 'factories churning out criminals'. See http://g1.globo.com/Noticias/Politica/0,,MUL155710-5601,00-CABRAL+DEFENDE+ABORTO+CONTRA+VIOLENCIA+NO+RIO+DE+JANEIRO.html.

(3) Brazilian statistical office (IBGE, the Instituto Brasileiro de Geografia e Estatística) currently defines a favela as 'a settlement of 50 housing units or more located on public or private property and characterized by disordered occupation without the benefits of essential public services'. None of these features, however, are exclusive to the favelas, being illegality and precariousness more the rule than the exception within a historical context of non-compliance with urbanistic legislation in Brazil.

(4) In practice, the 'pacification' process works like this: the Special Police Operations Batallion (BOPE) initially occupies the favela and undertakes special operations of armed confrontation and tactical dismantling of the drug trade networks, thus clearing the path for their replacement by specially trained and first-year officers recently graduated military police (to avoid the corruption endemic in the more experienced echelons of the force). The police occupy the strategic areas of the favela and stand guard almost permanently.

(5) The survey was conducted by FGV-Opinião applied social research group, which specialises in quantitative and qualitative research and is coordinated by Professor Márcio Vilarouca. The study was carried out by two teams, each consisting of six interviewers and one supervisor. Applying the questionnaire took, on average, between 15 and 20 minutes.

(6) In the non-probabilistic sample, it was likewise not possible to use stratification quotas, due to the lack of knowledge of the population parameters.

8 Chinatowns as Tourist Attractions in Australia

Jock Collins

Introduction

Ethnic tourism is a field relatively undeveloped in the international tourist literature. Ethnic tourism can be defined as tourism driven by the presence of immigrant minorities in host countries. Immigrant minorities shape the cultural landscapes of the built and social environment in their host cities, with places of worship (temples, mosques, churches, synagogues and others) and shops and restaurants decorated with ethnic iconography and adorned with signs in foreign languages, the most visible market of this minority immigrant community presence. This happens most often in cities because most immigrants are attracted to the cities of Western (Castles & Miller, 2013) and non-Western societies (Saunders, 2010) because of the employment opportunities on offer, though non-metropolitan areas in many Western nations such as Australia (Hugo, 2008; Jordan *et al.*, 2011), the USA (Massey, 2010) and Canada (Clemenson & Pitblado, 2007) often have an immigration history and increasing contemporary immigration to regional and rural areas.

Very few nations, cities or regions in the world today do not have an immigrant presence with contemporary patterns of immigration (Goldin *et al.*, 2011), suggesting that global people flows are increasing in numbers and diversity. As Jan Rath (2007: xvi), editor of one of the few books dedicated to canvassing the contemporary dynamics of ethnic urban tourism in the immigration gateway cities of Western nations puts it: 'More and more travellers, leisure seekers and business investors in gateway cities are indulging in ethnocultural events and festivals, and are gravitating to centres of immigrant ethnic commerce, The urban tourist economy is thus becoming one of the interfaces between immigrants from all strata of society and the wider economy'.

Despite this, the international tourism literature has only recently begun to explore in detail the interface between immigration, ethnic diversity and tourism (Aytar & Rath, 2012; Hall & Williams, 2002; Rath, 2007). Given Australia's long immigration history as one of the world's major settler immigration nations, ethnic tourism has particular salience.

Australia has, in relative terms, one of the world's largest and most diverse immigration populations – one in four (24.6%) of the Australian population are first-generation immigrants, while 43.1% are either first- or second-generation immigrants – with around 60% of the population Sydney, Perth and Melbourne first- or second-generation immigrants. These immigrants come from all over the globe, so that Australia has the world in one nation and its largest cities are cosmopolitan in character where the tourist can find the world in one city (Collins, 2013).

While the Australian immigration experience has been subject to detailed research, the links between Australian immigration, cultural diversity and tourism are surprisingly neglected as a field of study (Collins *et al.*, 2007, 2010; Collins & Jordan, 2009; Jordan & Collins, 2012). Large and diverse immigrant communities are linked to national and international tourism in a number of ways. Many immigrants first experience their new host country as a tourist before deciding to emigrate. For example, a study of immigrant teachers in Australia found that a number had decided to apply for a permanent or temporary visa to teach in Australia after visiting Australia as a tourist (Reid *et al.*, 2014: 68–80). Second, relatives and friends of immigrants visit a country on international tourist visas because of these social links: a host country like Australia looms large on the tourist imagination when they hear about the experiences of family and friends. In this way, tourism is driven by international social networks (social capital). Similarly, those who arrive in Australia on a temporary visa as a skilled worker, international student or working holidaymaker often return to Australia on international tourist visas to reconnect with their friends and/or family after their temporary visa expires. For example, young Koreans (the second-largest group of working holidaymakers in Australia) often return to Australia as tourists after completing their working holiday. Third, destinations like Australia become attractive to international tourists because of the appeal of their cosmopolitan character, itself a direct consequence of a large and diverse immigration programme. While this is a more indirect link between immigration, ethnic diversity and tourism, it is relatively unexplored in the literature and is the central concern of this chapter.

One of the consequences of large and diverse immigration intakes into Australia has been the emergence of cosmopolitan cities such as Sydney (Collins & Castillo, 1998) and Melbourne (Collins *et al.*, 2002), and within these cosmopolitan cities, clusters of immigrants of minority ethnic background, or *ethnic precincts*, emerge in downtown areas and suburbs. Each Australian city, like most global cities in the world, has developed a Chinatown. Similarly, some neighbourhoods become a Little Italy, Little Greece, Little Vietnam or Little Korea. Others take on more pan-ethnic identities such as Asia-towns.

The photo on the front and back cover of Martin Selby's (2004) book, *Understanding Urban Tourism*, is of two Chinese dragon dances performed for a largely Chinese crowd at the front of the welcome gates of some (unnamed) Chinatown. This chapter takes Chinatowns in two of Australia's largest cosmopolitan cities – Sydney and Melbourne – as case studies to explore further the immigration/ethnicity/tourism interface. The aim of this chapter is to explore in more detail the links between ethnic precincts in Australia and international tourism. In order to do this, it first looks at the Australian and international literature on tourism in urban places and spaces that are identified with immigrant minorities. The remainder of the chapter draws on fieldwork conducted in Sydney and Melbourne Chinatowns to explore their historical development, their characteristics and changing development and, finally, their links to international tourism before reflecting on the implications for a theory of ethnic tourism.

The Immigrant Other as Tourist Attraction

The commodification of ethnic diversity in a city has become increasingly important to contemporary cultural landscapes of tourism (Selby, 2004; Urry, 2002), particularly urban tourism. Cosmopolitan cities generate diversity and excitement (Florida, 2002: 227) and tolerance of difference (Florida, 2005: 6), though outbursts of racial conflict can disturb this tolerance as riots in Los Angeles (1992), Paris (2005), Sydney (2005) and London (2011) attest. Zukin (1995) points to the role of ethnic diversity in shaping place and space, and then relates this to a tendency to commodify cosmopolitan lifestyles in cities, often involving what MacCannell (1973, 1999) calls a 'reconstructed ethnicity'. This is obviously the case in the world's great immigrant cities. Recent data (The Economist, 2014) show that nearly 60% of the population of Miami are first-generation immigrants (that is, foreign born) as are over 45% of the Toronto population and 40% of Vancouver's population. Other great immigrant cities are London and New York (about 37% foreign born), Paris (23%) and Montreal (32%). This is consistent with other data on the immigrant population in cities across the world (Price & Benton-Short, 2007), which add major immigrant cities in Australasia (Sydney, Melbourne and Auckland), Asia and the Middle East to the list. These immigrant cities are also major global tourist destinations.

There is a long history that links the emergence of immigrant places and spaces as tourist attractions, particularly when these immigrant cultures are very different from that of the mainstream host society. For example, Lin's (1998: 174–176) account of how middle-class New Yorkers in the 1880s liked 'to go slumming in China Town', riding in 'rubbernecker vehicles' (also known as 'gape wagons') attracted by the chance to glimpse, from a safe distance, the gambling, prostitution and drug culture that was associated with 'exotic' Chinese culture. The term 'rubbernecker' (for a gawking tourist) entered into American parlance during this era.

Chinatowns are an almost universal form of this *ethnicised* place in contemporary Western cities (Anderson, 1990, 1991; Fitzgerald, 1997; Fong, 1994; Kinkead, 1993; Lin, 1998; Zhou, 1992). But ethnic precincts also emerge associated with other communities of the immigrant other. Ethnic precincts such as 'Little Italy' (Conforti, 1996), 'Little India' (Chang, 2000; McEvoy, 2003), 'Little Bavaria' (Frenkel & Walton, 2000), 'Little Sweden' (Schnell, 2003) and 'Finntowns' (Timothy, 2002) have emerged in countries across the continents. A key feature of these ethnic precincts is the provision of ethnic food and ethnic restaurants (Gabaccia, 1998; Warde, 1997; Warde & Martens, 2000), while most ethnic precincts are also sites where ethnic community organisations are located and their activities, including ethnic festivals, are staged. These urban ethnic precincts often undergo an 'ethnic makeover' with ethnic iconography, signage and symbols giving these places a distinctly different feel, smell and appearance to other parts of the city. It is this difference that is the attraction to local and national and international tourists alike.

Ethnic precincts are one example of the spatial dimensions of the commodification of ethnic diversity in cities (Rath, 2007). Ethnic precincts are places in the city that combine both private and public spaces and where the cultural and symbolic economy gain prominence shaped by the interaction of producers (ethnic entrepreneurs), consumers and the critical infrastructure (regulators, community leaders, critics, place-marketers) (Zukin, 1995). The private spaces are those of the ethnic and other entrepreneurs that exist in the forms of restaurants, cafés, shops and other businesses that are the main attractor of people to the ethnic precinct. The public spaces are the streets, footpaths, malls, squares, pedestrian thoroughfares and transport nodes outside the private businesses in the ethnic precinct. They have been developed to include ethnic iconography, symbols and design to reflect the ethnicity of the precinct, a public spatial form of the commodification of ethnicity.

Ethnic precincts are fundamentally contradictory sites (Collins, 2006). First, there is the problem of the credibility and authenticity of the ethnic precincts, which involves who is 'authorised' to claim authenticity, how that authenticity is symbolised and what employees and employers in ethnic enterprises have to do to generate that authenticity. Second, how legitimate can a precinct be in the eyes of the co-ethnic community, other locals and tourists if it has been developed by deliberate regulation, planning and government intervention? Third, there is the problem of control and the ways that crime in ethnic precincts threatens the safety of the ethnic tourist experience.

One of the critical parts of an ethnic precinct is its outer façade. What constitutes an authentic Chinese/Italian/Vietnamese place and how do you develop it? Bryman (2004: 52) refers to the centrality of *theming* in contemporary consumption places and the contradictions inherent in such theming attempts. Critics of theming often disapprove of the use of symbols of nostalgia for thematic cues. Drawing on faux designs and histories, theming in terms of nostalgic references is often depicted as presenting a sanitised history, one that removes any reference to hardship and conflict in the cause of consumption. The processes by which the public façade of ethnic precincts is developed, the authenticity of these ethnic precincts and the contradictions that emerge are explored in the rest of this chapter by a study of ethnic precincts in Sydney.

Immigrant entrepreneurs cluster in these ethnic precincts. Their restaurants and retail outlets at the street level are adorned with appropriate cultural façades and language, creating the 'ethnoscape' of the precinct. Their main customers are co-ethnics and other locals and tourists. Upstairs, professional immigrants provide medical, legal and cultural services largely directed to the co-ethnic market who seek culturally and linguistically familiar services. As Selby (2004: 24) reminds us, 'ethnic tourism enclaves' are presenting many countries with opportunities: 'The potential for "ethnic tourist attractions" is now widely recognized by local governments and tourist boards, encouraging the development of areas such as Brick Lane in London, Little Italy in Boston and the Balti Quarter in Birmingham'.

For example, McEvoy (2003) presents an excellent insight into the formation of the *curry mile* in what effectively is a Little India, in the town of Rushholme, Manchester, UK, and the key role of the ethnic entrepreneurs – not Indians, but *Pakistanis* – in its emergence as an ethnic precinct. Similarly in Sydney, Korean immigrant entrepreneurs cluster in a few blocks of the central business district (CBD) and in the suburbs of Strathfield, Eastwood and Campsie where Korean immigrant settlers concentrate. There are 55 Korean-owned restaurants and food shops in Strathfield alone. While many of these Korean-owned restaurants are Korean BBQ and Korean cuisine, many others are Japanese sushi restaurants. In many cities around the world, pizza restaurants are run by Turks, Greeks and Poles rather than by Italians.

This raises the issue of authenticity in the tourist experience of the immigrant other in Western cities. What constitutes such an 'authentic' ethnic tourism experience within the city? This question is embedded within the cultural stereotypes that exist of the immigrant other. As Fainstein *et al.* (2003: 246) put it: 'The tension between differentiation and homogeneity makes for a contradiction and conflict in urban tourism regimes'. The problem with the concept of authenticity when applied to the ethnic economy is that it is subjective (Cohen, 1988; MacCannell, 1973). Thus, what constitutes an 'authentic' ethnic or cultural eating or tourist experience could vary according to the different standpoints of those who participate in the daily life of the ethnic precinct. What symbols are appropriate, who decides and how? There is a fundamental contradiction emerging here from the coincidence of outdated ethnocultural stereotypes and tourist iconography in countries of immigration that usually depict a static homogeneity of immigrant or ethnic experience and the dynamic diversity of contemporary life in countries of immigrant origin. For example, contemporary China has a very heterogeneous population and its regions and towns experience uneven development: What then is the appropriate cultural iconography of a Chinatown? As Meethan (2001: 27) has put it, symbols 'are multivocal, that is, they have the capacity to carry a range of different, if not ambiguous and contradictory meanings'. Meethan (2001) reminds us that authenticity is a matter of negotiation and ascribed meaning.

Sydney's Chinatown and Tourism

Sydney's Chinatown is the largest Chinatown in Australia, and one of the largest in the world. It is located in downtown Sydney, a few hundred metres from the city's main railway station. Although the precise boundaries of Chinatown are unclear and not officially designated, the concentration of Chinese businesses takes up roughly 10 city blocks, between Pitt Street to the east, Barlow and Thomas Streets to the south, Harbour Street to the west and Liverpool Street to the north. The Dixon Street mall remains Chinatown's symbolic centre.

As an urbanised space with a clear, visible concentration of symbols reflecting the cultural attributes of a (loosely defined) ethnic group, Sydney's Chinatown can be characterised as an 'ethnic precinct'. Indeed, it is probably Sydney's best-known ethnic precinct, and one of the few promoted as tourist attractions by the state tourism authority, Tourism New South Wales.

Sydney's first 'Chinatown'[1] developed in the 1860s in 'the Rocks' area where Chinese migrants established lodging houses, furniture makers, tailors and cook shops. By the 1880s, most of Sydney's Chinese were settling further south around Campbell Street, following the relocation of the city's fruit and vegetable markets to this end of town. By 1900, 86% of Sydney's Chinese population lived in this area (Fitzgerald, 1997). During the 1920s, the city council moved the fruit and vegetable markets and, combined with 'slum clearance' operations in the existing Chinatown, this encouraged the movement of Chinatown to its current location of Dixon Street, a few blocks further west (Fitzgerald, 1997).

During the 1930s and 1940s, businesses in Chinatown struggled with the combined effects of the depression (Fitzgerald, 1997) and the 'White Australia' policy, which saw the Chinese population in Sydney dramatically decline. Those who remained spread to the suburbs and, by the early 1960s, less than 15% of Sydney's Chinese population lived in Chinatown (Fitzgerald, 1997).

By the 1970s, Chinatown's fortunes were changing. The White Australia policy was being dismantled, multiculturalism was replacing assimilation as the official policy towards migration and Australian attitudes were changing. While the more adventurous (or less salubrious) Caucasian clientele had long-frequented Chinatown's restaurants, mainstream consumers, spurred on by features in popular women's magazines, began to see the consumption of Chinese goods as enticingly 'exotic'.

The city government saw potential in reinvigorating the area as a commercial precinct and in 1971 established the Dixon Street Chinese Committee, drawn from the local Chinese business owners, to plan the redevelopment. Some saw the idea as 'contrived and backward-looking' (Fitzgerald, 1997: 151), while others disagreed about how the redevelopment should proceed (Anderson, 1990). But when the city invited public comment, many submissions were broadly supportive and donations came in from several Chinese businesses. 'Chinese' street lighting and rubbish bins were installed, Dixon Street was closed as a pedestrian mall and Chinese arches were built at both ends of the street. Chinese earth was buried under one of the arches to signify that Sydney's Chinese community was here to stay (Fitzgerald, 1997).

The redevelopment was commercially very successful. It coincided with exogenous changes that saw investment in Chinatown rapidly increase: federal immigration laws had changed again to attract wealthy business migrants; and the decision made in 1984 to hand control of Hong Kong to China led to a rush of investment from Hong Kong in overseas property such as Sydney's Chinatown (Fitzgerald, 1997). The Chinese immigrant population continues to grow: the China born comprised 2.8% of the Australian population in 1996 and 6.5% of the Australian population in 2011 (DIAC, 2013: 125).

Under the Sydney City Council, further redevelopment was carried out in the lead-up to the 2000 Olympic Games, including the installation of themed street lighting and public art. Today, the main point of contact between the City of Sydney and Sydney's Chinese community is the Chinatown Cultural Advisory Committee which, as the successor to the Dixon Street Chinese Committee, is the only ethno-specific committee under the auspices of the city council. The City of Sydney sponsors the Chinese New Year Festival, with many activities centred in Chinatown. Each year the number of events in the festival, the participants and the number of tourists that it has attracted has increased. Events include the biggest Chinese New Year parade outside of Asia, Chinese opera, dragon boat races, special banquets, art exhibitions, film screenings and history tours.

Today, 89% of the enterprises in Chinatown are owned by ethnic Chinese entrepreneurs and investment by local and overseas Chinese has continued to expand. The residential population of the downtown area of Sydney is on the rise, with an increasing number of ethnic Chinese living in or nearby Chinatown in new high-rise apartment blocks. Residents and entrepreneurs have come from Hong Kong, Taiwan, Malaysia and Indonesia, among other countries, as well as from various regions within China.

While Dixon Street remains Chinatown's symbolic centre, the precinct has grown considerably. It has become a popular entertainment area, particularly for its dozens of Chinese restaurants. A 1994 International Visitor Survey ranked Chinatown as the ninth most popular tourist destination in New South Wales (NSW), behind the Sydney Opera House and Darling Harbour, but ahead of museums, art galleries and zoos. Visitors from China and Hong Kong are the largest single tourist group to Sydney, representing 14% of all international tourists to Sydney in 2012. Sydney's Chinese New Year attracts 150,000 tourists from China and other Asian countries over a six-week period (Souros, 2012).

The Chinese Garden of Friendship, built next to Chinatown in 1988, is also heavily promoted as a tourist attraction and in 2005 there were around 200,000 visitors to the Garden (Chinese Garden of Friendship, 2006). It is a replica of an 11th-century Chinese garden. It was billed as a 'gift' from China to the people of NSW, although it was paid for by public funds in NSW. The plans were gifted from China along with a landscape architect and artisans. A Chinese-born Australian architect did the conceptual design and authorities consulted with Chinese community leaders. There were 200,000 visitors to the Garden in 2005. It is interesting that most visitors are non-Chinese (11% say they have Chinese heritage). The low number of Chinese visitors may be because the Garden is too familiar to them. On weekdays, 55% of visitors are international tourists. On weekends, this figure drops to 28%. Overall, 32% of visitors say they found out about the Chinese Garden of Friendship from walking past it, 23% through word of mouth and 15% from an English-language brochure (which is placed in hotels and at monorail stations) (Chinese Garden of Friendship, 2006).

There has been little research involving tourists in Sydney's Chinatown. One pilot study of 100 tourists approached at random at various times and days and key informant interviews conducted with Sydney City Council and Chinatown's Chinese community and business stakeholders (Collins et al., 2007) gives some insights into the Chinatown tourist experience. The key findings are reported in the following paragraphs.

Most respondents were young and single (46%). A further 12% were young/midlife couples with no children. In total, 52% of respondents were between the ages of 18 and 34. The next largest group was older, working, married people (13%). Of the respondents, 20% were in their fifties, with only 7% aged 60 or above. Only 4% of respondents were parents with young children aged under 5. Of the survey respondents, 24% self-identified as being Chinese or Asian; 12% identified as being Anglo or Caucasian. The vast majority of visitors to Chinatown were from Greater Sydney ('local').

Of the overseas visitors, almost half were from Asia; 24% of respondents were 'tourists', defined as those having been away from home for more than one night; 55% of respondents were male. Most respondents were visiting Chinatown to eat (35%) or shop (16%) or for sightseeing and general interest (14%). When asked how they had heard about Chinatown, 32% said that they were told by friends and family; 33% reported that they had always known about Chinatown. Among the 'other' category, several respondents indicated that they knew there was a Chinatown because 'there is one in every city'.

Visitor responses to Chinatown were largely positive. When asked if they would like to visit Chinatown again, 92% of respondents agreed or strongly agreed; 83% agreed or strongly agreed that they would recommend Chinatown to others. However, only 58% of respondents agreed or strongly agreed that Chinatown had met their expectations. A further 22% somewhat agreed with this statement. When asked what they liked most about the architecture and physical features of Chinatown, most respondents said that they liked the Chinese arches, the trees, the Chinese signage and the 'Chinese feel'. When asked what they disliked about the general atmosphere of Chinatown, many respondents said that it was dirty and smelly and needed cleaning up. Many also disliked the 'spruikers' outside the restaurants in Dixon Street trying to encourage them to eat at their restaurants. Almost all respondents (92%) reported that they felt safe in Chinatown. Among those who responded in the 'other' category, most reported that they felt safe in the day but less safe at night. Suggested improvements to Chinatown included cleaning and 'revamping' the streetscape, making Chinatown bigger and improving parking. A number of international tourists wanted more information on the history of Chinatown and the Chinese in Sydney as well as information booths or maps that directed them to points of interest or guided them to shops and restaurants in Chinatown.

Sydney's Chinatown is used differently by different groups. For example, many Chinese migrants from the suburbs continue to use Chinatown to access Chinese goods and Chinese-speaking service providers. Tourists from China use the site for duty-free shopping. Local and international visitors come to Chinatown to dine out, while Chinese students visit the karaoke bars or utilise the space simply to walk and get 'fresh air'. Together, these activities create a vibrant tourist site. These various interests must be catered for. For example, while key informant interviews suggest that Asian tourists may not be interested in learning about the history of Chinatown, our visitor surveys indicate that many international tourists do want more information on the history and culture of Chinatown. They would also like more assistance in guiding them to points of interest and popular shops and restaurants in Chinatown. Providing this information at the site (such as through information booths, maps and a Chinese history museum) would increase the tourist appeal.

Melbourne's Chinatown and Tourism

Melbourne's Chinatown is in the downtown area of the city and consists of the eastern quarter of Little Bourke Street, plus the 23 lanes, places and alleys that intersect with Little Bourke Street between Spring Street and Swanston Street. Melbourne's Chinatown is well defined with Chinese gates and lanterns at each end of the precinct. Chinese characters on signage for shops and other businesses are prominent. The narrow street and the even narrower alleyways give the feel of a traditional Chinese *hutong* (narrow street or alley). The precinct is dominated by restaurants, although there are a variety of businesses including hotels, hairdressers (both Asian and European), fashion boutiques, banks and money exchanges. In Little Bourke Street alone, there are at least 38 restaurants between Spring and Swanston Streets. All are Asian with the majority, a total of 24, being Chinese. Melbourne's Chinatown emits a commercial feel with evidence of little overt tourism product beyond eating, drinking and, to a lesser extent, shopping. During the Lunar New Year Festival, Chinatown spills into Russell Street, between Bourke and Lonsdale Streets. This section of Russell Street is blocked to vehicles during the event and is the main focus of the festivities.

The Melbourne City Council has been central to the formal establishment of a Chinatown in this area of Melbourne and its subsequent redevelopment over the decades till today. In the 1970s, initiatives by the Melbourne City Council and the Chinese Professional and Business Association of Victoria led to moves to give the area an ethnic Chinese makeover in order to develop it into a formal 'Chinatown' tourist precinct. This led to the introduction of 'celestial arches', Chinese lanterns and other Chinese iconography that was seen in Chinatowns in Australia and other countries. Immediately the controversial issue of the Melbourne Chinatown's ethnic authenticity arose, with parts of the Chinese community challenging the formulaic Chinese streetscaping that reflected a stereotypical and outdated 'White western gaze' (Anderson, 1990). Further enhancement of the area as a tourist precinct in the 1980s included the creation of a lunar New Year festival and the establishment in Cohen Place of the Museum of Chinese Australian History in 1985 with a grant from the Victorian Tourist Commission.

Like Sydney's Chinatown, tourism to Melbourne Chinatown is linked to ethnic festivals and the history of Chinese immigration as well as the day-to-day tourist attraction of Chinese restaurants that cluster in the area. The development of Melbourne's Chinatown as a mainstream restaurant hub for the non-Chinese community began in the 1960s and rapidly developed through the 1980s. The area is now known as a centre for Chinese cuisine but has also developed significant new retail activities in videos, magazines and fashion, catering to the new ethnic Chinese student population resident in and around the city. Tourist activities and events in the district comprise a Feng Shui tour of Chinatown, the Museum's Chinatown Heritage Walk, the Chinese New Year Festival and the Asian Food Festival conducted by the Melbourne City Council, the Chinese Restaurateurs Association of Victoria and Chinatown Precinct Association. The district still hosts some traditional political, religious and cultural activities associated with the Chinese community.

There has been little research involving tourists in Melbourne's Chinatown. One exception is a research project, conducted in 2006, which involved observation fieldwork, a survey of 100 tourists and key informant interviews with Melbourne City Council and Chinatown's Chinese community and business stakeholders (Collins *et al.*, 2007), which gives some insights into the Chinatown tourist experience. These research findings are summarised below.

Most respondents to the survey (55%) were aged 18–34, with those in their twenties comprised over one third (38%) of the sample total. The ethnicity of participants was evenly divided, with 32% defining themselves as Chinese or Asian and 35% claiming European or 'European–Australian' background. The gender division was 45% female and 55% male. Two thirds of those surveyed were locals while 15% were with interstate visitors and 20% international visitors.

One key question relates to the reasons that locals and tourists visited Chinatown. Almost one third of respondents (30.8%) claimed to visit Chinatown for the restaurants. This was followed by those present for sightseeing/general interest (17.9%) and shopping (14.5%). Another key question relates to how locals and tourists found out about Chinatown in the first instance. For one quarter of the non-local survey respondents, knowledge of Chinatown came largely from friends/family, another 14% of respondents 'just wandered in', while only 5% claimed that formal tourist information encouraged them to seek out Chinatown. Local Melbourne residents 'had always known about [China Town]'.

What did tourists and locals think of their visitor experience in Chinatown? Most respondents reported a positive experience in Chinatown, with two in three respondents strongly agreeing, agreeing or somewhat agreeing that their visit had been 'memorable'; 80% of informants said that they would recommend a visit to Chinatown to others and 88% claimed that they would like to visit again. The Chinese-style lights and gates and the general Asian inspiration of the streetscaping were the most appealing aspects of Chinatown's architecture and physical features. Visitors described these as 'striking', 'colourful' and 'eclectic'. The small scale of the streetscape was also valued along with a perception that the area was 'different to the rest of the city' and 'a haven'. The heritage buildings were not strongly regarded as significant in the overall appeal of the site. These were described as 'run-down' and 'old and boring' by some users, while others found them to be 'inauthentic' and 'lacking in character'. The majority of negative commentary regarding Chinatown's physical experience was directed at the narrowness of the footpaths which made walking difficult and the apparent 'dirtiness' of the area. Rubbish bins in laneways were regarded as particularly unsightly and noisome. Graffiti was also mentioned as destroying the 'Chinese character' of the district along with other 'negative influences of the west' such as heavy use of inappropriate signage on historic buildings. The existence of cars in Little Bourke Street was also seen as significantly undermining the quality of the experience in the precinct.

Survey respondents indicated that Chinatown's 'busyness' was significant in contributing to the generally vibrant atmosphere of the district. The sense of 'lots of people and activity going on day and night' imbued Chinatown with dynamism for visitors and a sense of difference from the rest of the city. For those tourists visiting from Asia, Chinatown 'reminded me of home', while for non-Asian visitors the district was 'familiar but exotic' and several felt 'reminded of Asia'. Other favourable contributing features were the 'cultural character' and 'cross-cultural feeling' of the destination. One respondent described their enjoyment at seeing 'people with a lonely planet look on their faces' visiting the area. For a small number of respondents, the existence of the Museum also added to what was described as the 'cultural atmosphere' of Chinatown.

Factors that were seen as hindrances to a pleasant atmosphere in Chinatown were overwhelmingly traffic related but also referred to the dirty state of the streets and the sight of rubbish bins. There were several requests to have Little Bourke Street turned into a mall as the traffic and trucks in particular made visiting the area dangerous and disagreeable for pedestrians. A second, less-dominant theme related to an apparent 'lack of Chinese character' and suggestions that Chinatown was 'not cultural enough', while a lesser number of respondents complained of the presence of 'drug dealers' and 'seedy laneways'.

Safety is a big issue in ethnic tourism, particularly in Chinatowns where the attraction historically has been to see the vice, gambling and drug culture often associated with Chinese immigrant minorities (Collins, 2006; Lin, 1998: 174–176). Nearly all those surveyed perceived Chinatown as non-threatening, particularly during the day, and a frequently voiced perception that 'Asians are safe people' or 'not intimidating' added to visitors' sense of security. Several respondents compared Melbourne's Chinatown with similar districts overseas, describing it as 'safe compared to others' and referring to Melbourne as 'generally safe'. Asian visitors also enjoyed the security that their cultural familiarity gave the area. Overall, Chinatown was described as 'a big asset for Melbourne', as adding 'vibrancy to the city' and as comparing well with Chinatowns in Sydney and other non-Asian destinations. Aside from its role as a major restaurant hub, Chinatown was perceived as an important destination for non-Chinese to learn about

Chinese culture although, for one respondent, 'China Town is too western and does not educate'.

Inevitably, the chief improvements to Chinatown suggested by respondents reflected previously stated concerns about the quality of the environment and the authenticity of the experience for visitors. 'Clean up the area' and 'remove rubbish bins' were the most frequently voiced improvements followed by reducing the impact of vehicles in the area and the conversion of Little Bourke Street into a pedestrian mall. Several respondents suggested a street market should be introduced as a means of improving the pedestrian flow, adding variety to the retail options currently available and enhancing the sense of an authentic 'Chinese' streetscape for visitors. There were significant numbers of requests relating to improving the ethnic nature of the experience such as 'more Chinese culture', 'reduce the western influence' and 'expand Asian cultural events beyond lunar New Year'. One respondent suggested the need for a visitor centre with maps and a history of the destination placed in a prominent position for visitors, while several requested Chinese music to be broadcast in the streets and for the opening of Asian nightclubs and 'authentic Asian cultural facilities other than just restaurants'. One respondent suggested having older Chinese residents 'volunteer as guides either on walking tours or in an information booth. Have them share stories'. However, another warned against turning the area into a 'theme park' and advised letting 'business control tourism development'. Signage on the heritage buildings in the area was more frequently criticised as being too difficult to read or too easily missed. These buildings were also claimed to be in need of 'refurbishment' by several respondents.

Immigrant Minorities, Ethnicity and Tourism

Tourism is becoming an increasingly competitive marketplace. Countries, cities, regions and towns compete to attract national and international tourists by offering some unique, unforgettable and different tourist experience. Ethnic tourism appears to have the potential to attract increasing numbers of tourists. All countries of the world are attracting more immigrants today than at any previous time in history. These immigrants transform the cities, towns and neighbourhoods of the host country in which they settle. Ethnic eating places and shopping establishments are the prime attraction for many tourists as are the ethnic iconography of ethnic precincts and neighbourhoods and the ethnic festivals held there. The attraction is the promise of an 'exotic' and unique experience of the ethnic 'Other', spicing up the tourist experience at a number of levels. However, ethnic tourism is underpinned by a number of contradictions as the cases of the Chinatowns of Sydney and Melbourne highlight.

One contradiction relates to the authenticity of the ethnic tourist experience. Chinatowns in cities across the world all look alike, but they do not look like contemporary Chinese towns or cities. Does this matter? To most Western tourists the Chinatown experience is what they expect, but to some Chinese tourists there is a kitschy air of unreality to the Chinatowns of Sydney and Melbourne. Nevertheless, these Chinatowns are a central port of call for Chinese and Asian tourists, particularly during the Chinese New Year festivals when a large range of authentic Chinese cultural and artistic events fill the events calendar.

Local government authorities, like the Sydney and Melbourne City Councils, decided to formally develop, brand and market a particular area of the city as a Chinatown, drawing on the history of Chinese immigrant settlement in the cities to do so. They also consulted the local Chinese community about their plans for an ethnic makeover or redevelopment of the ethnic precinct, though here another contradiction emerges: there are over 100 Chinese ethnic community organisations in Sydney alone. Which organisation represents *the* legitimate Chinese voice? Another interesting contradiction relates to the approach of marketing authorities to the promotion of ethnic tourism. During the fieldwork in Sydney and Melbourne reported in this chapter, state government tourist authorities were consulted. The NSW tourist authorities said that they did not promote Chinatown or other ethnic precincts in Sydney in their international tourist campaigns because they focused on images of what was uniquely Australian and specific to Sydney: the harbour bridge, the opera house, Sydney Harbour and Bondi Beach. On the other hand, the Victorian tourist authorities had long developed campaigns that promoted the ethnic diversity of Victoria and Melbourne to national and international tourists. The problem here is that the ethnic tourist experience cannot by definition be unique to one country or city: cosmopolitanism is by definition an international experience.

Note

(1)   The term 'Chinatown' only gained widespread use in Sydney in the 20th century. While Chinese businesses were concentrated in the areas described here, the pattern of Chinese residential settlement was always more dispersed (Fitzgerald, 1997).

Part 4: Development Policies

Introduction

Past and present urban development or regeneration schemes often fail to take into consideration the role of local communities in policy and strategy making. This situation is even more pronounced in the case of minority or ethnic communities. However, Hamnett (2003) estimated that the ethnic minority population of cities like London would be more than 40% by 2010. Florida (2005: 39) emphasised the importance of diversity in the development of creative cities, stating that 'more open and diverse places are likely to attract greater numbers of talented and creative people – the sort of people who power innovation and growth'. Recent developments in many cities have shown that there is a growing interest among policymakers, planners and tourists alike in marginal and ethnic cultures, with the increasing promotion of ethnoscapes, ethnic festivals and gay quarters, for example. Although such attractions often develop organically, there is a need for a greater focus in urban planning on addressing some of the difficulties inherent in the development and promotion of ethnic and minority tourism. Shaw *et al.* (2004) outlined some of the potential problems of developing for leisure and tourism what Appadurai (2000) termed 'ethnoscapes' or places associated with tourists, refugees, exiles, guest workers and other mobile groups and individuals. There are major ethical considerations which should be addressed relating to commodification, objectification, appropriation, invasion and displacement, among others. Increasing numbers of visitors can be intrusive and disturb the rhythm of everyday life, diminishing spontaneous intercultural and interethnic encounters; a degraded environmental quality; few employment or income generation prospects; the raising of property prices followed by the displacement of low-income groups; and commercial gentrification, which may drive out small businesses.

Planning for Urban Communities

Until the 1970s, there was little understanding of the role that communities could play in urban planning and development. Mumford (1968) suggested that individual urban groups and communities had very little effective control over their own destinies. The degree of local integration and consultation depends on context and the role played by various stakeholders. Not surprisingly, there seems to be a direct correlation between power and influence and the education and class of the stakeholders, for example, Owen (2002) suggests that:

> Some communities are more able than others to form effective resident actions groups, and these are typically the well-resourced, better educated, higher socio-economic communities. (Owen, 2002: 334)

This means that ethnic and minority communities are likely to have relatively little power and influence in the context of urban development and regeneration.

Sorkin (1992: xiv) suggested that cities became increasingly fragmented as a result of impersonal planning, which does not focus on human connections. Planning ideally needs to be strictly regulated by governments, integrated into the existing urban fabric and sensitive to local needs. Conflicts of interest are of course inevitable; however, extensive consultation of relevant stakeholder groups is becoming a more integral part of the planning process. The rhetoric of regeneration in Britain, for example, frequently includes terms like 'community empowerment'; therefore, mechanisms are often implemented to achieve this. There is also increasing evaluation and monitoring of community development projects in order to assess their real impacts. Miles (1997) suggests that the concept of empowerment is a complex but necessary process. As stated by Shaw (2004: 1998) 'Without a balanced and open dialogue between municipalities and the diverse communities who live and work in inner-city areas about the development of urban tourism, the process may exacerbate rather than defuse tensions in areas that, in many cases, have long and violent histories of intolerance towards minority groups'.

Lefèbvre's (1974) concept of lived space and Soja's (1996) concept of Thirdspace imply that the focus of urban developments should be the everyday lives of local residents and their role in helping to shape space and create place. Lefèbvre describes the production of space as an active, creative process in which physical, mental and social spaces are interconnected. Lefèbvre's 'spatial triad' consists of 'representations of space' (e.g. space as conceived by actors and agents such as planners, developers, architects, urbanists), 'spatial practices' (e.g. the ways in which physical space is perceived symbolically) and 'representational space' (e.g. peoples' lived spaces and interactions therein). Soja's (1996) Thirdspace embodies this concept of 'everyday life' as described by Lefèbvre (1974), wherein the individual can transcend the oppression and banality of the city. De Certeau (2002) also describes how everyday life in the city is tactically manoeuvred by governments, corporations and other institutional bodies, but citizens create their own spaces nevertheless. In Habermas's (1989) 'lifeworlds', peoples' cognitive horizons and values are shaped by institutions and regulations as well as customs and traditions.

In Lefèbvre's lived space and Soja's Thirdspace, citizens can transcend restrictions and manipulations through culture in the form of the arts, literature and festivals (Lefèbvre) or cultural politics (Soja). The role of culture is significant as Soja suggests that Thirdspace is informed by post-modern cultural politics. For example, he refers to the chosen marginality of the cultural theorist bell hooks and her Thirdspace of resistance. He also cites Homi Bhabha's Thirdspace of hybridity, where alternative enuncia-tions can be constructed. These theories are especially relevant to ethnic communities. In his later work *Postmetropolis*, he refers to a new cultural politics of difference rather than equality where the agenda is opened up to questions of identity and representation. The work of Lefèbvre and Soja asserts that a Thirdspace approach to planning can bring together diverse and disparate voices, viewpoints and representations, not in a consensus but rather a crystallisation. That is to say that numerous articulations are recognised even if they are not always compatible with each other.

Florida (2002) insists that cities need to have a 'people climate' as well as a 'business climate'. This means addressing issues of inequality, intolerance and safety, as well as creating a vibrant atmosphere and an experiential economy. It also means 'community building' and engaging in civic action. It is generally believed that the involvement of local peo-ple can enhance development and regeneration, especially if planners can go beyond the tangible physical and economic outcomes of development. Consideration of some of the more intangible elements of everyday life such as identity, image, sense of place, local character, authenticity as well as typical activities and patterns of everyday people within the locality are arguably equally important. This can ideally serve to improve quality of life. Fenster's (2004) research on the personal experiences of two cities' inhabitants concludes that so-called 'quality of life' can mean a combina-tion of comfort, belonging and commitment. She argues that one of the prime challenges of planning should be to make people feel 'at home' in globalised urban spaces. She describes how different models of planning have been used in attempts to achieve this, for example, advocacy plan-ning, whereby several plans are developed (instead of one master plan), each of which represents the interests of the group that the planner repre-sents; equity planning, which focuses on trying to bridge urban inequality gaps; radical planning, which aims to empower the disempowered focusing on the voices of the 'other'; and communicative action planning, wherein local knowledge is incorporated and local voices are heard. The positional-ity of the planner is always crucial (e.g. whether he or she comes from the local area or community, and his or her role as key actor or facilitator).

Sandercock (1998) refers to 'insurgent practices' within a planning con-text, which allow 'a thousand tiny empowerments' to flourish. She cites the work of Foucault, stating that if power is anchored in the micro prac-tices of everyday life, then this is where emancipatory and oppositional politics need to begin. Power relationships that are built into everyday practices can be deconstructed and reconstructed through political planning. Fenster (2004) suggests that 'professional planning knowledge' is still based on power relations and the superiority of white, Western knowledge. Thus, this type of knowledge is seen as 'scientific' and 'universal', whereas local knowledge is seen as being less significant. However, Sandercock (1998) argues that some of the most radical planning paradigms emerge from people, agencies and organisations, which challenge existing power structures. Such new paradigms rely on a familiarity with the life ways of communities, as well as new kinds of cultural and political literacies. These may be led by visionary 'mobilisers' just at the level of a neighbourhood, but they are generally based on collectivity, consensus and care for communities. Communication, a strong commitment to social values and citizenship are central to this philosophy of planning. So too is an ability to listen to the voices of difference. Sandercock (2000) suggests that new ways of planning should be 'therapeutic', involving negotiation, mediation, facilitation and consensus building. We can see here the gradual unfolding of local participation and the potential role of local culture and place within a development context.

From the 1990s onwards, urban development and regeneration strategies tended to prioritise environmental issues and the concept of sustainable development. Present-day strategies are also once again starting to recognise the needs of local communities, especially minority groups. Some theorists acknowledged the complexity of planning for different cultures. Sandercock (1998: 183) strongly advocates that 'the cities and regions of the future must nurture difference and diversity through democratic cultural pluralism'. She describes how the foundations of postmodern planning praxis should be built on the acknowledgement of multiple publics. She describes how the 'voices from the borderlands' – i.e. those of the marginalised, displaced, oppressed or dominated – are increasingly being listened to. Cultural differences should not simply be tolerated, they must be valorised, which requires a new kind of 'multicultural literacy'. An important part of this is a familiarity with the multiple histories of urban communities, especially where these intersect with struggles over space and place claiming. This includes the histories of 'imagined communities' such as gays, lesbians and women, as well as ethnic and diasporic communities.

A Cultural Planning Approach to Urban Development

Many urban theorists and practitioners now advocate an anthropological or community-based approach to planning. A sense of place and animation is arguably created through and by the people resident in an area, coupled with the social and cultural programmes that are provided for and supported by them. Public spaces need animation, perhaps through the development of cultural festivals or the presence of public art. One definition of cultural planning (Creative City, 2006) suggested that the process is now inherently community orientated:

> Cultural planning is a process of inclusive community consultation and decision-making that helps local government identify cultural resources and think strategically about how these resources can help a community to achieve its civic goals. (Creative City, 2006: 7)

Shaw (2007) emphasises how, with careful planning and management, the development of the cultural tourism and visitor economies can help to foster the role of ethnic and minority entrepreneurs as active agents of regeneration. Many authors have advocated a more creative approach to regeneration in order to combat standardisation and serial reproduction, and to support cultural and community diversity (e.g. Richards & Wilson, 2007). Florida (2002) shows clearly that the most attractive and economically successful cities tend to be those with the highest concentration of creative and bohemian people (including gays). Nevertheless, care must be taken not to gentrify regeneration areas to the extent that original residents and artists are priced out.

The concept of cultural planning takes into consideration the issue of diversity. The origins of cultural planning go back several decades; however, the concept has only existed in its current form since the mid-1990s. Cultural planning aims to transform physical space and is technically about the way in which governments or planners integrate cultural resources into the everyday lives of people, and considers the diverse benefits that cultural resources can bring to a community if planned for strategically. Cultural planning has the following main characteristics:

- People-orientated approach to development.
- Consultative and inclusive.
- Pluralistic and diverse.
- Promotes importance of access and tolerance.
- Aims to improve quality of life.
- Recognises the importance of place and character of environment.
- Includes intangible and symbolic aspects of culture.
- Advocates creative approaches to development.
  (After Bianchini & Ghilardi, 1997; Evans, 2005; Ghilardi, 2001; Mercer, 1991)

Culture is mainly defined by practitioners in the context of urban development and regeneration (e.g. politicians, policymakers, planners and consultants) as formalised activities (e.g. heritage, visual and performing arts, museums, festivals and events). The consideration of culture as everyday life and the way that this is articulated by local people is rarely given as much consideration as, for example, business development, conservation or tourism. Thus, cultural developments are often not well integrated into local areas and local residents can fail to engage with them fully, if at all. Of course, it is much harder to identify or define culture which is integrated into everyday life practices, as it is not explicitly articulated as it would be in a work of art or an exhibition, for example. There are much more subtle elements such as a sense of one's personal history and ancestry, a sense of community or identity, identification with certain practices, traditions or activities, even a feeling of being 'different' if one is from a minority culture or ethnic group. Questions therefore need to be asked of individuals or groups of residents in local areas for their own articulations of culture rather than using standardised definitions (it might even be more appropriate not to use the word culture, but instead to refer to other indicators such as common activities, feelings of belonging, likes and dislikes, etc.). This is especially important for ethnic groups who do not have a tradition of written culture (e.g. Gypsies).

The following table provides a more detailed summary of the approaches that could be taken in urban development and regeneration, which focuses on communities, especially ethnic and minority groups.

Consideration of local, multiple culture(s)	• Local (including marginal) cultures at the centre of and integral to planning. • Takes account of cultural diversity (including religious diversity). • Recognition of multiple histories/heritages. • Multiple representations (e.g. in museums, galleries, festival programming, marketing). • Recognition of hybrid and multiple identities (including those of second- and third-generation immigrants).
Involvement and empowerment of local stakeholders	• Democratic and community-orientated (including ethnic and marginal communities). • 'Bottom-up approach. • Gives a voice to all stakeholders. • Predominantly anthropological and ethical in approach. • Supporting local (including minority and marginal group) participation in the arts and cultural activities. • Fostering civic pride, a sense of local identity and ownership.
Emphasis on everyday life practices	• Emphasis on 'quality of life' (including safety and security). • Awareness of intangible aspects of culture (e.g. oral histories and 'hidden' traditions). • Access to public spaces (physical and psychological, e.g. safe spaces for women or gays).

	• New, more 'tolerant' spaces for social interaction (e.g. community centres, support groups, female-only events, gay bars). • Spiritual and 'sacred' spaces (e.g. multifaith). • Emphasis on place identity and place marketing (incorporating ethnic diversity). • Retention of local 'authenticity' (i.e. supporting traditions, customs, celebrations).
Creative and experiential approaches	• Creative approaches to development (e.g. with input from different cultures). • High 'creative' and 'bohemian' indices (including the Gay Index). • Animation of cities through culture and creativity (e.g. ethnic festivals, carnivals). • More exhibitions and events that confront dissonance in new ways (e.g. slavery, the Holocaust, homophobia, sexism).

Adapted from Smith (2010)

These four main categories form the basis of a cultural planning framework with the first three categories being a prerequisite for more locally orientated, people-centred development. However, the fourth category adds an important dimension once these prerequisites have been met, which is to provide unique and exciting experiences, which help people to transcend the 'ordinariness' or mundanity of everyday life (e.g. through the arts, architecture, festivals or creative industries). These have the benefit of attracting tourists to a location and developing an external place identity that is attractive and competitive. It is also important not to shy away from some of the more dissonant aspects of cultural experience that most marginal groups face on a daily basis, including racism, sexism and homophobia. This includes the heritage of dissonance, such as slavery, which Harvey (2007) suggests has been ignored or downplayed in tourism-led regeneration projects. It is also difficult for urban development, tourism or regeneration agencies to deal with racism or homophobia; however, cultural activities (e.g. exhibitions, festivals) can be used to showcase different cultures and ways of living, thus rendering them more familiar and less threatening for local populations and tourists alike.

The development of ethnic festivals can sometimes help to raise the profile of local community groups, leading to a greater understanding of and interest in their culture. They can also be highly attractive for tourists, as well as acting as catalysts for urban regeneration. Carlson (1996) provided an interesting analysis of the significance of performance for traditionally marginalised groups, such as women, homosexuals and ethnic minorities. Tensions between self and society might be explored, including issues relating to objectification, exclusion and identity. The development of larger audiences for ethnic or minority performances and events can help to raise the profile of such groups. However, audience development for ethnic and minority events can be contentious, with claims that Caribbean carnivals and similar events have become 'whitewashed' or over-touristed (e.g. Errol, 1986). Local events can also outgrow their areas, for example, the Notting Hill Carnival in London. Burr (2007) listed the problems of crowd congestion, organisational and procession chaos, an increase in crime and violence, occasionally even murders, health and safety issues from litter and urination in the street and deafening noise. Nevertheless, suggestions to move the event to another location were met with protests from the local African-Caribbean inhabitants of Notting Hill, who consider its origins in that area of London to be important for cultural continuity. Like Caribbean carnivals, Asian melas have come to symbolise all that is 'colourful' about diaspora, transforming ethnicity into a cultural showcase for growing numbers of white and tourist audiences. This similarly engenders fears of cultural dilution, distortion and 'othering' (Smith & Carnegie, 2006).

Ethnic and Minority Cultural Quarters of Cities

Ashworth (1995: 76) suggested that most European cities suffer from a high degree of homogeneity, which closely follows worldwide fashionable trends. Within his framework, tourism can play a dual role either as 'a celebration of unique place identities, or an instrument of homogenization' (Ashworth, 1995: 77). Ethnic quarters can give cities a certain amount of uniqueness. However, this could not usually be described as 'local' culture, as many of the ethnic groups are immigrants or diaspora rather than indigenous peoples. As a result, many of the world's cities have developed ethnic quarters like Chinatowns, which are perceived to be somewhat generic. One of the problems is that ethnic or minority groups may feel the need to conform or aspire to the dominant culture in a process of integration or assimilation, thus losing elements of their traditional culture such as customs or language. This is true of the Gypsy communities in Hungary, for example. As stated by Aitchison et al. (2000: 27), the rhetoric of equality and social inclusion often 'emphasise hierarchies of difference and can serve to militate against notions of cultural diversity and heterogeneity'. Graham et al. (2000: 125) suggest that heritage policies 'would ideally work towards a balanced, proportionate inclusion of minority elements and interpretations, the objective being to obtain social profit from celebrating – and economic gains from selling – heritage diversity'. However, they also note that it is more important to promote social harmony than to pursue profit at its expense.

Ethnic quarters of cities are often referred to in common parlance as 'ghettos'. Ghettos have been described in various ways, including as 'an ideogram of salient non-white others' (Linke, 2012: 297), often in derelict cores and inner suburbs (Davis, 2007). However, this term is used far more in North America than in Europe, as post-Holocaust the word 'ghetto' has taken on somewhat different connotations connected to the partial incarceration and immiseration of Jewish communities during World War II. However, like the term 'slum', 'ghetto' has also taken on a mainly negative or pejorative association, except when it is used in connection with music or fashion, and then it is appropriated by the middle classes in a romanticised rather than a real sense (Linke, 2012).

The marketing of ethnic heritage and culture tends to be somewhat selective. Phua *et al.* (2012) discuss how Singapore uses its multicultural society and racial/ethnic heritage in its branding. Since the late 1980s, three areas have been the focus of tourist interest: Chinatown, Little India and the Malay village. However, Phua *et al.* (2012: 1256) state that 'The presentation of Singapore as a multicultural society does not necessarily mean that each of these three ethnic groups have equal representation. The emphasis of each ethnicity in the materials is related to and a reflection of the population and power distributions of these groups'. This is perhaps typical of many multicultural cities. It might be based on numbers of citizens within the ethnic group, how vocal they are, the degree of economic power they have, or political support. In the case of Singapore, it seems that the Chinese culture dominates, but this does not imply a lack of social harmony with the other ethnic groups.

A number of cities both in Europe and internationally can claim to have a gay quarter which has a thriving evening economy, not to mention daytime leisure and retail provision. This is certainly true of Madrid, Amsterdam, San Francisco, Sydney, Rio, to name but a few. The increasing popularity of gay areas, especially with women and heterosexual couples, has sometimes led to concerns about the 'de-gaying' of certain spaces, in much the same way that Notting Hill African-Caribbean residents are concerned about the increasing white, middle-class presence. For example, Hughes (2002) wrote about The Village in Manchester, UK, a gay quarter full of bars and restaurants which is used by both gay and straight visitors but where the 'de-gaying' of space has sometimes been a cause for concern, especially for lesbians (Pritchard *et al.*, 2002). The Village has been viewed as a success in terms of economic development and tourism and enhancing the image of a former industrial city, but as noted by Hughes (2002) gay life and space should be organic and community based, not commodified and used for other purposes. Here, as in other cities, the Village serves to demonstrate the 'progressiveness' of the city and the gay community may feel more mainstream as a result. However, Hughes (2006) noted in the case of Manchester's yearly Lesbian, Gay, Bisexual and Transgender Festival that there may be a need to reduce the tourism element in the future if the festival is to retain its meaning for the gay community.

Poverty Alleviation and Pro-Poor Tourism

A cultural planning approach may be less simple in the case of slum tourism. Slum tourism discourse tends to centre on poverty but it is valorised as such and is almost expected by the tourists as part of the experience (Burgold *et al.*, 2013). Frenzel (2013: 125) even describes it as a 'romanticisation and fetishisation of poverty'. If slum tourism were a successful strategy for poverty mitigation, it would ironically undermine its own premise (Steinbrink *et al.*, 2012). However, slums naturally call for political action in the form of urban development policy and planning. Nuissl and Heinrichs (2013) suggest at least three dimensions to which the problems associated with the slums can be related:

- the material dimension refers to the physical urban structure and infrastructural layout of slum areas;
- the social dimension takes up the hardships that life in the slums entails and the lifeworld of slum dwellers;
- the institutional dimension refers to the multitude of formal and informal rules that regulate the life of slum residents.

Many slum dwellers are illegal occupants and live in constant fear of being evicted. It means that they cannot invest or plan for the future. Resettlement can sever economic and social relationships and networks. There have been some slum upgrading programmes, but generally a black–white dichotomy of 'slums of despair' and 'slums of hope' is presented (Nuissl & Heinrichs, 2013). Ironically, the former may not even be visited as they are perceived as unsanitary or unsafe for tourists. Indeed, many of the slums that are visited by tourists tend to be wealthier than others. Frenzel (2013) describes how slum tourism is most frequently pursued in countries that have made strong economic advances in the last two decades, i.e. Brazil, South Africa and India. For example, in comparison to other favelas in Rio, Rochinha is relatively rich! Although the conditions of the Dharavi slum in India are quite poor, it is a place of significant industry where many inhabitants work, therefore it cannot be considered as a place of extreme poverty in absolute terms (Dyson, 2012; Meschkank, 2010).

Koens (2012) suggests that township tours in South Africa do not visit the poorest townships, and that the complexities of poverty exceed any measure of purely quantifiable terms. The South African Tourism Organisation includes township tourism in its cultural, historical and heritage tourism category (Booyens, 2010). The figure for domestic tourists who make a cultural, historical or heritage visit was only 3% of the total in 2011. Since there are no separate figures for township tourism, it means that there are no accurate figures for the money spent by township tourists

(Gold, 2012). Indeed, Gold's (2012) research showed that numerous projects for township tourism have been announced with much fanfare under the banner of pro-poor tourism, followed by expensive feasibility/business plans but that they rarely come to fruition. Booyens (2010) conducted research in Soweto and concluded that township tourism can promote socio-economic regeneration and pro-poor development, but only if it is developed responsibly and the benefits are spread widely. However, his research showed results that were far from successful. The most negative findings pertained to the lack of opportunity for participation in tourism and the inequitable distribution of economic and employment benefits. Residents also felt disempowered by their lack of control over tour operators and the opportunities for participation in tourism. To sustain township tourism, it was suggested that the local people should have more decision-making power which would promote a type and scale of tourism development that would allow them to uphold, respect and nurture their cultures and share in the economic benefits of tourism development. Rather than bringing new wealth to the community, township tourism seems to leave little to the majority of the local residents as organisers and entrepreneurs keep the profits from the tours. Tours are often in white ownership and tend to be run by those from outside the townships (Butler, 2012). On the other hand, Nkemngu (2012) presented evidence from the Soshanguve community suggesting that community benefit from township tours included some financial benefit in addition to sociocultural and environmental benefits, including a high percentage of young people involved and interested in the industry.

Frenzel (2013) quotes Scheyvens (2011) who analysed the tourism–poverty nexus. He suggests a 'post-structuralist' or 'post-developmental' approach to poverty alleviation and tourism where its measurement cannot be reduced to quantitative indicators. Pro-poor (PPT) academics propose to consider non-monetary, qualitative aspects of tourism's role in poverty relief; however, in practice the evaluation seems to tend to move back to positivist, quantitative indicators (e.g. a headcount of people who move beyond the poverty line). Frenzel (2013) advocates using Zhao and Ritchie's (2007) set of qualitative indicators, including the concepts of 'opportunity', 'empowerment' and 'security' to evaluate tourism in slums. This includes analysing local participation in the workforce and roles as entrepreneurs and local residents. They also proposed to analyse stakeholders and in particular the tourists' role in shaping tourism in relation to poverty (including volunteering or charity work). However, Frenzel (2013) suggests that tourism is probably not the best strategy for alleviating poverty in slums, as it is too small scale to have a major impact. This might unfortunately be true of many forms of ethnic and minority tourism, but mass tourism to such areas is clearly not a solution either.

On the other hand, mega-events can bring thousands of visitors into very close proximity with slums. Steinbrink (2013) examines how urban policy deals with slums in the context of cities staging mega-events, for example Rio with its 2014 FIFA World Cup and 2016 Summer Olympics. The conventional policy strategy has traditionally been demolition and eviction, especially in countries in the south. For example, New Delhi (India) was supposed to be 'slum-free' by the opening day of the Commonwealth Games in 2010. There are often fears of crime, for example in the case of South Africa in 2010 and negative image creation prior to or during the event (Sochi 2014 is a good case in point regarding some of the ethical and human rights dimensions of the event, not to mention corruption). Steinbrink (2013) makes the point that the main target groups of many so-called festivalisation policies are not the residents, especially the poorer ones, but instead the billions of global TV viewers, international tourists and investors. However, in Rio, it is difficult to conceal the presence of the 750 or so favelas. Steinbrink (2013) states that:

> Due to their exposed locations, they are very visible on the city's front stage, and their appearance is difficult to reconcile with the striven-for world-class city image. Due to their dense and apparently chaotic building structures, the favelas rather emblematically stand for attributes (poverty, bad governance, social stratification etc.) the elimination of which is meant to be presented to the world. (Steinbrink, 2013: 133)

There are also serious concerns about the high crime rate in Brazil. Typical policy interventions may include 'invisibilisation', which may mean not indicating favelas on tourist maps, for example. They may just be indicated as 'green spaces'. Favelas are usually left out of any promotional campaigns too, including photos and advertising videos. A 'pacification' process has also been started which means a crackdown on crime especially drug trafficking and armed violence in the favelas using special police forces. Another step is 'aesthetic remodelling' and 'beautification', which means improving the outward appearance of the favelas. It could just mean 'facadism' but it might also include demolition and displacement of inhabitants. Of course, in many cases there have been protests from the local residents about developments which are clearly not in their interests and may even be extremely detrimental to them. Finally, the tourist gaze is selectively directed towards 'pacified' and 'spruced up' favelas. Overall, it seems that the urban policy of mega-events in regard to slums is largely outwardly directed towards short-term promotion and tourism, not to the people who will be most affected in the long term by these changes. This is not surprising in the light of previous research, but it is certainly disheartening.

Conclusion

This section shows that there is an increasing move towards community and local empowerment in urban planning, but that it is by no means simple to optimise the use of tourism as a tool for development or poverty alleviation. It is also clear that the 'success' or 'failure' of ethnic quarters or slums cannot simply be measured in economic or quantitative terms. On the other hand, it is important that local people have the means and the wherewithal to increase their role in tourism development through entrepreneurship for example, rather than mere entertainment. Although the arts and festivals play a major part in attracting tourists to ethnic quarters, these activities may not be enough to provide sustainable benefits for more than a few individuals. There are growing examples of entrepreneurship in the food sectors especially in ethnic quarters, evening entertainment (e.g. gay quarters) and accommodation and tour guiding (e.g. townships).

The chapters in this section consider a number of development issues which are specific to ethnic and minority tourism. Nelson Graburn provides examples of numerous tourism development projects in China, many of which have been successful and have led to poverty alleviation. However, others have been focused more on prestige, image or the attraction of international tourism. Some developments have simply failed because they are too remote to attract enough tourists, thus the trend of bringing ethnic rural culture to cities, often in the form of theme parks. This and some of the values surrounding heritage and culture in China may be slightly at odds with Western and especially European development models. For example, improving and embellishing culture and preserving and 'fossilising' heritage only for tourism purposes is encouraged as a professional practice. Melanie Smith and Anita Zátori analyse the challenges inherent in creating Jewish tourism based on partly absent communities and material culture, balancing remembrance and memorial with entertainment, and interpreting and representing Jewish heritage and culture for different audiences. Development policies are often needed to preserve the remaining tangible heritage (e.g. buildings) or to guard against the kind of appropriation of Jewish culture that has taken place in some cities in the absence of a Jewish community. Esti Venske analyses the complexity of developing gay tourism in a multi-ethnic environment. Despite South Africa's gay-friendly, post-apartheid constitution and development policies for the Pink Village in Cape Town, gay tourism is still dominated by white, middle-class gay men. In addition, there are fears that the nearby Cape Malay quarter which is predominantly Muslim is being infiltrated by non-Muslim and gay residents and visitors. For this reason, it has been necessary to focus on sustainable development policies and initiatives promoting mutual respect.

9 Ethnic Tourism in Rural China: Cultural or Economic 'Development'?[1]

Nelson Graburn

Chinese *minzu*: Ethnic Tourist Villages

China's population of 1.3 billion includes 55 'minority' nationalities or ethnic minorities (*shaoshu minzu*, i.e. non-Han [Chinese] peoples) who comprise 70 million people or 1.8% of the total, many of whom are concentrated in the southern and western provinces, such as Yunnan. The *minzu*, formally thought of as 'primitive' people, have inhabited Han Chinese consciousness for centuries. The minority *minzu* are feminised in the sense that they play a passive role vis-à-vis the Han (Schein, 2000; Swain, 1990); in addition, the sexual attraction of minority women, as women, is illustrated by the fact that some Han Chinese women prostitutes wear Dai ethnic dress in the Xishuangbanna tourist region of Yunnan (Hyde, 2007). In some Chinese metropolitan regions, ethnic groups are represented in 'folk culture villages', a kind of theme park which brings together typical artefacts and crafts, features life-size models of rural village homes and homesteads and demonstrates various folk cultural performances for the expectant urban, Han tourists (Gordon, 2005; Oakes, 2006).

Much of the recent political and commercial development of tourism in China has focused on the poorer regions of the country, to the west and south-west, and within those, on the ethnic minorities, or *shaoshu minzu*, who are among the poorest in the regions, and whose difference and exoticism fascinate the urban and mainly Han Chinese who form the vast majority of the tourists. Although independent travel of the 'backpacking' kind is growing among China's urban middles class (Lim, 2009), their travel is generally on the same circuits to 'scenic spots' (Nyíri, 2006) as more organised mass tourists. Serious ecotourism or the penetration of 'wild nature' itself has been less attractive to many Chinese but there have been some developments in western China run by non-governmental organisations (NGOs) such as the World Wildlife Fund and the Nature Conservancy which appeal mainly to Western tourists.[2] Throughout the country, there are certain nodes where Western tourists gather to experience ethnic minority cultures, but these communities in turn manipulate the representation of identities, especially of through material souvenirs, for their own benefit.

At a national level, tourism development in rural, ethnic minority regions has been promoted widely in the decades since 'Reform and Opening' in the late 1970s (Donaldson, 2007; Oakes, 1998; Schein, 2000). As a policy, ethnic tourism in rural China has gained even greater attention and prominence since the 2000s, first with a national programme for economic development called 'Open Up the West' (*xibu da kaifa*), beginning in 2000, and then in the mid-2000s with the campaign to 'Build a New Socialist Countryside' (*jianshe shehui zhuyi xin nongcun*), introduced as a key element of the 11th Five-Year Plan (Chio, 2014; Harwood, 2013; Oakes, 2011). These programmes for rural tourism development in ethnic minority villages and regions across western and south-western China have involved the efforts of multiple stakeholders, including: corporate investors who establish and operate destinations (selling tickets, managing security, etc.) through contracts with local government agencies; regional and provincial tourism bureaus who produce promotions, organise events and seek out investors; local-level (village or township) associations and leaders who participate in tourism training programmes and manage day-to-day village affairs; construction bureaus and subcontractors who obtain contracts to build roads, bridges, hotels and other necessary infrastructure; and national and international development agencies, including the World Bank, who are funding many of the larger-scale tourism projects across the nation. In all of this, the impact of tourism development on the everyday lives of ethnic minority people in rural China should not be overlooked, or overstated. While tourism work has become a viable and profitable option for many rural ethnic Chinese, whose home villages are now destinations for urban tourists, the ongoing consequences of modernisation and development in rural China extend into bigger issues of educational opportunities, social integration, economic stability and changing cultural subjectivities.

Rural Minorities and Ethnic Tourism

The case studies of ethnic and rural tourism in this chapter are mainly found in Xinjiang Uyghur Autonomous Region in the far west, and in Yunnan and Guizhou in the south-west. The cities of Kunming (in Yunnan) and Shenzhen (near Hong Kong) are sites of ethnic theme parks. But we must remember that in spite of the enormous growth of rural ethnic tourism, the vast majority of rural ethnic villages are beyond the reach of regular tourism, as they are too far from urban centres or they are not connected by roads. Nevertheless, many communities aspire to tourism and many local authorities may see tourism as a practical means of rural development and hold out hope that success will eventually come their way.

Absent and incipient tourism

But tourism is only one means of rural development. Many local and regional governments try to help or develop rural ethnic villages in other ways by improving their infrastructure.

In one Buyi village I visited in Qingyi County, Guizhou province[3] all traffic in and out is on foot, and ordinary tourists and their vehicles cannot reach it. The villagers are partly dependent on the local market. Pigs are taken to market in baskets carried on people's backs. The government has assisted development in other ways: it introduced electricity and built a system in which methane gas from the pigs' manure is piped up to be used for cooking. The animist religion survived the communist purges of the 1960s and 1970s by going underground, and the local spirit-gods are again visible as 'paper gods' in the village shrine.

Not all tourism development in ethnic areas is aimed to include the local ethnic peoples. For instance, in Tuyuk, a Uyghur village in the Turfan Depression of Xinjiang,[4] there is minimal involvement of the local people in officially supported tourism.[5] Officially sponsored, state tourism investment and facilities are directed to the sacred drawings of Buddhas in caves in the hills left by the Buddhists over 1000 years ago when this was an active part of the Silk Road. The regional government built a covered parking area in the village with a long wooden walkway to the caves, which are in the desert area outside the village (Graburn, 2008).

Quite separately from official tourism, religious tourists/pilgrims, mainly Uyghurs, travel to Tuyuk to visit the mosques and make donations. The seven tomb/mosques are the graves of the founder-prophets who set out from Yemen in the 8th century. These magical founders were originally killed and buried but came alive again hundreds of years later. These magical occurrences make them powerful attractions for the region's religious tourists or pilgrims who visit informally and make donations which maintain the fabric of the structure and pay the local religious leaders. The government does not encourage the local *mazar* Islamic tourism (Dawut, 2007) for fear of raising pan-Islamic consciousness.

Ethnic villages: Marginal to tourist developments

Not all government efforts to develop tourism are motivated solely by poverty alleviation. International prestige and the attraction of international tourists are also motives. The very poor Hani ethnic minority of Qingkou village in the mountainous Yuanyang region of southern Yunnan[6] maintains immense terraced rice-growing slopes, which the national and regional governments have proposed as a UNESCO World Cultural and Natural Heritage Site (Wang, 2008). These sculpted terraced fields are already well known as tourist attractions, although there are more accessible regions in China, such as the Longji Terraced Fields Scenic Area in the Guangxi Zhuang Autonomous Region (Chio, 2014). Qingkou is very far from urban areas, but tries to advertise itself on main road. The tourist map of the village highlights traditional and animist features.

The village consists of thatched houses, known as 'mushroom houses'; the government pays the villagers an annual fee not to replace them with metal or flat roofs in order to keep the place looking picturesque. This village was the stage for a television drama that did not pay the villagers for the use of their community and left its plaza full of fake 'altars', attempting to enhance its 'primitive' look. The TV company told the villagers that the 'advertising' effect of appearing on TV was their 'payment'. There is also a small local museum, with a government-trained Hani guide. A few wealthy tourists (including anthropologists!) occasionally bring opportunities to sell local handicrafts. Tourist groups are very rare, but a lone Japanese backpacker tourist visited the craft store while we were there. The village leaders complained to me that they are exploited by hundreds of photographers who come to photograph the dramatic rice terraces but they see very little of the money that must be made (by sales of photos for calendars, books, travel magazines and so on). In fact, Wang (2008) reports that the local Hani thought that they might be better off flooding the rice terraces all year long instead of just in the spring, because that seemed to be the main thing that the tourist-photographers wanted to see. Calling this 'pushing rice for water', they thought that they might become wealthier by doing this because more tourists would come to the village and the villagers could buy the rice they needed cheaply on the open market!

Sometimes, tourism development projects are attempted and fail completely, and leave the place worse off. There is a small ethnic Yao village in the very remote hills of Guangdong province. The big horn (a musical instrument made of white ox horn) is their totem, and a giant replica was made as an icon next to the village entrance gate; it is common that a 'symbol' of animistic or totemic religion serves as a marker of the special culture of attractive minority villages. A company had invested about 5 million yuan in a tourism programme, but it was failed because very few tourists ever went there. The most dramatic thing was that the kids, the little boys, asked visitors to pay 5 yuan whenever they took pictures! Previously, these Yao people didn't have any commercial tradition or customs. Even though it failed the tourism programme, the programme along with the advent of TV, changed their whole view of money and the world.

Ethnic villages and controlled/collaborative tourist development

Guizhou province is a region with many culturally varied rural minority groups (Zhang & Liu, 2006), most of whom are poor even by Chinese standards. But the provincial government has been increasingly successful in promoting poverty alleviation through tourism. The Tourism and Rural Poverty Alleviation branch of the provincial tourism bureau has been successful in raising World Bank money and international non-governmental organisation (NGO) help in focusing on the poorer ethnic groups. The Bala River rural tourism demonstration project[7] organised seven Miao villages in south-eastern Guizhou over 15 years for gradual, collaborative tourism development, using money and expert advisors from the World Bank and NGOs outside China (World Bank, 2007). Each village chose its own course for development, such as having a restaurant or a museum or small hotels, in consultation with the government and foreign experts. But in all villages, it is the Miao young women dressed on 'traditional' clothing who attract and welcome the tourists (offering rice wine) while the men, in their less visually spectacular traditional clothing, provide the *lusheng* music in the background.

The foci of tourist attention are the usual set developed for ethnic tourism in most of the world. These include: performances of dancing and music, wearing distinctive traditional costumes,[8] traditional craft demonstrations and sales, and regional foods and cuisine. The tourists are encouraged to participate in many of these at some point. In Upper Langde village, the performers dance around the ladder/tree of life in the village square. Elderly women are 'on show' to demonstrate their special skills at spinning cotton and weaving to younger local people and to visitors. However, tourists often try to buy directly the presumably more authentic traditional textiles and clothing being worn by the local women!

Local food and cooking are often featured, served by women in traditional costume. In Maomaohe village, a restaurant is located upstairs in an old house. At the time of my visit in 2004, British textile expert Gina Corrigan (2001) was very warmly welcomed because she had visited many times before and because the locals realised that they benefited from being featured in her travel and textiles books. In the Bala project, great attention is paid to training the local people in hygiene, washing their hands, cleaning the food and the dishes. Often, running water and toilet facilities have to be built. Tourism is still secondary to rice agriculture in the village economies; although throughout the project's duration in the mid- to late 2000s the influx of funding and government support for tourism resulted in increased numbers of tourists to some villages (Blanchard, 2007; Chio, 2009, 2014), the overall distribution of profits to individuals was still relatively small. In a sense, the distribution of 'profits' resembles a half way between the previous work points communal system (in which people were assigned 'points' depending on the importance of their roles, and the communal profits were split accordingly), and the present and often rampant private business model (Zhao & Getz, 2008). Attempts have been made to seek outside investors to help fund the construction of higher-end hotels and facilities, but since 2008, tourism to the Bala River region has declined somewhat with the redevelopment and opening of nearby Xijiang 'Thousand Households' Miao village (*Xijiang qianhu miaozhai*) through large investments from the Leishan county government, provincial authorities and an private tourism development corporation which has taken over the management of the area. Thus, while this village cultural development model may appear a socially integrated effort for the revival, maintenance and display of the local minority culture, we should not imagine that this is a political revival stemming from an internal resistance to the national state culture.

Rural villages with developed tourism: Routinisation of performance

Some minority villages have come to specialise in tourism as an economic basis. These villages are often close to towns with good transportation, near spectacular scenery or have received visits from the highest government officials. Xiawutun township, a typical Buyi village in the Qingyi County of Guizhou, with well-organised tourism, is set in photogenic karst mountain scenery. A typical welcome party at the gate includes, as usual, women dressed in traditional clothing and two women performing craft demonstrations, spinning cotton.

A welcome banner gives the district's name and acknowledges the guidance of the communist ideology. The local animist religion is tamed and exoticised in recently sculpted 'religious totems' inscribed 'Heaven and earth'. Bilingual tourist information boards are typical of official tourism developments, not necessarily because they expect foreign tourists, but as markers of modernity and progress. There is the mandatory Buyi craft demonstration, weaving the local cloth that is used in local clothing and in souvenirs.

Nearly all dance performances are said to be courting couples. Romantic 'wooing couples' dance on stage. Tourists are always encouraged to join in later, either to 'court' the local young women or, as in the case of myself and Professor Peng Zhaorong, to dance and play the local musical instruments. Local and exotic foods are another focus of the tourism system. Tourists take part in pounding the 'sticky rice' said to be found only in south-western China and in Japan. One of the tourists was actually Professor Zhang Xiaosong, the anthropologist working for the Guizhou Rural Tourism and Poverty Alleviation bureau. Buyi women stuff the sticky rice balls with bean paste to share with the crowd of visitors.

Some tourist villages are 'famous for being famous'. Na Chan, a nationally famous Buyi tourist village in Zhenfeng County originally became known for its setting in the unique karst mountain scenery. After it was visited by then President Hu Jintao on New Year's Day 2005, it became even more famous. There is a huge commemorative billboard in the parking lot telling tourists that they have come to a famous place, and the village entrance road is marked with festive banners. Outside the village there is a huge stone dance stage with 'religious totem poles' and stadium seating was specially built for President Hu's visit; this is only an oversized version of a 'dance stage' common in tourist villages.

Ethnic Tourism without Ethnicity

In the rich, fruit-growing countryside of southern Guilin, other experiments with rural ethnic tourism developments are taking place in Gong Cheng County. These involve training and providing facilities for the Yao minority, who are farmers, to add to their incomes by running small guest houses. Ping An Heng Shan is one of these villages. The county government has built three-floor, apartment-like holiday lodges on what was once a rich landlord's estate. The old landlord's house serves as the centre and as a hotel. New facilities have been built, including a theatre 'on the lake' for cool evening shows. An old pagoda decorates the grounds and nostalgia is invoked by the remains of agricultural implements that are on display, much as in the guest houses and restaurants of many European rural tourist areas. Local Yao farmers set up a market in the tourist parking area, again preserving a nostalgic feeling of rurality. But Yao ethnicity itself is not on display: the Yao are 'modern' in Oakes's (1998) sense and the ethnicity of display is more like a generalised 'folkloric rural China'.

Nearby another experiment involves more control by the minority Yao people. In the newly developed Hong Yan ecological village built near a traditional Yao village of stone houses, small modern 'hotels' have been erected on the riverfront. The local county government contracted with the village to supply the materials to build these bed and breakfast hotels, training the farmers to build them with their modern facilities such as electricity and running water. The hotels face the waterfront where there are also many Yao-run floating restaurants. The village corporation chose the farmers who with their families moved into the ground floor of the hotels, and wives do the cooking and cleaning etc. The ground floor also holds the 'restaurant' where tourists can eat, as well as a small store. The upper floors contain modern bedrooms and flat-screen TVs. The housework is done by the farmer's wife who calls on other villagers to work part time – thus spreading the wealth – in the busy season. I was told that one of the most enterprising families had managed to pay off their whole 14,000 yuan debt (for the construction) in one year. Outside each house is a fish tank, and above it is a mercury-vapour lamp which is turned on at dusk, attracting and stunning insects which then fall in and feed the fish that are later taken to feed the guests and the family.

Urban Ethnic Tourism: Lijiang and Theme Parks

For some Westerners it might seem that urban ethnic tourism in places such as Lijiang in Yunnan province is a paradox, for its architecture resembles traditional Chinese houses. However, the nature of 'ethnicity' or minoritiness in China does not completely follow the model engendered by the situation of North America or Australia, where a majority settler-nation has imposed itself on indigenous peoples with very little cultural commonality to the majority. Much of minority ethnicity in China resembles more that of Europe or the Middle East where there have been hundreds or thousands of years of mutual cultural influences. For instance, Naxi polity of Lijiang reproduced the hierarchical polity of medieval China when granted semi-indirect rule; the local Mu dynasty was granted authority in the Tang Dynasty. The palace is now a tourist attraction where local Mandarin-speaking Naxi guides are available. Naxi cultural institutions have preserved aspects of medieval Chinese (Han) culture such as music played by the Dongba Orchestra, sometimes called a 'living fossil'. This orchestra is part of a revival of many aspects of the local religion and associated arts and crafts, traditionally associated with Naxi culture. Whereas young men from the countryside used to be brought to Lijiang for training as Dongba priests and return to their communities as part-time religious and healing specialists, nowadays the majority remain in Lijiang to practice visible aspects of their traditional arts and rituals for tourists (Zhu, 2012), while their functions back home are taken by more modern institutions. And these have become tourist attractions for Han Chinese who are in fact, as many acknowledge, viewing part of their own cultural past which they have given up. Wang Yu (2007), working with home stay tourists and hosts in the ancient core of the Naxi (minority) city of Lijiang, found that both tourists and locals subverted UNESCO's hopes that 'World Heritage' status would ensure the maintenance of authenticity. Tourists looked for non-traditional 'home' comforts and the entrepreneurs were happy to provide them with an intermediate form of 'customized authenticity'. The commercialisation of 'Old Lijiang' has in fact allowed many Naxi to cede their heritage homes by renting them to outside business people and to give up much of their 'authentic' visible culture to go and live in the more convenient parts of the newly built town, invisible behind the hill from the UNESCO-protected old town (McKhann, 2001).

Minority ethnic *minzu* identity is a key component of Chinese regional identity in the north-west and south-west. In addition to the tourist villages, an ethnic theme park was established in Kunming, the capital of Yunnan, providing a condensed version of the province for tourists. To a large extent, the ethnic theme park in Kunming[9] advertises itself as a metonym of the diverse populations of Yunnan.

In her introduction to the section on Kunming's nationalities village, Gordon (2005: 31:30–32:35) says

> *Minzu Cun*, Yunnan's nationalities village, is a state run gateway in to this multicultural and ecologically diverse province. The entrance to the park is a space known as Unity Square. Here, visitors watch a performance of all the nationalities in one place and at the same time. The Dance of the *minzu* is a snapshot of the states official discourse about minorities and the role they play in the united multiethnic state. The policy states that people of all ethnic groups jointly and with one heart and mind promote the development and prosperity of the nation. Minorities are directed to oppose ethnic splits and safeguard the unification of the country.

These ethnic performers perform in a very different context from the Miao and the Buyi described above. In the theme parks of Kunming (and Shenzen), as well as many of the other 'ethnic shows' organized by outside companies, such as at theme park in Jinghong city, Xishuangbanna, Yunnan, they are professional performers who have learned roles for a choreographed 'show' which is constantly being developed by commercial directors, a difference pointed out as distinguishing in general between Guizhou and Yunnan styles of ethnic tourism development (Donaldson, 2007).

Discussion

What can we learn from this initial and brief look at contemporary ethnic tourism in China?

(1) One can note that though the choice of what to represent in these villages and parks varies from the most 'backward' of domestic minorities to urban communities, everything is represented in a '*folkloric regime*', which draws upon a somewhat idealised nostalgic past, not on today's world with its problems and anomalies. The 'inhabitants' of the Chinese ethnic villages and theme parks are supposed to wear recognisably traditional clothing which not only marks age and gender, as do contemporary Chinese and Western clothing, but also 'ethnicity'. Their dress is 'traditional' and used on special occasions rather than everyday wear, one might say, to mark special occasions. The buildings show a similar nostalgic and idealised style: this is most obvious in the Chinese villages where traditional styles and appearances must be kept

for presentation (Chio, 2014), whereas in many other rural minority villages they are giving way to 'modern' forms of construction and more general regional styles.

(2) In the more rural ethnic villages, it is overwhelmingly the young women who are presented and present themselves. Young women paradoxically represent 'tradition' – they are the 'keepers of the culture' by being more home bound and less likely to be out competing in the modern urban world; and in their youth, they have not been 'corrupted' and assimilated to the outside world. Of course, many of the more successful and capable young women (and men) working in tourism have in fact gained experience and skills as migrant workers elsewhere, before returning to rural villages (Chio, 2011). Furthermore, the minorities themselves are gendered and sexualised as feminine as Schein (2000) has shown: though the marriage-less and free-loving Mosuo women are the extreme target of Chinese fascination and men's desires (Hyde, 2007; Walsh, 2005), nearly all minority women are under 'sexual pressure' in the tourist encounters.

(3) China, the 'Central Kingdom', has in recent decades as for much of its history, been more concerned with internal struggles and less with outside threats. Domestic tourism in China approaches the western and the south-western regions as places that are less securely part of their country and as an integrated developed nation, as evidenced in the campaign to 'Open up the West'. At the same time, there are concerns that the people in western regions are less securely part of the modern nation than are the majority Han Chinese – this is especially true for Tibet and the Muslim populations of Xijiang, Ningxia and nearby provinces. Mass tourism shows the majority what and who their western flank consists of, and at the same time it overwhelms the minorities demographically and economically, and teaches by repetition that all minority peoples are together, equally, part of the great nation, and that they should cooperate as allies to the nation.

One nationalist saying is 'Only together can we build a mountain'. Though the emphasis on retaining national differences as they work together may appear to resemble Durkheim's 'organic solidarity', we must remember the guiding principle for minorities which the former commissar for nationalities of the USSR, the late ethnic Georgian Joseph Stalin propounded 'Nationalist in form but Socialist in content', i.e. differences are superficial and the bonding principal is mechanical solidarity of Socialist structures.

(4) The re-enactment of stereotyped traditional performances for tourist purposes is not only a lesson in reinforcing minority equality, it is, as Oakes (1998) has shown for the Miao of Guizhou, through these performances of tradition that tourism is supposed to bring or to impose

modernity on the hinterland *minzu*. It is by drawing attention to their 'traditions' that they show *what not to be* – except when performing for paying tourists.

'All the world's a stage' (Shakespeare): The stage is a common metaphor with which to think about tourism. MacCannell (1976) developed the concept of staged authenticity following the dramaturgical sociology of his mentor Erving Goffman. It is in consideration of the concept of authenticity and reproduction that some of our Western ideas are most challenged. The Chinese assertion that 'authenticity' can be greatly improved upon by professionalisation does not coincide with common Western notions of either creativity or intellectual and artistic integrity. The *authenticity* of minority *minzu* village cultural expressions has no value except as a source of inspiration for entertaining and commercial performances. Recent research by both Li (2003) and Chio (2009, 2014; see also Chio dir., 2013) shows that the local minority people (Dai in Li's study; Miao and Zhuang in Chio's) gradually see themselves not as 'enacting their culture' but as acting a modern role in Chinese society, a role which happens to involve their successfully looking like and acting the attractive and visible parts of their traditional culture, and *learning to improve upon them*. Indeed these successful 'professionals' have come to look down on the ordinary co-ethnic members of their villages who still have to make a living practicing agricultural and other mundane occupations. Tourism has brought modernity to the countryside and rural people are excited to embrace aspects which suit and flatter them and play out their new lives on a more cosmopolitan stage (Swain, 2001).

Notes

(1) This paper was originally presented as they keynote address at International Conference on 'Tourism and Indigenous People/Minorities in Multi-cultural Societies', organized by the Institute of Anthropology, Yunnan University, and the Department of Anthropology, Chinese University of Hong Kong, 21-24 December 2007, Xishuangbanna, Yunnan. It was illustrated in part by clips taken from the video Global Villages (Tamar Gordon 2005). A version was published in Chinese as 'Chinese Ethnic Tourism in Global Perspective' (Graburn 2011). I extend many thanks to Dr Jenny Chio for her recent editorial advice.

(2) Information originally obtained in 2001 during a visit to the World Wildlife Fund (WWF) office in Lijiang, Yunnan, at that time under the direction of researcher Heather Peters.

(3) For visits to all the rural ethnic villages of Guizhou in 2004, 2005, 2011 and 2012, I must thank anthropologist Professor Peng Zhaorong of Xiamen University who put me in touch with Mme. Yang Shenming, director of Tourism and Rural Poverty Alleviation for Guizhou and Professor Zhang Xiaosong who works with her. At least two, sometimes three, of these people accompanied me to all the villages mentioned.

(4) My thanks go to Berkeley graduate student Cindy Y. Huang for hosting me and Professor Marie-Francoise Lanfant during our visit to Urumqi, Tuyuk, and other villages and sites in 2005; and in turn we thank Professor Rehile Dawut, Ms. Huang's professor at Xinjiang University, for her hospitality and guidance, and to Ms. Huang for accompanying us to Tuyuk.

(5) By 'officially supported tourism', I mean destinations that are specifically developed for tourism by government offices (usually regional and provincial-level tourism bureaus) and thus officially recognised by the government as a 'scenic spot' (*jingqu* or *jingdian*, see Nyíri, 2006.)

(6) For my knowledge of this village and the UNESCO-related developments, I must thank anthropologist and Duke University graduate Wang Yu who is from this region and who completed her doctoral dissertation on this topic (Wang, 2008). I particularly thank her for introducing me and Berkeley graduate Jenny Chio to the people of this village and to the authorities and stakeholders of this region in July 2006.

(7) I was first introduced to this project in the fall of 2004 after a conference on Rural Tourism Development and Poverty Alleviation in Guiyang by Mme. Yang and Professors Peng and Zhang (see Note 3). Jenny Chio (2014) studied the village tourist development process in one of the Bala River villages, Upper Jidao.

(8) I specifically use the word costume here, instead of clothes or garments, to indicate that they are special purpose and not (or no longer) everyday clothes; I also imply that they may not be strictly traditional but modified to express eye-catching versions of the traditional.

(9) I first went to Kunming in 1999 when invited to the conference 'Tourism, Anthropology, China' whose proceedings were published in two volumes (Tan *et al.*, 2001a, 2001b); I returned in 2001, hosted by Professor Zhang Xiaoping and Professor Yang Hui (and again in 2006) and was taken around the Nationalities Village by Wang Yu, then a student of The Chinese University of Hong Kong.

Acknowledgement

Thanks go to anthropologist Wang Yu for introducing me and my wife to Lijiang and to the WWF office.

10 Jewish Culture and Tourism in Budapest

Melanie Smith and Anita Zátori

Founded by the Romans, destroyed by the Mongols and oppressed by the Ottoman Turks, Budapest has reinvented itself time and again, flexible in the flux of time. It has also served as a laboratory of sorts for varying political ideologies, from National Socialism to Fascism to Communism.

Follath, 2013

Introduction

This chapter analyses the role of Jewish culture and heritage in tourism in Budapest. Despite the tragic history of Jewish communities in Hungary and continuing and growing anti-Semitism, Jewish culture is flourishing in Budapest and the community is the largest in central and eastern Europe. The heritage area, which served as a ghetto for a short time during World War II, is one of the most attractive and popular areas of the city, the Great Synagogue is the second-largest non-Orthodox synagogue in the world and there are many cultural events, such as the summer festival, which celebrate contemporary Jewish culture. Several Jewish heritage tours are offered, including those that provide alternative narratives to the mainstream Holocaust-related tours. Of course, the Holocaust and its memorials are also important attractions in Budapest as elsewhere in Europe, especially for those Jewish tourists with Hungarian ancestors.

Using a combination of qualitative research methods, the authors provide an overview of the history, development, preservation and celebration of Jewish culture in Budapest and its role in tourism. The methodology includes participant observation on five Jewish tours of Budapest, visits to all of the Jewish sites and events mentioned in the text, in-depth interviews with three specialist Jewish tour guides, an online interview questionnaire with seven Jewish cultural and tourism organisations and netnographic research of TripAdvisor reviews.

Jewish Heritage and Tourism in European Cities

Eastern European Jewish life generally is here to stay. That was not at all apparent
before the collapse of the Iron Curtain.
Gruber, 2009

It seems that despite the decline in numbers of Jewish communities following World War II, there has been something of a rebirth of Jewish culture in many European cities in recent years. Nevertheless, Sandri (2013) suggests that Jewish heritage in cities has remained a marginal topic in the tourism debate despite being 'valuable cultural capital on the global market of city tourism' (Ruethers, 2013: 675). One reason given by Gruber (2002) is that Jewish heritage, especially memorials, cannot be treated in the same way as other tourist attractions. Remembrance and commemoration must precede entertainment, and interpretation is frequently contentious (e.g. Auschwitz as documented by Tunbridge and Ashworth [1996] among others). Another problem in central and eastern Europe and the Baltic States was that the Nazis attempted to eradicate all traces of Jewish material culture in a process of so-called 'ethnocide' (Lemée, 2009). Collective remembrance was also suppressed under communism in many central and eastern European countries until after 1989 and former Jewish quarters of cities often became derelict.

Sandri's (2013) work focuses on Kracow and Vilnius. Vilnius was once known as the 'Jerusalem of Northern Europe' but the whole Jewish community was virtually annihilated during World War II and the Jewish quarter was badly damaged, whereas in Kracow it was not destroyed. As a result, Kracow attracts far more tourists to its Jewish heritage attractions than Vilnius, but this is also because Auschwitz is relatively nearby and the film *Schindler's List* in 1993 enhanced its image. However, until recently, Kracow was frequently described as containing a Jewish quarter without any Jews, as Jewish heritage and culture was often appropriated by and even reinvented by those who were not Jewish (Cabot, 2009; Gruber, 2002; Lehrer, 2007; Salamensky, 2013).

Podoshen and Hunt (2011) write of the 'animosity' of many Jewish people towards countries which were perpetrators of the Holocaust or failed to protect their Jewish citizens and suggest that:

In the case of the Holocaust, we believe that some Jews may avoid travel to Poland and/or Germany because they believe that today's relatively small exemplar of Jewish life in Eastern Europe (comparatively speaking) is a result of still-prevalent (and cognitively accessible) anti-Semitism. (Podoshen & Hunt, 2011: 1333)

Their research also showed that many Jewish people find it too painful to visit, that they do not think it necessary to be at the physical site of the

Holocaust to learn about it and some resent the economic benefits that are created at sites of suffering for the host country that was partly responsible. This could be true of other central and eastern European and Baltic countries too, although some other authors have suggested that visits to these regions are a kind of pilgrimage of memory for many Jewish people (Stier, 1995) and an 'obligatory' secular ritual (Kugelmass, 1994). The Israeli government actually organises class trips for students in their final year of high school to visit Poland and Auschwitz. It is considered to be a very important part of their education.

Sandri (2013) highlights the problems typical of many Jewish heritage quarters of cities, which are often seen to be inauthentic, idealised or even like a kind of Disneyland. Salamensky (2013) refers to 'Diaspora Disneys' which include two phenomena which she describes as 'Jewface' and 'Jewfacade':

> Jewface encompasses music, dance, theater, and extra-theatrical modes of performance, in which non-Jews dress up and act like 'Jews,' as historically imagined; Jewfaçade encompasses museum-type installations, as well as architectural and decorative constructions, depicting imagined 'Jewish' life. (Salamensky, 2013: 21)

Gruber (2002) suggests that Jewish culture is frequently represented through 'pseudonostalgia', which can lead to historical inaccuracy, false remembrance and commodification. Nevertheless, the contemporary Jewish culture in some European cities has recently been revived. Gill (2013) suggests that Kracow's Jewish life is starting to thrive again, partly due to young Polish Jews, ex-pats and returning ancestors. Sklarewitz (2012:1) expresses his surprise that even Berlin has once again become a home for Jews, especially for young, secular Israelis: 'Beyond the memorials and the synagogues, it's not hard at all to spot examples of lively rebirth of Jewish social, gastronomic and artistic life in Germany's capital'.

Budapest is another city where Jewish culture and heritage play an important role in the life and tourism of the city. Vörös (2001) writes that Jewish life in Hungary is centred in Budapest, but that there are increasing attempts to revitalise the Jewish communities of other towns as well. She states that 'Jews and "Jewishness", whichever way we define them, are inseparable from the image as well as the history of Budapest, just like any other Central European city' (Vörös, 2001: 93). However, Gruber (2008: 12) suggests that 'There is a big—and important—difference between its revitalization and that of most of the other Jewish quarters in East-Central Europe. For in Budapest, unlike the other towns and cities in the region, there is a large and viable Jewish community'. She also notes that the majority of Jewish Hungarians are totally assimilated.

The History of the Jews in Hungary

Vörös (2001: 88) suggests that 'The history of Hungarian Jewry has been a neglected and somewhat isolated chapter of the general history of Central and East European Jewry'. This may be because of the difficulties of translating the Hungarian language. On the other hand, there is a body of international literature focusing on the Holocaust in Hungary which is growing all the time as more materials are being translated into English (e.g. Braham, 1994; Cesarani, 1997; Cole, 2011; Vági *et al.*, 2013). Although this chapter does not deal with the Holocaust in depth, its spectre is ever-present in any discussion of Jewish culture in Budapest like it is everywhere in central and eastern Europe.

As elsewhere in Europe, the history of the Jews in Hungary and Budapest is an extremely tragic one. Jews had lived in Hungary since the time of the Roman Empire and the community flourished especially in the second half of the 11th century, although social restrictions were placed on them by the Christians. There were several tolerant kings until the 14th century. During the 15th century, large numbers of Jewish immigrants started to settle in the city of Buda. Jews were treated well under the Ottoman regime from 1541; however, when the Habsburgs captured Hungary in the late 17th century, anti-Semitism grew and Jews were expelled from cities. When Hungary was granted independence in 1867 and the Austro-Hungarian monarchy was formed, the Hungarian parliament accepted a law that declared the equality of Jewish citizens in their political rights. The political situation, the economic boom and the city's rapid growth attracted more Jewish settlers from the outskirts of the monarchy and neighbouring countries. Meanwhile, strong nationalism and wealth supported a massive assimilation process of Jews into the Hungarian nation. A new branch of Judaism called Neolog Judaism was formed, which, as a mild reform movement, adopted the Hungarian language and its followers viewed themselves as Hungarians of Jewish religion. In 1895, Judaism was accepted as one of the national religions (Vörös, 2001).

By the late 19th century, there was still political anti-Semitism but the population grew to 910,000 by 1910, and 55–60% of all merchants were Jewish by World War I. Similar to the situation in Austria at this time, many members of the intelligentsia were also Jewish, including artists and writers. Around 10,000 Jews died on the front line in World War I, but a further 3,000 died because of the so-called 'White Terror' massacres in 1919 when Jews were blamed for the communist regime (Vörös, 2001). Throughout the 1920s and 1930s, anti-Jewish sentiments did not wane, numerous anti-Jewish laws were passed and, by 1939, the majority of Jews were prohibited from participating in liberal professions, administration and commerce. A total of 250,000 Hungarian Jews lost their source of income, so many even converted to Christianity (Jewish Virtual Library, 2013). Interpretation Panel in the Holocaust Memorial Centre (Researchers' own visit, 2012) states that 'Hungarian Jews were expelled from society with a speed unparalleled in the Holocaust', a fact that is also noted by many historians (e.g. Cesarani, 1997; Cole, 2011). One example of an anti-Semitic 1940s' poster stated that 'You can't make bacon from a dog! You can't ever make a Hungarian out of a Jew'.

By 1941, there were around 850,000 Jews in Greater Hungary; however, many were massacred by Hungarian or SS troops or died in the battlefield against the Soviets. By 1943, Jews were no longer involved in Hungary's public or cultural life, and 400,000 were confined to ghettos. Jews were forced into the Budapest ghetto in December 1944, where conditions were so bad that many died. Deportation began in October 1944, with the majority of Jews being sent to Auschwitz. Of the original 825,000 Jews before the war, 260,000 Hungarian Jews survived and 565,000 died. At the end of the war, 69,000 Jews remained in Budapest's central ghetto and 25,000 remained in a smaller ghetto in another part of the city. Approximately 25,000 Jews came out of hiding in Budapest (Jewish Virtual Library, 2013).

After the war, most Jews moved to the capital Budapest or emigrated. Under communism, Jewish life was restricted, so 20,000 left Hungary during the 1956 Revolution. By the 1970s, there were only 60,000 Jews in Hungary, 50,000 of whom lived in Budapest. However, it was estimated that there were 80,000–120,000 in Hungary by the 1980s, but the numbers are not clear (Vörös, 2001). Vörös (2001) writes of how Jewish identity, culture and history were taboo topics in socialist Hungary until the mid-1980s when debate started to re-emerge. She also notes that many scholarly works on all aspects of Hungarian Jewry became available in Hungary except those dealing with the Holocaust period.

Anti-Semitic attacks took place in the early 1990s by nationalists and skinheads, and a 2012 survey on attitudes towards Jews in 10 countries showed that more than 70% of Hungarians think that Jews are 'too powerful' in the business and financial world, and 63% think that they talk too much about the Holocaust (Davies, 2012). In 2012, a Jobbik (far-right) politician called Márton Gyöngyösi urged the government 'to tally up people of Jewish ancestry who live here, especially in the Hungarian parliament and the Hungarian government, who, pose a national security risk to Hungary', which caused international outrage.

Unfortunately, at the time of writing this chapter in 2014, anti-Semitism had once again become perceptible in Hungary. Hungary's far-right Jobbik party staged a rally in central Budapest in protest at the capital's hosting of the World Jewish Congress (WJC) in May 2013. Ironically, the event aimed to highlight the growing problem of anti-Semitism in several European countries including Hungary (BBC News Europe, 2013). Currently Hungary's third-biggest party with more than 10% of the seats in parliament, Jobbik is openly anti-Jewish and accuses Israeli businessmen of buying up property in the country wholescale. There have since been several controversies including the potential naming of a street after an anti-Semitic author (Tzur, 2013) and the erecting of a statue of Horthy in the centre of Budapest, Hungary's wartime leader and a controversial figure. Some say that he restricted deportations from Hungary (Cole, 2011) but others disagree (Braham [1994] comments more on this). Kurtz (2013) notes that although 2013 was full of planned memorial services to mark the 70th anniversary of some of the worst atrocities in Hungary during World War II, with joint events planned between the Israeli and Hungarian governments, this was seen by some as an effort to dampen international outcry about Hungary's increasingly public far-right anti-Semitic movements. This could have an impact on tourism, especially Jewish tourism.

On the other hand, in April 2013, the annual March for Freedom by the Danube attracted a record turnout from people angry at the rise in anti-Semitism in Hungary (Euronews, 2013). Despite what has happened to them, 100,000 Jews live in Hungary, the largest number in east-central Europe (Jewish Virtual Library, 2013). Jewish heritage and culture continue to be some of the most interesting and popular attractions in Budapest with both Jewish and non-Jewish tourists alike.

Jewish Culture and the Historical Jewish Quarter in Budapest

> *The stones will tell you stories here. But so will the faces which you see. The beautiful past is still here, when vibrant Jewish life filled the quarter. The not so beautiful past is present too, when fear ruled over these streets. The present building on the ruins of yesterday is also at hand.*
> Gyárfás et al., 2013: 6

When asked how Jewish culture and heritage is viewed in Hungary today compared to elsewhere in the world, one interviewee said that it was often considered from a racial or historical point of view rather than a cultural, mystical or religious one. This was seen as similar to the other countries around Hungary in central Europe (e.g. Poland, Czech Republic). However, another interviewee considers that:

Jewish culture and heritage in Hungary is nurtured and highly esteemed. As Hungary prides itself in one of the largest Jewish communities in Europe, maintaining the values and remaining assets is one of the top priorities both for the community and on a government level.

It is perhaps important to note here that most of the interviewees were aged between 30 and 65. One interviewee in her fifties stated that 'the younger generation is more hopeful, open to the world and wears his/her

Jewish identity with pride'. Another interviewee confirmed this view, and added that while the older generation has more vivid memories about and identity connected to the Holocaust, among the younger generation, many view being Jewish as a positive identity. While the first and second generation of Holocaust survivors rather have a denial approach, the younger generations are actively interested in Jewish culture and heritage. This links to Katz's (1990) notion that today several kinds of Jewish identities may exist in Hungary.

Vörös (2001) suggests that it is difficult to define what a Jewish quarter is in Budapest. She describes how historically, there were several areas of Budapest which had higher concentrations of Jewish communities or where the buildings were owned by Jewish people (e.g. in the 1920s). However, she concurs with other authors that there is only one real Jewish quarter in Pest besides the earlier ones in Buda. The so-called Old Jewish Quarter in the centre of Budapest has become a major tourist attraction. Gyárfás *et al.* (2013: 6) describe how 'this is where Budapest's Jewry lived its most beautiful and dreadful days'. Before World War II, the Jewish population was not concentrated here; they also lived in other parts of the city, e.g. Districts VI and VIII. When the ghetto was established in 1944–1945, non-Jews had to move out and Jewish people were forced to move in. 'The Quarter, which was filled with so many happy memories turned into a setting for terror, fear, starvation, illness and death' (Gyárfás *et al.*, 2013: 32).

It is stated by two interviewees that the so-called Historical Jewish Quarter (the former World War II ghetto area) is quite a new identification for the area. After 100 days, the war ended, and the survivors of the ghetto either emigrated or moved to other parts of Budapest, but the historical and memorial value of the area remains. Several synagogues can be found here, and the area is also the centre of Budapest's Orthodox Judaism. The gentrification of the past decade turned the Jewish quarter upside down: younger generations moved in, the ruined buildings were reconstructed and creative industries appeared along with a multitude of community places, bars, pubs and restaurants.

Private developers are often given free reign by the city's municipalities to destroy old buildings and to build new ones (i.e. housing). Ironically, many of these are Jewish or Israeli! (Lebor, 2008). According to Kraske (2007), investors achieved astronomical returns of about 40% in the old Jewish quarter in 2006. This can increase rents and force out traditional businesses and inhabitants. The Jewish quarter is an area which requires greater heritage protection. Lukács (2005) stated that:

The Jewish Quarter in Budapest survived the World War and the Communist era. However, just now, after the establishment of democracy in Hungary, this outstanding complex of building is disappearing at an alarming speed. (Lukács, 2005: 1)

A small activist group known as 'ÓVÁS' ('Objection') is a civilian group which was established to prevent the further demise of the old Jewish quarter. They succeeded in gaining 'area of historic significance' status for the area, which meant that historically valuable buildings could not be destroyed even if they seemed in poor condition. UNESCO experts added their support. ÓVÁS also created a memorial space in 2010 with a plaque on a wall in three languages to show the map of the ghetto in November 1944. The memorial is visited by thousands of visitors each year (Gyárfás *et al.*, 2013); however, it is a well-hidden tourist attraction, located in the closed backyard of a building where the original ghetto wall stood, which makes it hard to find without a guide.

Lukács (2005: 1) explains that civil action groups are not only upset because of the lack of respect for the ghetto and its victims, but also because it is still a living Jewish quarter which could provide excellent opportunities for youth and alternative culture. The past decade led to a development in this direction. Already in 2007, Popper suggested that the ghetto was getting a 'facelift' with the opening of 'hip' new Jewish bars and nightclubs. He states that 'The seventh district is becoming Jewish again, but on very new terms'. Gruber (2008) suggests that they form the hub of an alternative Jewish youth scene that is eons removed from synagogue services or Jewish community centre programmes.

Many of these bars, clubs and restaurants are owned by Jewish residents and are following Jewish traditions or representing the culture. Gradually, the Jewish quarter has become a significant meeting place for young and creative people. A large number of non-Jewish bars, pubs, restaurants and wine bars have opened their doors too. Their close concentration makes it an ideal place for bar hopping. This includes the so-called 'ruin pubs' like Szimpla Kert, voted the best bar in Budapest and one of the best bars in the world on TripAdvisor in 2012, which plays the role of a catalyst in turning the area into a creative and entertainment district. The quarter contains 180 restaurants and coffee shops and 31 pubs and bars in a relatively small area (where everything is within short walking distance). This kind of development was facilitated by low property prices compared to other parts of the city centre. This small city quarter further includes 220 cultural heritage and architectural monuments, 25 hotels, 15 galleries, 22 design shops and 25 dentist and other medical clinics. As a cooperation between private and public sectors, a cluster was formed to reinforce the development of an attractive place for all stakeholders including businesses, residents and tourists too. The cluster, called KultUnio, chose a slogan to define itself as 'Budapest's Multicultural Quarter' (www.kultunio.hu, 2013).

There are a number of Jewish festivals throughout the year in Budapest, the most famous one being the Jewish Summer Festival which uses the Great Synagogue as one of its main venues. This was described by one interviewee as the main attraction for Jewish tourists to Budapest. However, there are several other smaller events such as the biannual Quarter6/Quarter7 cultural festival, a festival organised twice a year on major Jewish holidays, having a cultural and community profile, welcoming both Jewish and non-Jewish visitors; Judafest – a culinary and cultural festival aimed at audiences interested in Jewish communal life; and the Spinoza Café's Summer Festival and Music Festival. There are also growing numbers of design and crafts fairs in the area, such as Gouba in the Gozsdu-udvar. The quarter might be described as 'a performative space within the framework of a commemorative landscape' (Ruethers, 2013: 672).

Jewish Tourism

The unofficial, alternative sightseeing tours and strolls organized into Budapest's old Jewish Quarter are always a great success
Lukács, 2005: 5

As a result of public pressure from groups like ÓVÁS, the municipalities in Budapest have been partly forced to halt the destruction of heritage buildings by developers. However, at the time of writing this chapter, the Budapest municipal authorities and national tourist office were not actively involved in promoting Jewish attractions or tourism in Budapest, the initiatives mainly coming from individuals, entrepreneurs, small businesses and Jewish cultural and tourism associations. For example, Jewinform (2012) a travel guide and magazine promoting Jewish cultural-historical hotspots includes specialised Jewish heritage tours. Most of these tours visit the Jewish quarter or former ghetto; the main synagogues; Jewish cemeteries and memorials; the Jewish Museum; the Holocaust Memorial Centre; and Kosher restaurants and cafés. They also sell tickets for the Jewish Summer Festival in August/September, which includes concerts, exhibitions, dance, book fairs, films and kosher food. Famous Hungarian Jews are also listed in the guide.

The questionnaire interviewees agreed that one could speak of 'Jewish Tourism' in Budapest, with one interviewee stating that 'it is a flourishing segment'. The same interviewee estimates that 200,000 tourists arrive annually in Budapest for Jewish culture and heritage, but most especially for the annual Jewish Summer Festival. This event alone attracts 80,000 Jewish and non-Jewish visitors. The main markets quoted in the interviews are American Jews with some European roots, for example, survivors of World War II, their children or grandchildren tracing ancestors or visiting relatives. Lemée (2009) describes this form of tourism as 'historico-memorial' as it follows the history, identity and memory of the Ashkenazi worlds in the Baltic and central Europe before and during the Holocaust (Jewish people from the Austro-Hungarian and Balkan areas are sometimes referred to as

Ashkenazi). She notes that this is becoming even more important as the last survivors of the Holocaust are dying out. There is a Hungarian Jewish Archive in Budapest founded in 1994 where numerous documents can be found. One interviewee who is a tour guide estimated that 80–85% of the tourists on guided tours in English are American Jews. However, the number of French and Spanish tourists visiting the Great Synagogue is also increasing, and numerous TripAdvisor reviews about Jewish sites are written in Italian. The main motivations might also include joining family members for Jewish festivals, holidays or events.

An analysis of 2013 TripAdvisor reviews, ratings and comments for the main Jewish attractions in Budapest revealed the information shown in Table 10.1, where rating refers to how satisfied tourists were with the attraction out of a possible 5 and ranking shows how popular it is out of 210 identified attractions in Budapest.

According to the netnographic analysis of reviews, the National Jewish Museum is described as a 'most moving experience', 'very poignant' and 'informative'. However, the museum is also seen as small and cramped with poor signage with the Holocaust Memorial Centre receiving better reviews overall. On the other hand, it should be noted that the Holocaust Memorial Centre serves a very different function and it is not necessarily appropriate to compare a cultural site with a memorial site. The Holocaust Memorial Centre is difficult for many tourists to find and it is not as well signposted or promoted in the same way as the Great Synagogue, Jewish tours or the Jewish quarter. This is not the fault of the excellent managers of this site but rather the city authorities who do not provide adequate and visible signage. However, visitors are extremely impressed by their experiences there, with many describing it as a 'must-see' site in Budapest, 'an excellent memorial' and even 'the best memorial I have ever been to'. Some reviewers noted that there is nothing like it in Hungary's neighbouring countries, all of which were also involved in the Holocaust. Of course, it is also perceived as a 'harrowing', 'haunting', 'shocking', 'humbling' experience and 'not for the faint-hearted or squeamish'. One quotation from a non-Jewish visitor summarises the memorial extremely well:

Table 10.1 TripAdvisor reviews of Jewish sites in Budapest

Attraction	No. of reviews	Rating (/5)	Ranking (/210)
National Jewish Museum	32	4	49
Holocaust Memorial Centre	305	4.5	12
Shoes on the Danube promenade	1486	4.5	9
Great Synagogue	1006	4.5	25

It provides an excellent historical perspective on the Holocaust and roots of Hungarian and European anti-Semitism. It also integrates the attempt to annihilate the gypsies as well. Better than any other museum exhibit I have seen in Budapest, this one puts the Holocaust into perspective; it didn't arise from nowhere...... I congratulate this museum for not sugar-coating history – especially when anti-Semitism is on the rise in Europe again and particularly in Eastern Europe. This museum is a must to get a good handle on history. It will fill in a lot of gaps left by visits to other historical exhibits. (TripAdvisor Reviewer, 2013)

Another memorial which is often found by chance is the shoe monument on the banks of the Danube. This symbolises the spot where the Arrow Cross shot 8,000–10,000 Jews into the river. Again, tourists lament the fact that it is difficult to find and that there is no information about the meaning of the memorial in English. As a result, some tourists behave inappropriately there, trying on the shoes, etc. However, the reviews are almost entirely positive and one reviewer stated that it is 'One of the most heart-rending Holocaust memorials we saw on a trip to Prague, Budapest and Vienna'.

However, it is the Great Synagogue which attracts the majority of visitors and many of the Jewish tours are conducted from this starting point. The architecture outside and inside is deemed impressive, with various reviewers claiming that 'This building is by far one of the most beautiful synagogues I have seen', 'a must see!! absolutely stunning', 'The interior decor is unique and unmatched anywhere in the world' and 'It would be a pity for anyone visiting Budapest to miss out this site'.

Learning from history is a major focus of many of the reviews of the Jewish sites, including comments by history teachers. The sites are described as 'a must for Jews and Israelis and for people which are concerned about racism and global violence'.

Jewish Tours

The role of tour guides in Jewish tourism in Budapest is quite significant. Although there is a new (2013) Jewish quarter guidebook especially for youngsters, entitled *Jewnior Guidebook: The Pocket Guide to Budapest's Jewish Quarter*, and maps and app tours can be downloaded too, many visitors comment on the importance of tour guides, saying such statements as 'You should use the tour guide as small interesting details can be missed' and 'Guided tours are the best way to get the full impact and story'. It was thought by the interviewees that a Jewish guide might be able to identify himself/herself with the painful past he/she is explaining. However, most of the interviewees suggested that an open mind, interest and knowledge of Jewish culture and heritage in Budapest were more important than being Jewish. Although many visitors appreciate it if their guide is Jewish and had a personal experience, e.g. 'given that our guide is a survivor himself, we really appreciated him taking his time and sharing part of his life'.

There are many Jewish tours of Budapest, which can last anything from two hours to one day. When asked about the differences between these seemingly similar tours, one interviewee stated that 'The major part of the tours are all the same and show important highlights such as the Great Synagogue and the former ghetto', but another said that each tour is 'tailor-made to suit the tourists' needs'. This of course depends on the numbers and interests of a group. Most are walking tours, but one or two are by bus (partly because the shoe memorial by the Danube and the Holocaust Memorial Centre are a bit out of town compared to the Great Synagogue, the Orthodox Synagogue and the Jewish quarter). The one-day tours often include a synagogue service and meeting members of the local Jewish community. One free tour includes visits to 'authentic' pubs and Jewish party places. The researchers' own experience of two three-hour heritage tours included the Jewish Museum, the Great Synagogue, the cemetery, a walk in the Jewish quarter and refreshments in a kosher café. Other members of the group on two of the tours were American Jews who were doing a tour of Jewish heritage in central and eastern Europe. However, another tour which offered an alternative view of Jewish heritage in Budapest took the researchers and the other tourists to different parts of the district including other synagogues which were hidden from sight in a historic courtyard. One interviewee described One interviewee described how they tried to make a tour which is a story rather than being fact based and showing life now and then which is integrating, informative and fun for both Jewish and non-Jewish tourists. Some of the tours are organised in Hungarian for locals, with the aim to educate them about Jewish culture and heritage.

One interviewee stated that most visitors are interested in taking guided tours to learn more about the Holocaust in Budapest and the stages and sites it involved. The Holocaust is inevitably a focus of the Jewish heritage in Budapest as it is elsewhere in central and eastern Europe. As stated by Lemée (2009: 143) 'the Ashkenazi identities, more than other Jewish identities, are today (re)defined through the prism of the Holocaust'. One interviewee considers that the Holocaust history and memorials are very important for visitors and that the former ghetto area/Jewish quarter is an essential part of the tours. However, one Jewish guide stated that he also tries to give visitors a longer history going back several centuries in time. Nevertheless, it is not uncommon for tourists to ask guides to focus specifically on recent history and most especially the Holocaust, as happened during one of the tours experienced by the researchers.

It is important to include positive stories too, for example, those who tried to save and protect the Jews (e.g. Raoul Wallenberg). Other interviewed guides (two of an 'alternative' Jewish tour and one of a private tour) make a conscious effort to promote positive and contemporary aspects of Jewish culture and not only the Holocaust. As alternative tourist attractions, the interviewees suggested the Jewish heritage found in other districts of Budapest such as District VIII, Óbuda and Buda. Some interviewees suggested taking other topics into consideration for the interpretation of Jewish heritage – such as Jewish customs, sports and typical professions.

Mobile applications focusing on Jewish heritage in Budapest were recently launched. A walking tour based on a mobile app allows the user to discover the quarter's heritage. It guides the user on a two-hour walk, and provides information about not only the Great Synagogue, but also two smaller and equally intriguing synagogues. It aims to explore both the physical and philosophical space while providing information about the quarter's contemporary Jewish life. The tour finishes in a restaurant renowned for its modern Jewish cuisine. It seems that a certain degree of mediation is important and experience enhancing for Jewish tourism in Budapest, whether it is actual and personal (a tour guide) or virtual and generic (an app or TripAdvisor reviews).

Conclusion

There is a revival of interest in the Hungarian Jewish past as there is elsewhere in central and eastern Europe. The growing, thriving and vibrant Jewish community in Budapest makes it different from some of the cities in Poland or the Baltic States, where the Jewish population was more diminished after World War II. Although Budapest may still fail to attract some Jewish tourists because of animosity and other reasons as discussed by Podoshen and Hunt (2011), it may also be seen as a place for 'historico-memorial' tourism such as tracing ancestors (Lemée, 2009), or a secular ritual linked to the Holocaust (Kugelmass, 1994). On the other hand, it might also be seen as a place for the celebration and positive promotion of Jewish culture, something which the festival organisers and alternative tour companies have tried to develop. The growing emphasis on the 'alternative youth scene' and creative business development also contributes to changing perceptions of the former ghetto area of Budapest.

Most of Budapest's Jewish tourism still centres around tangible heritage such as buildings, museums and exhibitions. It is interesting to note that Jewish heritage sites and memorials feature in the Top 50 attractions in Budapest on TripAdvisor for Jewish and non-Jewish tourists alike, with three of them being ranked in the Top 25. What is less positive is the fact that they seem to be underpromoted, poorly signposted and difficult to find.

It is surprising that the shoe monument on the Danube is ranked in the Top 10 attractions in Budapest despite being discovered mainly by chance.

However, Vörös (2001) suggests that there is also an 'invisible Jewish Budapest' which consists of the artistic and intellectual contribution of Jews to Hungarian culture (e.g. architecture, art, literature). Although the Nazi ethnocide attempted to eradicate these, significant legacies remain and could be explored further. There is also much hidden heritage in other former Jewish quarters of Budapest which warrant a visit. Jewish festivals already celebrate much of the intangible living culture with 'real' Jewish performers, unlike the 'Jewface' performances in some other cities of Europe where the appropriation of Jewish culture and heritage is more common, resulting in a greater tendency towards what Salamensky (2013) describes as 'Diaspora Disneys'. In other central and eastern European and Baltic State cities with smaller Jewish populations, invisibility is more about absent communities than intangible culture.

Much of this research suggests that Jewish tourism needs to be based as much on the intangible as the tangible, and as much on people or personalities as places (as stated earlier, Jewinform has already started promoting famous Hungarian Jews). For this reason, tour guides play an important and valued role in mediating the tourist experience. They do not necessarily need to be Jewish nor do they need to have experienced loss in the Holocaust to provide an interesting picture of Jewish life and culture in Budapest, as some of the younger and alternative tour guides prove. Nevertheless, while ancestors of Holocaust victims or survivors are still alive, the Holocaust will continue to be an important focus of Jewish tourism in Budapest just as it is elsewhere in Europe.

Overall, Vörös's (2001) assertion that Jewishness has always been central to Budapest continues to be true. The renegotiation and expression of Jewish identities on the part of Hungarian Jews (Katz, 1990) mean that the culture remains dynamic. The increasing emergence and translation of documents relating to both Hungarian Jewish history and culture can lead to greater understanding of this often misunderstood but truly significant minority. This can hopefully have positive implications not only for tourists but also for the Jewish citizens themselves.

Acknowledgements

The authors would like to thank all of their interviewees, especially János Bakti, an historian of Jewish History and tour guide, for his interest in and contribution to this chapter and Vera Vadas, director of the Jewish Summer Festival, and Judit Markovitz for their useful comments.

11 Pink Tourism in Cape Town: The Development of the Post-Apartheid Gay Quarter

Esti Venske

Introduction

Since the 1994 post-apartheid liberation movement's strategic decision to focus on equality, inclusive of the protection of gay rights (Croucher, 2011: 159), Cape Town has become one of the world's top 'pink' destinations and has branded itself as a liberal and accepting city towards the gay market (Oswin, 2005). This has led to the development and growth of Cape Town's gay quarter, De Waterkant, which, as Africa's ultimate gay village, allows the city to benefit from the lucrative gay tourism market (Visser, 2003a, 2003b, 2004). The gay quarter's expansion falls partially within a rich historic national preservation area known as the Bo-Kaap, which preserves the traditional Malay/Muslim sociocultural heritage of the majority of the residents as well as the unique architecture of the area.

This chapter provides an overview of the impact of South Africa's post-apartheid constitution on the gay minority group and explores Cape Town's success as a top international pink tourist destination. The chapter then discusses the historic context relevant to the gay quarter's development and explores the multi-ethnic community that contributes to the area's unique cultural appeal. The city's gay tourism products and services offered to pink tourism visitors are briefly analysed, along with considerations for responsible tourism, taking cognisance of the country's continuous promotion of racial, gender and religious freedom and equality for all minority groups. These include the Malay/Muslim residents that fall within and border on the De Waterkant gay village. The chapter argues that although various initiatives have been undertaken by Cape Town Tourism to capitalise on gay tourism opportunities (Tebje & Ozinsky, 2004), the establishment of effective collaboration between gay tourism developers and the Malay/Muslim residents of the area remains imperative to ensure De Waterkant's success as both a gay and a socioculturally responsible tourist attraction. In conclusion, the chapter reflects on the benefits of sociocultural responsiveness and collaboration in responsible tourism development between the ethnic Malay/Muslim residents and the gay community of the area.

Post-Apartheid Gaiety: Towards Pink Tourism in Cape Town

Implemented in 1948, the South African apartheid system attempted to regulate sex, sexuality and the spaces where this could be realised (Visser, 2002: 85) and discriminated against sexual and gender minorities in such a way that any person who could possibly be identified as homosexual could be subject to sanctioned repression, persecution and arrest (Steyn, 2006: 138). To avoid homophobic harassment from the government and society at large, homosexual minority groups were forced, as a matter of personal safety, to employ a level of censure or denial regarding their sexual orientation (Steyn, 2006: 138).

The 1990s saw the rapid demise of the hugely inefficient and restrictive apartheid system (Sonneborn, 2010), and the sociocultural conservatism of the apartheid rule was replaced by the main liberation movement's quest for a new, equitable, democratic, non-racist and non-sexist society. In 1994, South Africa celebrated the start of its first years of democracy and political liberalisation and embarked on the revision of the county's constitution in support of a society free from all forms of oppression and discrimination. During this time, South African gay social movement organisations united to develop the National Coalition for Gay and Lesbian Equality Project, which fought for the inclusion of gay rights in the new legislation, including the right to permit same-sex couples to legally marry (Oswin, 2007: 651). The country became the first in the world to include the protection of sexual orientation in the equality provision of the country's post-apartheid constitution (Cock, 2003: 35) and at this time a new national culture of equality and non-discrimination was widely adopted by South African society at large, setting a context for the development of Cape Town as a popular, gay-friendly tourism destination.

Cape Town's gay community also capitalised on the euphoria of the unexpected constitutional recognition of gay rights in 1994; gays celebrated their sexual difference by proudly showcasing the gay culture to the world through gay festivals such as the Mother City Queer Project (MCQP) (Steyn, 2006: 105), while Cape Town Tourism utilised these events to enhance the city's image as a gay-friendly destination to the local and international gay leisure markets. Cape Town's array of successful gay events has boosted pink tourism to the destination, and has led to the recognition of the importance of the gay market by Cape Town

Tourism and the continuous development of gay attractions, including the urban gay quarter known as De Waterkant (Rogerson & Visser, 2007: 20), an area where gay and lesbian people have a sense of community and freedom of expression without fear of censorship (Gay Net Cape Town, 2013).

Gay tourism has experienced continued international growth since the 1990s and the increase in gay tourism may, among others, be attributed to the acceptance of gay tourism by many national governments, the use of the internet by gay tourism product and service providers to promote pink travel and the increased availability of gay-friendly accommodation in gay-friendly destinations (Waitt & Markwell, 2006: 10). With the increased number of gay-friendly international destinations since 2000 (Guaracino, 2007: 4), the South African Gay and Lesbian Travel Alliance (SAGLTA), an organisation representing South Africa's gay-friendly tourism products and services, adopted a more aggressive promotional approach to attract international pink tourists to South Africa, and Cape Town specifically.

The status of Cape Town as the 'pink capital' of the African continent is known worldwide owing to the liberality, gay-friendliness and branding of Cape Town. Furthermore, gay travellers to South Africa have noted the development of the country's urban areas without their losing their 'African-ness' as a key attraction for visitors (UNWTO, 2012). Gay travellers from international destinations favour Cape Town, also known as the 'pink city' of South Africa (SouthAfrica.info, 2013), because of the city's scenic beauty, colourful diversity and local gay population; Cape Town is also one of the world's Top 20 gay travel destinations for 2013 according to a survey conducted by Out Now Business Class, who specialise in the lesbian, gay, bisexual, transgender (LGBT) market (Barford, 2012). Table 11.1 provides the Top 10 things to do in gay Cape Town according to the official Western Cape Gay Portal (Cape Town.tv, 2013) and compares, in order of preference, the Top 10 general tourist attractions with gay-specific attractions.

Cape Town's Gay Quarter: De Waterkant, the Pink Village

The presence of a fixed gay space is an important consideration when gay travellers select their holiday destination (Ballegaard & Chor, 2009: 17) and contributes to the overall appeal of Cape Town as a pink destination. The well-established gay village, De Waterkant or the Pink Village, has become 'the most visible expression of queer [gay] life on the African continent' (Visser, 2003a, 2003b) and offers a cluster of upmarket gay leisure facilities to the gay community. Gay tourism attractions in the De Waterkant area include bars and nightclubs, bathhouses and spas, massage studios and upmarket escort agencies, accommodation establishments,

Table 11.1 Top 10 things to do in gay Cape Town

Top 10 general tourist attractions within Cape Town and the surrounding areas	Top 10 gay attractions within Cape Town and surrounding areas
(1) Table Mountain: Considered Cape Town's most famous attraction, one of the seven natural wonders of the world.	(1) MCQP: Mother City Queer Project (MCQP) is Cape Town's major themed gay costume party that is staged annually in December.
(2) Victoria & Alfred (V&A) Waterfront: This shopping area is one of Cape Town's foremost attractions with an estimated 20 million visitors annually, situated alongside the well-known Two Oceans Aquarium with over 3000 living animals.	(2) Cape Town Gay Pride: Cape Town Gay Pride runs once a year for a week from the end of February and includes a number of festivals and events celebrating the city's wonderful diversity, and creating awareness around issues impacting on the South African gay community.
(3) Robben Island: Declared a UN World Heritage Site, the museum is most famously known as the prison where Nelson Mandela was imprisoned and is a reminder of South Africa's struggle for democracy.	(3) Pink Loerie Mardi Gras & Art Festival: Hosted in the surrounding Western Cape Garden Route town of Knysna, this colourful event takes place annually around late April, and is a week-long gay art festival.
(4) Penguins at Boulders Beach: Since 1982, this colony of playful African jackass penguins has become a major attraction at Boulders Beach.	(4) De Waterkant Gay Village: A trendy selection of gay clubs, shops, bars and accommodation venues located in the upmarket suburb of Green Point and the cultural Bo-Kaap district.
(5) The Wine Route: With over 200 grape and wine producers in the beautiful Western Cape region, it is famous for its world-class gastronomic tourism experiences.	(5) Clifton Third Beach: This internationally renowned beach is the most popular beach frequented by the gay community.
(6) Cape of Good Hope Nature Reserve: Situated at Cape Point, this top tourist attraction offers unrivalled scenic beauty and wildlife on the coastal tip of southern Africa.	(6) Sandy Bay Nudist Beach: Sandy Beach is Cape Town's only nudist beach with a mix of straight and gay visitors; however, there is a prime area at the end of the beach where the gay community prefer to relax and tan.
(7) Kirstenbosch Botanical Gardens: Known as one of the greatest botanic gardens in the world with over 22,000 indigenous species and fynbos.	(7) Cape Peninsula Helicopter Ride: This helicopter ride provider caters for romantic trips to and around the Cape Peninsula's scenic locations.

(8) Bo-Kaap/Cape Malay Quarter: The Bo-Kaap community are mostly Muslim/Malay descendants of East Indian slaves brought over by the Dutch. Their influence on Cape Town is seen through-out the area's colourful architecture, food and language.	(8) Sunset on Table Mountain: Table Mountain offers scenic views of the African sunset over the Atlantic Ocean to tourists enjoying a 360° view of the city from cable cars.
(9) Shark Cage Diving: This favourite activity among travel-lers allows close-up encounters with the great white sharks in their natural habitat.	(9) The Wine Route: The various wine estates offer gay-friendly food and wine tastings in the beautiful Cape Winelands countryside.
(10) Cape Whale Coast: Known for its excellent whale-watching opportunities, travellers can view south-ern right whales from land or by boat.	(10) V&A Waterfront: This shopping area also offers upmarket gay-friendly penthouse complexes sur-rounding the V&A Waterfront and char-tered yacht trips for gay travellers depart daily from the harbour complex.

Source: Adapted from Cape Town.tv (2013)

restaurants and cafés, and specialist shops, and the area plays host to various annual gay events of which a number are officially cited in the Pink Map, Cape Town's official gay guide (Cape Town Tourism, 2012b). The Pink Map is one of the city's official high-profile promotion cam-paigns aimed at attracting the LGBT tourism market and indicative of Cape Town's commitment and desire towards pink tourism growth. Table 11.2 indicates the gay products and services offered specifically in the gay quarter.

The Pink Village is marketed to international visitors as a liberated urban utopia within a non-discriminatory community (Oswin, 2005) and while this message is for the most part a true reflection of the gay space, it does however depreciate gay Cape Town's lack of consideration towards racial, class and cultural differences. De Waterkant has in many instances not considered the inseparability of sexuality, race, gender and class, and consequently the particular dominance of gay white males within the Pink Village may raise questions about whether the physical space considers the inclusive rights of all oppressed communities and the extent to which pre-existing privileges (such as the white male privilege) have influenced the area's demographic composition. Directly linked to the legacy of apart-heid is the possibility that coloured and black men in particular may risk exclusion from socialising in certain Pink Village leisure spaces because

Table 11.2 De Waterkant gay quarter products and services cited in the Pink Map of Cape Town

Gay guide category	Product and/or service located in De Waterkant gay quarter and immediate surrounds	Product and/or service description
Places to stay	Glen Boutique Hotel	Cape Town's gay four-star hotel with chic individually styled rooms
	De Waterkant Village	Situated on Loader Street, De Waterkant Village offers a variety of urban-living options for gay travellers
	Amsterdam Guest House – For Men	The four-star award-winning gay guesthouse
Wine and dine	Beefcakes Burger Bar	A retro-chic diner that offers gourmet burgers, a cocktail bar and entertainment
	Café Manhattan	Popular restaurant/bar with regular art exhibitions and parties
Health and grooming	Dr Nico Botha – dentist	An aesthetic dentistry practice
Travel and leisure	Cape Info Africa – travel and tourism centre	The one-stop pink travel centre facilitates all tourist information and travel arrangements
Retail therapy	Cape Quarter Lifestyle Village	Offers a unique shopping and lifestyle experience in a piazza environment
	Philip Wulfsohn Jewellery	A welcoming jewellery design studio and workshop offering exquisite jewellery
	Prins and Prins Diamonds	Bespoke jewellery on offer in a relaxed atmosphere with private consulting rooms
Pubs, clubs and entertainment	Amsterdam Action Bar	Popular for drinks after work and offers a cruising section upstairs with private cubicles and a dark room
	Crew Bar Cape Town	One of the city's premier gay action bars with bar dancers and sexy barmen; the bar offers monthly events and features top South African DJs
	Madison	Features a sexy light show and stylish décor that make it one of Cape Town's most popular pink dance clubs
Steam baths	The Hothouse Steam & Leisure	A trendy and modern sauna with an upmarket atmosphere including a lounge with bars, two video lounges, private cabins, a maze and showers

Source: Adapted from Cape Town Tourism (2012b)

of the colour of their skin, which is not used as a racial indicator or to define so-called economic disempowerment, but because of their inability to conform to the area's particularly powerful and exclusive cultural identity: the epitome of the upmarket white urban gay male (Tucker, 2009). De Waterkant's communication message emphasises the tourism aspects and aesthetics that are typically attractive to the international white gay male visitors and this abstracted façade hinges significantly on previous exploitations and racism emanating from the country's history of racial inequality (Nast, 2002).

The categorisation of gay people in South Africa is not homogeneous and quite complex, being black, gay and middle class is very different from being white, gay and middle class (Donham, 2013) and inequalities still exist in the country, and consequently in the Pink Village itself. When the privileged gay white male dominance of the area is coupled with the superior buying power of the notable amount of German and British men who frequent and permanently reside in De Waterkant, the exclusion of middle-class coloured and black men is almost guaranteed as the white gay monopoly of the space radiates upmarket exclusivity (Visser, 2003a). The post-apartheid economic landscape has evolved in many ways with significant changes in the racial composition of middle and upper class and a remarkable increase in the black upper class (Visagie, 2013); however, De Waterkant remains dominated by affluent white gay men. Regardless the emergence of 'black diamonds', a phrase describing South Africa's post-apartheid very affluent non-white individuals, black and coloured gays are still in the minority in the area; therefore, economic affluence is but one of the possible reasons for exclusion. The ideology of apartheid continue to have an effect in Cape Town as relatively little mixing between coloured, black and white gays takes place in their respective communities, and one of the few spaces where all three groups can come together is the Pink Village. Coloured and black gays still favourably view the space as less inhibited, safer and freer than their residential areas, and hold it in high regard despite distinct factors that may constrain their access to the space, such as the distance of travel and the lack of affordable and safe public transportation between the Cape Flats and the Pink Village (Tucker, 2009). The Cape Flats is the combined geographic location where the majority of Cape Town's black and coloured people reside, and includes a vast and vibrant collection of segregated black townships and coloured communities, a living reminder of the demographic and geographic impacts of segregation. Many black and coloured gay South Africans still face exclusion from De Waterkant – in the past they were required to carry passes to allow access to certain areas; today, black and coloured gays require money, transportation and the correct attire to gain access to the Pink Village (Beebe, 2012).

This discrimination is partly caused by the white nationalist history of categorisation as De Waterkant's gay white patriarchy is rooted in historic white male privilege and supremacy. This practice of selective exclusion may be ascribed to the normalisation of pre-existing forms of inequality and exclusion promoted during apartheid (Tucker, 2009). The existence of gay white 'patriarchies' may indicate a continuance of a prejudiced gay society dictating who may be allowed or denied access. From a gay coloured perspective, for example, the homosexual history in apartheid South Africa is closely linked to Sea Point (bordering De Waterkant) and District six (bordering Bo-Kaap), the unofficial 'proto-gay neighbourhoods' for white and coloured gays, respectively. The white gay men at the time were influenced by fashionable and liberated overseas communities, while the most of the working-class coloured gays adopted aspects of gay life such as cross-dressing, drag and the speaking of Gayle, or *Moffietaal*, literally meaning homosexual language, a secret language spoken mostly among coloured gays during apartheid to safely identify and communicate with other like-minded individuals (Nyeck & Epprecht, 2013). Although some Gayle phrases and words have made their way into mainstream gay Cape Town, it is such aspects associated typically with coloured gays and non-white drag queens that may at times indirectly limit socialisation and promote exclusion as it does not fit the Pink Village's powerful cultural identity of white gay male patriarchy. This type of discriminatory practice may also exclude lesbians, or any other individual for that matter, who may distort the image of the leisure space, which only appears to be inclusive of all people. The marketing of De Waterkant as a gay space is largely founded on the ideals of freedom and non-discrimination; however, when only a privileged few control the space, it brings into question the true authenticity and multiculturalism of the space.

As the gay quarter partially extends into the Bo-Kaap (which literally means *Upper Cape*, since it is situated on the slopes of Signal Hill), also known as the Cape Malay Quarter, it inevitably comprises an interesting amalgamation of sociocultural communities. The Bo-Kaap is considered the spiritual home of the Cape's Malay/Muslim community as many of the residents are descendants of the slaves imported from countries like Indonesia, Java, the former Celebes and Bali by the Dutch East India Company during the 17th and 18th centuries (Cape Town Tourism, 2013). Similar to that of the South African gay community, the history of the Cape Muslims was influenced by the political processes of apartheid, as the Bo-Kaap was declared an exclusive residential area for Cape Muslims under the Group Areas Act of 1950, and people of other ethnicities and religions were not allowed to reside there (Cape Town Tourism, 2012a).

Until late in the 1960s, the areas of Bo-Kaap and De Waterkant beneath Signal Hill existed as a living link between the residents and the period of slavery when Cape Town's lower-class residents lived on the affluent colonial periphery (Grunebaum, 2011). The Bo-Kaap is now home to people of various origins and religions; however, the predominantly working-class population of the area continues to be a tight-knit Muslim community (Bokaap, 2013). As one of Cape Town's most vibrant and ethnically distinct parts, it affords tourists the opportunity to experience the unique Cape Malay culture in its historic and architecturally unique setting amid the numerous small, colourful cottages along the original cobbled streets. Table 11.3 indicates the main heritage tourism attractions in the Bo-Kaap (Cape Town Tourism, 2013).

Contrary to the largely hedonistic nature of gay tourism in De Waterkant, tourism in the Bo-Kaap is mainly centred around cultural tourism activities with a strong link to the community's Muslim heritage. While the development of Cape Town's pink tourism market has been inspirational and indicative of the country's commitment to non-discrimination towards minority groups, it is largely focused around leisure activities which have contributed to the physical transformation of the Bo-Kaap/De Waterkant area (Visser, 2003b). The possible positive and/or negative impacts of gay tourism (such as a critical analysis of the potential sociocultural impacts that gay tourism development may have on the characteristics of the

Table 11.3 Cultural tourism attractions in the Bo-Kaap

Tourism attraction	Description
Mosques	*Auwal Mosque* – South Africa's oldest mosque established by Tuan Guru in 1794 *Palm Tree Mosque* – South Africa's second-oldest mosque built in 1807 *Boorhaanol Islam Mosque* – declared a national monument in 1970
Museums	*Iziko Bo-Kaap Museum* – home to Muslims and emancipated slaves after the abolition of slavery and reflecting the existence of the community within the past sociopolitical and cultural context *Iziko Slave Lodge* – the second-oldest colonial building in the country which was built in 1679 for 500 slaves of the Dutch East India Company
Walking tours	The colourful houses, steep cobblestone streets, the muezzin's calls to prayer and children traditionally dressed for Madrassa, make this a unique cultural experience Visits to the kramats (graves of Muslim saintly predecessors) such as Tana Baru
Cape Malay Cooking Safari	An authentic culinary encounter where visitors prepare and enjoy typical Cape Malay dishes
Cape Coon Carnival	Originally introduced by the Muslim slaves to celebrate their only day off in the year, it now takes place annually on 2 January

Bo-Kaap) in South Africa have not yet been fully explored (Rogerson & Visser, 2005: 70).

The development and expansion of gay tourism have resulted in Cape Town's reputation as a leading gay city and this growth has in turn spurred the gentrification of the upmarket gay quarter and surrounding areas. When the country's Group Areas Act was repealed post-apartheid, the houses in the Bo-Kaap could be freely bought and sold in an open market (Todeschini & Japha, 2013). The prime location of the area in terms of its proximity to the central business district, the scenic views from the mountain slopes and the unique architectural environment reflecting the cultural influences of the area's early immigrant populations, made the Bo-Kaap attractive to wealthy non-Muslim and often gay buyers. For example, residents of the vibrant Cape Malay Quarter have been experiencing pressure as a result of aggressive development and accelerated gentrification (McDonald, 2008) and are often faced with pressure to sell their properties to take advantage of the high prices offered by potential buyers. Because of the new market values of the properties, the rate increases are also increasingly problematic. Some Malay Bo-Kaap residents have raised concerns that the influx of newcomers to the area, who are not Muslim, may possibly destroy the social fabric and tradition of the Cape Malay Quarter (Todeschini & Japha, 2013).

As a global city, Cape Town holds a number of gay pride celebrations similar to those in London and other cities well known for their cosmopolitan lifestyles and urban trendiness, which boost LGBT tourism to the destination. It is interesting to note the historic significance of the promotion of gay pride, which indirectly promoted all forms of societal tolerance and cultural diversity (Sarajeva, 2010). Accordingly, it is imperative to ensure that responsible gay tourism considerations are encouraged to promote the achievement of equality for all.

Often unintentionally, social and political inequalities may arise causing potential conflict over ethnic identity and territory in a destination (Hall & Brown, 2010). Cape Town's gay tourism industry therefore needs to express its commitment towards the welfare of all residents in this pluralistic area to ensure the tourism welfare of both the historic Cape Malay and trendy gay De Waterkant quarters. Respect for local cultures, lifestyles and traditions is an integral part of South Africa's responsible tourism practice. Figure 11.1 summarises some of the potential sociocultural impacts that tourism may generally have on the diverse communities living in the gay village and surrounding Muslim/Malay district of Cape Town (Spenceley et al., 2002). To privilege gay growth and prosperity at the expense of race, class or religion is to contradict the roots and reasons for oppression, invisibility and exclusion, and to allow fertile grounds for the continuation of such practices in liberated spaces such as De Waterkant (Beebe, 2012).

Potential positive socio-cultural effects of tourism on a destination's community	• Creates new opportunities for women and youth • Cultural traditions are preserved and community pride fostered • Brings about cultural exchange opportunities • Promotes the use and conservation of cultural resources • Supports preservation of indigenous languages • Encourages creative art • Creates improved economic stability and living standards
Potential negative socio-cultural effects of tourism on a destination's community	• May lead to cultural drift, loss of tradition and loss of language heritage • May increase the potential of cultural commodification • Tourists can offend local people (for example, by wearing revealing clothing or visiting private and sacred sites) • New forms of moral conduct, recreation and community organisation may lead to conflict among social groups • Increased tourism may lead to growth in prostitution, begging, alcohol and drug abuse

Figure 11.1 Potential sociocultural effects of tourism on a destination's community (Source: Adapted from Spenceley *et al.*, 2002)

Responsible Gay Tourism: Benefits and Considerations

In line with the aims of responsible tourism development of maximising economic, social and environmental benefits and ensuring that there is non-discrimination and access to tourism for all (City of Cape Town, 2009), Cape Town Tourism has established strong relations with gay travel associations and promotes gay tourism through national and international marketing initiatives. Some examples of how Cape Town has engaged with the pink tourism market include (Tebje & Ozinsky, 2004):

• The establishment of the Gay and Lesbian Association of Cape Town Tourism Industry and Commerce (GALATTIC) to formally represent pink tourism as part of the tourism industry.
• The development of the city's pink visitor's map listing Cape Town's gay-friendly tourism establishments and attractions.
• The inclusion of gay tourism as a recognised section in the official visitors' guide to the city.

- The collaboration of Cape Town Tourism with gay travel associations in order to promote pink tourism through international marketing initiatives.
- The outcomes of responsible gay tourism (Guaracino, 2007: 4) may include the following benefits for Cape Town Tourism:
- Communicating a positive message to potential tourists that form part of other minority groups as it is argued that if the destination is gay friendly, it will welcome other minority groups.
- Establishing a positive image and morale with gay employees in the tourism industry.
- Building a positive destination image; as gay travellers are often recognised as trendsetters, this can assist with the perception among other potential tourists that the destination is exciting and culturally bountiful.

For the pink tourism industry to continue to derive benefits from the city's responsible tourism efforts that protect and encourage social and cultural diversity, pink tourism developers, inclusive of the De Waterkant gay quarter, should employ cultural sensitivity through responsible tourism practices such as:

- Developing tourism products with dignity and respect, and nurturing local cultures (including religion) in the area, so that they enrich the tourism experience for all groups.
- Not compromising respect for the social, cultural and religious rights of all.
- Considering sites of slave occupation, festivals, struggle-related monuments and places, cultural monuments, food, drink, arts and crafts, music, dance and storytelling as important preservation areas (City of Cape Town, 2009).

From a responsible tourism perspective, the benefits of sociocultural responsiveness for Cape Town's gay quarter may include, among others:

- The sustainable use of the shared resources in the area – communal resources are utilised by many parties and acting in a socially responsible manner will ensure mutually acceptable use and multicultural cooperation.
- The success of De Waterkant as both a gay and a cultural heritage tourism destination – successful individual gay/cultural tourism enterprises are connected to the broader community in which they are situated and cooperation between tourism developers and the community will be beneficial to all.

- The collective and improved solving of problems within the area – for example, where community members, the local government and other role players formulate and implement united crime prevention strategies to benefit all.
- The fostering of mutual respect, as both gay and cultural tourism enterprises and tourists respect their neighbours, leading to improved communication and cooperation between community groups and tourists.
- The continued, reinforced positive image of Cape Town's gay village as trendy, inclusive and culturally diverse as a major competitor in the international LGBT market (Spenceley *et al.*, 2002).

Responsible cultural tourism in the gay quarter embraces the full range of human expressions that visitors experience through the lifestyle and heritage of all the diverse people and distinctive places that make up this tourism-rich space.

Conclusion

Post-apartheid equality and non-discrimination contributed towards the growth of Cape Town's international pink tourism market and the progressive development of the upmarket and trendy gay village, De Waterkant. The principles of equality and inclusivity that remain the driving force behind today's gay pride also relate to other minority cultural groups such as the Muslim/Malay inhabitants of the neighbouring Bo-Kaap. The development of the area by means of so-called 'pink money' from wealthy gay investors has led to a gentrified Muslim/Malay community in certain areas, as the descendants of slaves in the area have cultural wealth, but in general little economic wealth. There are various tourism attractions in the gay village area that may satisfy the contrasting needs of conservative cultural tourists versus the more liberal, hedonistic needs of gay tourists in general. The sociocultural responsiveness of tourism developers in the area remains vital to ensure that De Waterkant's image of an inclusive and tolerant gay community remains authentic and is reaffirmed in the eyes the international LGBT tourism market. From a local perspective, collaboration between the gay community of De Waterkant's gay quarter and the Bo-Kaap's Muslim/Malay quarter could lead to innovative and pioneering partnerships that may be a case in point for other destinations that strive to accomplish sustainability in similar diverse cosmopolitan tourism spaces.

Conclusions

This book examined from various perspectives the global phenomenon of ethnic, migrant and minority communities that face or choose tourism development. This approach integrates a broad variety of types of tourism, such as urban ethnic tourism, diaspora tourism, slum/favela/ township tourism, Jewish tourism, gay tourism, etc. While tackling the specificities of each of these forms of tourism, they also share many common and comparable features especially in terms of impacts. However, the analysis also shows the diversity inherent in the concept of urban ethnic tourism, where minority and migrant citizens are often perceived as belonging to homogeneous communities, but in fact can be very different from one another. There is no 'grand narrative' of urban ethnic tourism, as each district is shaped by different historical, spatial, social and cultural influences. Joshua Schmidt also demonstrates clearly in his chapter that different communities can have radically different perceptions and experiences of the same location depending on their economic, social and even religious status, not to mention the length of time lived there. Jock Collins notes that there can be as many as a hundred different organisations representing the Chinese communities in Australian cities, for example.

It can also be somewhat difficult to confine debates to the specifically 'urban', as many ethnic or immigrant groups may live on the fringes of cities in slums or shanty towns, or in outlying suburbs in 'ethnoburbs' (Li, 2009). Tacoli (1998) describes how the boundaries of urban settlements are usually more blurred than portrayed by administrative delimitations. Ethnic communities may be outside the jurisdiction of inner-city policies or located somewhere between the urban and the rural, for example, working in cities but living in rural areas where accommodation is cheaper. Products and goods may also be sourced from rural areas.

Nelson Graburn in his chapter notes how ethnic urban tourism in China can be surprising to visitors with its apparent representations of rural ethnic life and culture.

On the other hand, it is evident too that ethnic and minority citizens can have much in common, especially in terms of social attitudes and the degree of political support. Ethnic cultures may attract curiosity and hostility in equal measure. Although the former is more common in the case of tourism, many ethnic and minority communities are still treated as being marginal or undesirable by the mainstream society. Particularly, some groups are victims of discrimination, generally from their own fellow countrymen/countrywomen. For example, Zátori and Smith describe how the Hungarian population and media present the Gipsy community steadily in a bad light, labelling the Gypsy music played in restaurants as 'inauthentic' or 'kitsch', while tourists on the other hand are clearly delighted in most cases by their experiences and report very few incidences of Gypsy crime or harassment. For tourists, Gypsy music constitutes one of the representations of Hungarian identity contributing to the attraction of the country and being 'used' for the country's promotion by the public authorities.

Reisinger and Moufakkir summarise the situation as follows:

> The ethnicity which is portrayed in ethnic food and cuisine, ethnic dance, arts and culture is highly valued, appreciated and consumed; the ethnicity which relates to immigration remains a concern for public policy, politics and public opinion.

The paradox consists in the fact that on the one hand the majority culture expects and governments require integration and even assimilation of the migrant and diaspora communities, but on the other hand the same governments segregate and 'use' the communities to enhance and confirm a cosmopolitan image of the destination. Moreover, the characteristics of specific communities, such as music, gastronomy, shops with specific goods, and cultural events, are promoted in connection within a spatial entity such as a 'quarter'. Yet, as highlighted in the Community Perceptions Section of this book the ethnic or minority communities do not necessarily live in the spaces that are visited by tourists. This would be especially true of ethnoburbs as described by Li (2009). They are not technically hosts as they do not reside there and their culture may even be appropriated by other groups, especially governments and entrepreneurs. There may be Jewish quarters with few Jews (e.g. in Kracow) and gay residents do not necessarily live in the location where they socialise in gay bars and clubs. Reasons are myriad; inner-city areas may be unaffordable due to rising prices and gentrification; they may suffer from all of the quality of life issues of inner-city areas such as pollution, overcrowding, poor housing or noise; and they may even be undesirable because of the high numbers of visitors. It may also be the case that citizens of cities do not necessarily want to congregate, segregate or geographically isolate themselves. Some ethnic minorities may be forced to live close together in the cheapest areas of cities resembling slums, but it is sometimes more out of economic or financial necessity than social or cultural reasons. Often, the areas of poor housing and unsanitary conditions are not the areas that many tourists are choosing to visit with the exception of slums where the poverty is the main 'attraction'.

Poverty is undeniably an expected and even an inherent part of the tourism product especially in slums. The lens of postcolonialism still exists in many forms of tourism with white, middle-class tourists gazing on poor ethnic and migrant folk going about their impoverished daily lives. Shaw's chapter describes how ethnic quarters are the legacies of colonial relations and were established by migrants in the former colonising countries. He describes these as 'Oriental' enclaves of gateway cities, which are of interest to the majority culture, tourists from the homeland and international visitors. Relationships of inequality are perpetuated as the colonial gaze refuses to shift from a position of superiority and this includes many of the tourists, especially white, middle-class Europeans. Cloquet and Diekmann describe the situation in Matonge as a paternalistic colonial approach yielding few benefits for the communities there.

Tourists often have romanticised images of ghettos or slums based on films and novels (Diekmann & Hannam, 2012) as the home of joyful celebrations of culture, including dance or music, of heroes struggling for a decent life and freedom, but the daily lives of the residents there may be very different. Tourists may want to console themselves that residents' lives are better than they imagined which can serve to trivialise the poverty. On the other hand, Freire-Medeiros and Grijó Vilarouca show in their research that Brazilian tourists are not as perturbed by perceived poverty as the international tourists and their semantic associations are more positive. The positive experience related by many visitors is due to the fact that the tours are well organised and staged; tourists are taken to carefully selected favelas or slums which are relatively wealthier than others are and direct contact with the residents is subtly controlled by the tour organisers (Diekmann & Hannam, 2012; Dyson, 2012).

The major problem is that the poorest urban areas do not really benefit directly from the tourism activities, as with growing visitor numbers more and more private companies seek individual benefit, but do not contribute to improving the living conditions of the residents. Ironically, it is in the companies' interest to preserve the existing poor living conditions as they constitute the core business of the tours. The government in Brazil engaged in a process of aestheticisation of several slums in preparation for the mega sporting events of 2014 and 2016. But this often involved a form of facadism rather than addressing economic or social issues, and it also means that tourists are provided with an even more sanitised (and thus misleading) glimpse of slum living. Jock Collins' research shows that visitors were not happy with the dirtiness and smelliness of some urban Chinatowns, thus calling for greater sanitisation. Nimit Chowdary and Anya Diekmann discuss how the Indian government and some members of higher society would often prefer not to promote the slums as they give the country a bad reputation. In Budapest, Zátori and Smith show how tourists are taken on a visit to a Gypsy family of musicians, who are believed to have a higher social status and are more integrated into mainstream Hungarian society than other Gypsy groups.

Tourism offers selective snapshots such as short tours or cultural performances, and this explains why festivals and events are so popular, as they are ephemeral highlights in a calendar which is otherwise characterised by a high level of poverty and monotony. The 'frontstage' may represent the cultural performance, the 'backstage' rather the everyday drudgery. The latter is more authentic but less interesting for visitors. As a result, communities may choose to enhance or exaggerate what they have to attract tourism. Graburn's chapter shows how Chinese communities seem to engage quite actively in what Macleod (2013) calls 'cultural configuration' or the manipulation of culture for the purposes of tourism. Although this approach does not correspond to Western especially European notions of heritage and authenticity, it is also important not to fossilise cultures and see them as something dead or immutable. Jock Collins suggests that a form of inauthentic 'theming' is not at all uncommon in ethnic quarters such as Chinatowns, either. He also notes that most Chinese tourists are not that interested in visiting Chinese quarters or sites compared to foreign visitors who often want to learn something and understand Chinese culture better. In such cases, it may be important to present a version of Chinese culture that has retained at least some semblance of its original form.

However, it is already a good question as to how far one can speak of 'authenticity' of culture among second- or third-generation diasporic or displaced communities in global cities of liquid mobility and hybridised identities. Cultural traditions can change rapidly in a cosmopolitan global city. Fusion and hybridisation are part of the globalised/glocalised diasporic experience; however, most festivals and other presentations of culture are completely decontextualised or transformed. They are authentic to the diasporic community in as far as they can be in a new and different context, but they may be quite far removed from the traditions of the homeland practised several generations back in time. Festivals and events often become the focal point of ethnic or minority tourism because the communities are displaced or diasporic and have often left their material culture back in the homeland. In some cases, community traditions may be based more on intangible culture anyway (e.g. Gypsy culture), the material culture may have been partly destroyed (e.g. Jewish culture) or it may be non-existent. For example, one cannot really speak of 'gay culture' as such. Much of lesbian, gay, bisexual, transgender (LGBT) tourism is based on the visitation of safe spaces like bars, restaurants and clubs where freedom of expression is permitted or welcomed.

Some of this culture may also be appropriated by the majority communities, often sanitising it to make it feel 'safer' or more attractive for middle-class consumption (especially in the case of ghetto or slum culture). Shaw observes that ethnic minority entrepreneurs often adapt their products to the tastes of mainstream markets and international markets. This is especially true of food, where new dishes are created (e.g. the Balti pie in the UK) or dishes are rendered less spicy or edible to other cultural groups (e.g. halal or kosher Chinese). Ironically perhaps, many tourists now find it increasingly difficult to experience the 'host' culture in world cities like London, e.g. it is easier to find an Indian restaurant than an English one! Many ethnic areas of cities have become gentrified, even chic, and one growing trend in cities is for tourists to try to mingle with every-day citizens and engage in 'authentic' local experiences. This can include encroaching on safe spaces which have been created by the minority group (e.g. LGBT spaces). Ethnic or gay quarters of a city should ideally be a sanctuary for the communities who have chosen to live there, but the presence of visitors can have the opposite effect. For example, gay residents may feel that the whole city is full of heteronormative spaces which can be used by heterosexuals, yet they choose to 'invade' the gay space instead, creating a feeling of voyeurism or a human zoo. However, it may be more difficult to encroach on the living quarters of extreme poverty like slums or townships as the gap between tourist and resident is too wide and the tourists' safety may even be compromised. Tourist experiences there tend to be heavily mediated although there is arguably more freedom in large cities to pursue one's own agenda than in a remote Chinese village, a Brazilian favela or a South African township. Going beyond the tourist script is more common in cosmopolitan cities but the safety issue is still a major consideration, and tourists may be warned against wandering into districts which are locally perceived to be unsafe or hostile to outsiders. This is not, of course, true of most of the more commercialised ethnic quarters such as Chinatowns, Little Italies, Banglatowns or Jewish quarters. The worst that may happen is that tourists are disappointed by the inauthenticity of the experience, the lack of opportunity to meet 'locals' (who do not usually live there anyway!) or the poor quality of the 'local' food which has often been adapted for the tourists' palate.

In terms of urban policy and planning, a voice has increasingly been given to local communities, but some forces of economic development are stronger than the community voice and can lead to gentrification, displacement, marginalisation and worse. The poorest groups in society are unsurprisingly the least empowered and a class or caste system will further exacerbate the situation for ethnic and other minorities. Despite changes in the regime in post-apartheid South Africa, for example, the legacy of the system will take decades to overcome. In India, the status of and opportunities for lower-caste members of society will increase more slowly than the official policies would imply. Even societies which have hitherto been relatively tolerant (e.g. much of Western Europe in 2014) frequently adopt a 'scapegoating' stance of racism, anti-immigration and anti-Semitism in response to a lack of economic and social opportunities.

Interestingly, castigating minorities seems to be an easier focus of hatred and violence than the politicians who are usually to blame and who are actually in a position to take action! The role of governments and urban policies are paramount in shaping the development of ethnic quarters, as discussed in the Development Policies section of this book. Shaw notes the importance of not only the location and sociocultural composition of communities, but also land use, design, regulation and transport planning. Gentrification and rising prices may displace or alienate the local ethnic consumers, especially if the products and services are adapted significantly to external tastes. However, Jock Collins points out that too much planning, regulation and intervention on the part of governments and other agencies may serve to undermine the original character or authenticity of an ethnic quarter. Striking a balance is imperative but it is also challenging.

For example, there are socio-economic disparities within slums. They are not homogeneous entities, which can make policy and planning decisions complex. Political interventions can maybe improve slum conditions but it is important not to over-romanticise. They are still a major challenge to urban policy and planning, and tourism development can only have minimal impacts. The development depends on each destination. In some cases, the authorities support the development of tourism products, allowing them to control the message that is given to the visitors. In other places, the authorities are opposed to the organisation of slum tours, for instance in India. While in all current destinations, the initiatives of organising slum tours were started by either non-governmental organisations (NGOs) or charities with the aim of sharing the living conditions of the poor in order to find support to improve living conditions, nowadays a myriad of private agencies promote and organise tours. The same differences are valid for ethnic quarters, some of which have been initiators of tourism development (e.g. Harlem) while for others (e.g. Matonge) tourism development has been decided without the involvement of the destination community.

Ethnic and religious tensions between mainstream societies and minorities and also between minority groups have always existed, but in cosmopolitan cities of high mobility the need to coexist in relative harmony has never been stronger. Cultures have also benefited from hybridisation and fusion; it is not just a question of disempowerment and dilution. New cultural forms are often created which better represent the place of ethnic cultures in the mainstream society and are much more appropriate for the hybridised identities of second and third generations of immigrants, for example. Promoting social harmony is a much more important policy than promoting tourism. There might not be equal promotion of all ethnic or minority cultures in a city (e.g. in Singapore) but this does not mean that social tensions will be an automatic consequence. On the contrary, it may be through tourism that greater social harmony is created. For example, tourists may be much more sympathetic to the plight of poor local communities (e.g. slum dwellers, Gypsies) than national residents who have been indoctrinated with stereotypes and prejudice by politicians, family or peers. In the case of slums and townships, it is hard to measure the benefits of tourism as pure economic indicators do not take into consideration more intangible dimensions such as a sense of pride, education through cross-cultural exchange, renewed interest in traditions which may otherwise have died, etc.

Throughout the book, both the positive and negative aspects of tourism in ethnic, migrant and slum quarters are analysed. The positive view is that ethnic quarters showcase the contribution of ethnic communities to the cultural and economic life of cities, and can nurture creative fusions between different cultures in arts or food, for example. They can be catalysts for cultural exchange and mutual understandings. Shaw suggests that there has been a revalorisation of exotic streetscapes in recent years. This may seem to represent what he describes as 'a benign synergy between emerging visitor economies and a wider appreciation of ethnic heritage'. However, the negative side is that this can become a mask that disguises the fundamental inequalities, poverty, prejudice and social tensions that still exist. At the very least, many ethnic quarters offer what Shaw describes as 'formulaic sameness in their presentation of diversity'.

The management of quarters of extreme poverty such as slums and townships seems to be more challenging. The economic and social gaps between the residents and the tourists are generally significantly higher than in other forms of tourism, even if the slums visited are the relatively 'wealthy' (less poverty stricken) ones. This means that the degree of interaction is minimal and the experience is usually heavily mediated. Poverty alleviation can be a motivation for governments when developing ethnic and minority tourism, but as stated by Graburn in the context of ethnic tourism in China, 'Not all government efforts to develop tourism are motivated solely by poverty alleviation. International prestige and the attraction of international tourists are also motives'. There are few attempts to improve the fundamental economic and social problems contained therein. Cloquet and Diekmann show how the development and promotion of Matonge has been largely appropriated by the tourism authorities without much consultation with or involvement of the communities who are the focus of the tourist gaze. Visits are mediated by guided tours which are seen to be fairly intrusive and voyeuristic. There has been little improvement in terms of urban degradation and little integration of the residents in the tourism strategy. The residents are weary and even hostile because of the impersonal relationships with visitors, the lack of consumption in shops and the disrespect of culinary traditions in restaurants. Sometimes the government in China even pays communities not to modernise their houses so that they remain picturesque! On the other hand, few of the profits from tourism or TV dramas filmed there are returned to the communities. Even where tourism projects have failed because it is too difficult to get there, the development has changed the communities' mentality and attitude forever, with even small children becoming commercially minded. In the case of Gypsy tourism in Budapest, the tour company organising the tours is more socially responsible and ethical than any of the tourism authorities or government agencies who refused to support such initiatives.

In terms of existing and future research in the field of ethnic and minority tourism, it seems that the tourist perspective has been relatively under-researched, but so too has the host perspective which is even more complex to research without robust ethnographic or anthropological longitudinal studies. Even then, the research would tend to be on a case-by-case basis. Like in indigenous or tribal tourism research, it has been concluded after numerous studies that it is not possible to generalise about ethnic tourism and that research and development should only be considered community by community. For example, in Rio de Janeiro there are around 750 favelas and more than 20% of the population lives in them. Freire-Medeiros and Grijó Vilarouca therefore end their chapter by urging researchers and policymakers to consider the diversity not only within and across the favelas, but also their continuity with the rest of the city.

The different perspectives and approaches in this book (development policies, hosts, visitors and sociocultural developments) are all connected and each of them plays a crucial role in 'successful' and balanced tourism development. Some sociocultural developments are necessary to empower the community to become hosts who manage and control their destination and are not subject to commodification from outsiders. At the same time, the satisfactory experience of the visitor is also central to the sustainability of the tourism project. Policies developed in coordination with the community contribute to regulating the tourism encounter. However, balancing these different aspects is a real challenge for all stakeholders involved. Maoz's (2006) work on the mutual gaze suggests that the relationship between hosts and guests is not merely asymmetrical in terms of power and that hosts do not necessarily always adapt to the colonising gaze. Instead, they can exercise some choice and control and even gain power and agency if the conditions are right. Several scholars have discussed how tourism planning and/or interpretation practices could disrupt problematic relations of power between hosts and guests, hence tend towards a tourist valorisation and experience which would reinforce a feeling of togetherness instead of otherness (Amoamo & Thompson, 2010; Shaw, 2013 and this volume; Van der Duim *et al.*, 2005). Adopting a postcolonial approach, those authors view Bhabha's (1994) seminal work *The Location of Culture* as providing a potential way forward.

Indeed, Bhabha's key concepts of 'third space' and 'hybridity' suggest that it is possible to provide space for meaningful re-presentations of cultures. Overcoming Said's Manichean opposition of a 'static/essential "West" and an equally static/essential Other' (Hollinshead, 2004: 34), Bhabha identifies a 'third space', where transnational and transitional encounters take place and where minority groups can engage in processes of negotiation over differential meaning and value in hegemonic contexts (Hollinshead, 2004: 34). Amoamo and Thompson explain that:

> For Bhabha, the 'third space' renders ambivalent established structures of meaning and accepted points of cultural reference, disrupting the dominant sense of history, identity and culture. (...) Identities can no longer be stable and Self/Other relationships are a matter of power and discourse, rather than cultural 'essence'. Culture becomes newly syncre-tised as part of an inevitable ongoing process of global inter-connected-ness. (Amoamo & Thompson, 2010: 38)

As stated in the Development Policies section of this book, the move towards cultural planning for Thirdspace as identified by Lefèbvre (1974) and Soja (1996) can integrate these theoretical principles. In the third space, communication transposes the binaries them/us into you/me, enabling a hybridisation of the self (Amoamo & Thompson, 2010; Van der Duim et al., 2005). Examining the process by which tourism can participate in cosmo-politan formations, Salazar (2010) notes:

> It is not the mere act of travelling or the geographical places visited that help people figure out whom they are and the Other is. Rather, it is what happens psychologically within the traveller and tourism worker and interactionally between them that deconstructs or reifies the neat binaries modernity presents us with. (Salazar, 2006, as cited in Salazar, 2010: 178)

Although this alternative conceptualisation of interplays between hosts and guests seems idealised as it relies on a considerable shift in power and in thinking between 'Western' and 'ethnic' tourism stakehold-ers, the case of Green Street in Newham, London (see Shaw, this volume), a space fostering intercultural fusion, shows that it is not impossible. To create such 'third spaces' in a tourism-related context, Van der Duim et al. (2005) argue that the hosts need to be involved in decision-making and benefit from economic returns. Moreover, host–guest interactions need to be examined as part of a tripartite system, including hosts, guests and brokers: 'success or failure (...), especially in terms of sustainability, lies more substantially in the power of brokers and locals than in the power of tourist' (Van der Duim et al., 2005).

This book has attempted to raise and examine a broad range of issues related to ethnic and minority cultures as tourist attractions by looking into the sociocultural context, host and visitors' approaches as well as policies. While the interdisciplinary approach of this book hopes to contribute to existing research, we are aware that it is not possible to cover all issues at stake. Further research should focus on the role of events for ethnic and minority cultures and how they can contribute to bridging the gap between cultures. Moreover, it would be interesting to look into features such as architecture and the role of heritage in migrant quarters. Indeed, heritage of migrant quarters is revived in many places by second- and third-generation migrants with the aim of preserving their roots in the host country. Furthermore, the role of the 'promoted' ambiance in contrast to often decayed housing, in short the architectural contrasts, would deserve more in-depth research. More research would also be needed on entrepreneurship in ethnic and minority communities in the context of tourism. Indeed, in many destinations, be it ethnic urban quarters or slum districts, community entrepreneurs develop tourism activities. The impact and context of these have not yet been broadly studied; however, an enhanced understanding might help young entrepreneurs and policymakers. The concept of otherness has been analysed by many researchers, yet interdisciplinary research with psychologists, anthropologists and sociologists could help deepen the analysis and contribute to a better understanding of the stakes of ethnic and minority cultures within the dominant host country culture. The paradox between segregation (for tourism purposes) and integration (for political purposes) constitutes a real challenge to policymakers and needs broader attention by academics.

Indeed, ethnic and minority community-based tourism is fraught with contradictions and paradoxes. This includes the desire on the part of communities to retain some sense of culture and identity while being under pressure to integrate into mainstream society. The latter is very much desired by various authorities who may then lament the fact that diversity and unique cultural selling propositions are lost. Ethnic minority communities are often praised and promoted for their work in 'the arts' but are not supported equally in other spheres (i.e. political, economic and social). As a result, they may not even self-identify, which makes promotion of their culture challenging and even impossible. It has often been assumed that the tourist gaze is one way and essentially oppressive, but Maoz's (1996) work and some of the case studies in this book suggest that the quality and even safety of the tourist experience is very much dependent on a positive host gaze. Tourists may be searching for 'authentic' traditions while ethnic communities are busy creating hybridised and transformative lifestyles as part of the glocalisation process (Giulianotti & Robertson, 2007). It is not altogether clear anymore who is the 'self' and who is the 'other' especially in multicultural cities where the population can be up to 50% 'ethnic'. It cannot be assumed that second- and third-generation immigrants have the same living standards as their first-generation relatives, especially those who are resident in 'ethnoburbs' (Li, 2009). As Thirdspace thinking and planning imply, the rigid binaries that have traditionally existed not only in tourism literature but also in practice such as host/guest, self/other, rich/poor, us/them are breaking down and it is necessary to engage in a more equal and collaborative relationship of residents, tourists, governments and brokers or intermediaries from the tourism industry. All of this means working towards a feeling of togetherness rather than otherness, and integration rather than segregation.

References

AALDE (2013) Chinatown Then and Now: Gentrification in Boston, New York, and Philadelphia. Asian American Legal Defense and Education Fund, New York.

Aitchison, C., MacLeod, N.E. and Shaw, S.J. (2000) *Leisure and Tourism Landscapes: Social and Cultural Geographies*. London: Routledge.

Alonso, S. and da Fonseca, S. (2011) Immigration, left and right. *Party Politics* 18 (6), 865–884.

Amoamo, M. and Thompson, A. (2010) (re)Imaging Māori tourism: Representation and cultural hybridity in postcolonial New Zealand. *Tourist Studies* 10 (1), 35–55.

Anderson, K.J. (1990) Chinatown re-oriented: A critical analysis of recent redevelopment schemes in a Melbourne and Sydney enclave. *Australian Geographical Studies* 28, 131–154.

Anderson, K.J. (1991) *Vancouver's Chinatown: Racial Discourse in Canada, 1875–1980*. Montreal: McGill-Queens University Press.

Andersson, L. and Thomsen, B.S. (2008) Performative experiments and cultural replanning – Recapturing the spectacle of the city. *Nordic Journal of Architectural Research* 20, 39–51.

Ap, J. and Wong, K.K.F. (2001) Case study on tour guiding: Professionalism, issues and problems. *Environmental Management* 22, 551–563.

Appadurai, A. (1997) *Modernity at Large: Cultural Dimensions of Globalisation*. Minneapolis, MN: University of Minnesota Press.

Appadurai, A. (2000) Disjuncture and difference in the global cultural economy. In J. Benyon and D. Dunkerley (eds) *Globalisation: The Reader* (pp. 93–100). London: Athlone.

Appadurai, A. (ed.) (2001) *Globalization*. Durham and London: Duke University Press.

Appadurai, A. (2003) Sovereignty without territoriality: Notes for a postnational geography. In S. Low and D. Lawrence-Zuniga (eds) *The Anthropology of Space and Place: Locating Culture* (pp. 337–350). Oxford: Blackwell.

Arora, R. (2005) *Race and Ethnicity in Education*. Aldershot: Ashgate.

Ashworth, G.J. (1995) Heritage, tourism and Europe. In D.T. Herbert (ed.) *Heritage, Tourism and Society* (pp. 68–84). London: Mansell Publishing Ltd.

Ashworth, G. and Page, S. (2011) Urban tourism research: Recent progress and current paradoxes. *Tourism Management* 32, 1–15.

Athe Sam (2013) See http://www.athesam.hu (accessed 14 January 2013).

Australian Bureau of Statistics (2013) Perspectives on migrants. Department of Immigration and Citizenship. Canberra.

Aytar, V. and Rath, J. (eds) (2012) *Selling Ethnic Neighborhoods: The Rise of Neighborhoods as Places of Leisure and Consumption*. New York: Routledge.

Babits, M. (1939) A magyar jellemről. In G. Szekfű (ed.) *Mi a magyar?* (pp. 37–86). Budapest: Magyar Szemle Társaság.

Backer, E. (2008) VFR Travellers – Visiting the Destination or Visiting the Hosts? In Asian Journal of Tourism and Hospitality Research 2:1, 60–70.

Ballegaard, N. and Chor, J. (2009) Gay and lesbian tourism: Travel motivations, destination choices and holiday experiences of gays and lesbians. See http://studenttheses.cbs.dk/xmlui/bitstream/handle/10417/811/nina_ballegaard_og_jane_chor.pdf?sequence=1 (accessed 3 December 2013).

Barford, R. (2012) Top gay travel destinations: Cape Town recognised in Out Now survey, blog. See http://www.capetown.travel/blog/entry/

top-gay-travel-destinations-cape-town-recognised-in-out-now-survey (accessed 22 September 2012).

Bauman, Z. (2011) *Culture in a Liquid Modern World*. Cambridge: Polity Press.

BBC News Europe (2013) Jobbik rally against World Jewish Congress in Budapest. 4 May. See http://www.bbc.co.uk/news/world-europe-22413301 (accessed 10 October 2013).

BBC World News (2014) The changing face of New York's Chinatown. 4 February. See http://www.bbc.com/news/magazine-25988146 (accessed 15 February 2014).

Beebe, M. (2012) Whose Gay Town is Cape Town? An Examination of Cape Town's Gay Village and the Production of a Queer White Patriarchy. Independent Study Project (ISP) Collection. Paper 1280.

Beck, U. (2002) The cosmopolitan society and its enemies. *Theory, Culture and Society* 19 (1–2), 17–44.

Beeton, S. (2006) *Community Development through Tourism*. Melbourne: Landlinks Press.

Bell, D. and Jayne, M. (2004) *City of Quarters: Urban Villages in the Contemporary City*. Aldershot: Ashgate.

Ben-Porat, G. (2008) Political economy: Liberalization and globalization. In G. Ben-Porat, Y. Levi, S. Mizrahi, A. Naor and E. Tzfadia (eds) *Israel Since 1980* (pp. 91–116). Cambridge: Cambridge University Press.

Ben-Zadok, E. (1993) Oriental Jews in the development towns: Ethnicity, economic development, budget, and politics. In E. Ben-Zadok (ed.) *Local Communities and the Israeli Polity: Conflict of Values and Interests* (pp. 91–122). Albany, NY: State University of New York Press.

Berger, A. (2008) *The Golden Triangle: A Ethnic-Semiotic Tour of Present-Day India*. New Brunswick: Transaction Publishers.

Bernardo, F. and Palma, J.M. (2005) Place change and identity processes. *Medio Ambiente y Comportamiento Humano* 6 (1), 71–87.

Bernáth, G. and Messing, V. (2002) The neglected public: On the media consumption of the Hungarian Roma. In E. Kállai (ed.) *The Gypsies/The Roma in Hungarian Society* (pp. 107–125). Budapest: Teleki László Foundation.

Bhabha, H.K. (1994) *The Location of Culture*. London: Routledge.

Bianchini, F. and Ghilardi, L. (1997) *Culture and Neighbourhoods: A Comparative Report*. Strasbourg: Council of Europe.

Binnie, J., Holloway, J., Millington, S. and Young, C. (eds) (2006) *Cosmopolitan Urbanism*. London and New York: Routledge.

Blake, A., Arbache, J.S., Sinclair, M.T. and Teles, V. (2008) Tourism and poverty relief. *Annals of Tourism Research* 35 (1), 107–126.

Blass, M. (2009) Last Moroccan leaves the Netherlands. Radio Netherlands Worldwide. See http://www.rnw.nl/english/article/%E2%80%9Clast-moroccan-leaves-netherlands%E2%80%9D (accessed 10 January 2014).

Blau, P. (1977) *Inequality and Heterogeneity: A Primitive Theory of Social Structure*. New York: Free Press.

Blichfeldt, B.S., Chor, J. and Milan, N.B. (2013) Zoos, sanctuaries and turfs: Enactments and uses of gay spaces during the holidays. *International Journal of Tourism Research* 15, 473–483.

Bloomfield, J. and Bianchini, F. (2004) *Planning for the Intercultural City*. Stroud: Comedia.

Bock, P. (1970) *Culture Shock*. New York: Alfred Knopf.

Bokaap (2013) People. See http://bokaap.co.za/people (accessed 6 October 2014).

Boltanski, L. and Thévenot, L. (2006) *On Justification: The Economies of Worth*. Princeton, NJ: Princeton University Press.

Booms, B. and Ward, J. (1969) The cons of Black capitalism: Will this policy cure urban ills? *Business Horizons* October, 17–26.

Booyens, I. (2010) Rethinking township tourism: Towards responsible tourism development in South African townships. *Development Southern Africa* 27 (2), 273–287.

Boyd, N.A. (2011) San Francisco's Castro district: From gay liberation to tourist destination. *Journal of Tourism and Cultural Change* 9 (3), 237–248.

Braham, R.L. (1994) *The Politics of Genocide: The Holocaust in Hungary*. New York: Columbia University Press.

Branscombe, N. and Wann, D. (1994) Collective self esteem consequences of out-group derogation when a valued social identity is on trial. *European Journal of Social Psychology* 24, 641–657.

Brin, E. and Noy, C. (2010) The said and the unsaid: Performative guiding in a Jerusalem neighbourhood. *Tourist Studies* 10 (1), 19–33.

Brown, L. (2013) Travel for education: A force for peace and cross-cultural understanding. In Y. Reisinger (ed.) *Transformational Tourism: Tourist Perspectives* (pp. 199–211). Wallingford: CABI.

Bryman, A. (2004) *The Disneyization of Society*. London: Sage.

Budapest Beyond (2012) About Budapest Beyond Sightseeing. See http://beyondbudapest. hu/english/about_bp.html (accessed 13 January 2013).

Burgold, J., Frenzel, F. and Rolfes, M. (2013) Editorial: Observations on slums and their touristification. *Die Erde* 144 (2), 99–104.

Burr, A. (2006) The "freedom of the slaves to walk the streets": Celebration, spontaneity and revelry versus logistics at the Notting Hill carnival. In D. Picard and M. Robinson (eds) *Festivals, Tourism and Social Change: Remaking Worlds* (pp. 84–98). Clevedon: Channel View Publications.

Butler, R. and Hinch, T. (eds) (1996) *Tourism and Indigenous Peoples*. London: International Thomson Business Press.

Butler, R. and Hinch, T. (eds) (2007) *Tourism and Indigenous Peoples: Issues and Implications*. Oxford: Butterworth-Heinemann.

Butler, S.R. (2012) Curatorial interventions in township tours: Two trajectories. In F. Frenzel, K. Koens and M. Steinbrink (eds) *Slum Tourism. Poverty, Power and Ethics* (pp. 215–231). New York: Routledge.

Cabot, V. (2009) Jews everywhere – and nowhere: Remembrance, remorse stimulate Polish Jewish revival. *Jewish News of Greater Phoenix*. See http://www.jewishaz.com/jewishnews/980417/ (accessed 6 February 2009).

Cape Town Tourism (2012a) The Islamic Cape Town map. See http://www.capetown. travel/uploads/files/islamic-map1.pdf (accessed 3 December 2013).

Cape Town Tourism (2012b) The pink map: 2012 gay guide – Cape Town & surrounds. See http://www.capetown.travel/uploads/files/map-pink.pdf (accessed 3 December 2013).

Cape Town Tourism (2013) Bo-Kaap and De Waterkant. See http://www.capetown. travel/attractions/entry/Bo-Kaap_and_De-Waterkant (accessed 3 December 2013).

Carey, S. (2002) Brick Lane, Banglatown: A Study of the Catering Sector, final report. Research Works Limited. Hendon, London. Prepared for Ethnic Minority Enterprise Project and Cityside Regeneration.

Carlson, M. (1996) *Performance: A Critical Introduction*. London: Routledge.

Castles, S. and Miller, M. (2013) *The Age of Migration* (4th edn). London: Macmillan.

Catherine, L. (2006) *Wandelen naar Kongo. Langs Koloniaal erfgoed in Brussel en Belgïe*. Berchem: EPO.

Cave, J., Ryan, C. and Panakera, C. (2007) Cultural tourism product: Pacific Island migrant perspectives in New Zealand. *Journal of Travel Research* 45, 435–443.

Cave, J., Joliffe, L. and Baum, T. (eds) (2013) *Tourism and Souvenirs: Global Perspectives from the Margins*. Bristol: Channel View Publications.

Cejas, M.I. (2006) Tourism in shantytowns and slums: A new "contact zone" in the era of globalization. *Intercultural Communication Studies* 15 (2), 224–230.

Central Bureau of Statistics (2012) Geographical Information System. See http://www1. cbs.gov.il/reader/?MIval=cw_usr_view_SHTML&ID=567 (accessed 10 May 2013).

Cesarani, D. (ed.) (1997) *Genocide and Rescue: The Holocaust in Hungary 1944*. Oxford: Berg.

Chan, Y.W. (2006) Coming of age of the Chinese tourists: The emergence of non-Western tourism and host–guest interactions in Vietnam's border tourism. *Tourist Studies* 6 (3), 187–213.

Chang, T.C. (1999) Local uniqueness in the global village: Heritage tourism in Singapore. *Professional Geographer* 51 (1), 91–103.

Chang, T.C. (2000) Singapore's Little India: A tourist attraction as a contested landscape. *Urban Studies* 37 (2), 343–366.

Chinese Garden of Friendship (2006) Chinese Garden summary Factsheet 2006: Customer Awareness and satisfaction, unpublished.

Chio, J. (2009) The internal expansion of China: Tourism and the production of distance. In T. Winter, P. Teo and T.C. Chang (eds) *Asia on Tour: Exploring the Rise of Asian Tourism* (pp. 207–220). London: Routledge.

Chio, J. (2011) Leave the fields without leaving the countryside: Mobility and modernity in rural ethnic China. *Identities: Global Studies in Culture and Power* 18 (6), 551–575.

Chio, J. (2013) Nong Jia Le Peasant Family Happiness. Documentary. Berkeley Media LLC, Berkeley, CA.

Chio, J. (2014) *A Landscape of Travel: The Work of Tourism in Rural Ethnic China*. Seattle, WA: University of Washington Press.

Choli Daróczi, J. (1939) They took away the Gypsies. In G. Gömöri and M. Gömöri (eds) *I Lived on this Earth: Hungarian Poets on the Holocaust* (p. 63). London: Alba Press.

City of Cape Town (2009) Responsible Tourism Policy for the City of Cape Town. See http://www.capetown.gov.za/en/tourism/Documents/Responsible%20Tourism/ Cape%20Town%20Responsible%20Tourism%20Policy%20and%20Action%20Plan. pdf (accessed 3 December 2013).

Cityside (2002) Cityside SRB3 Final Report 2002. London: Cityside Regeneration Limited.

Clark, G. (1996) Beyond the great divide: Hollywood and race relations in the 1950s. *Howard Journal of Communications* 7, 373–382.

Clemenson, H.A. and Pitblado, J.R. (2007) Recent trends in rural urban migration. *Our Diverse Cities* No. 3 (Summer), 25–29.

Cock, J. (2003) Engendering gay and lesbian rights: The equality clause in the South African Constitution. *Women's Studies International Forum* 26 (1), 35–45.

Cocks, S. (2001) *Doing the Town: The Rise of Urban Tourism in the United States*. Berkley, CA: University of California Press.

Cohen, E. (1972) Towards a sociology of international tourism. *Social Research* 39 (1), 164–182.

Cohen, E. (1985) The tourist guide: The origin, structure and dynamics of a role. *Annals of Tourism Research* 12, 5–29.

Cohen, E. (1988) Authenticity and commoditization in tourism. *Annals of Tourism Research* 15 (3), 371–386.

Cole, T. (2011) *Traces of the Holocaust: Journeying In and Out of the Ghettoes*. London: Continuum.

Coles, T. and Timothy, D.J. (2004) *Tourism, Diasporas and Space*. London: Routledge.

Collins, J. (2006) Ethnic precincts as contradictory tourist spaces. In J. Rath (ed.) *Tourism, Ethnic Diversity and the City* (pp. 52–67). London and New York: Routledge.

Collins, J. (2013) Rethinking Australian immigration and immigrant settlement policy. *Journal of Intercultural Studies* 34 (2), 160–177.

Collins, J. and Castillo, A. (1998) *Cosmopolitan Sydney: Exploring the World in One City.* Sydney: Pluto Press.

Collins, J., Mondello, L., Breheney, J. and Childs, T. (2001) *Cosmopolitan Melbourne: Exploring the World in One City.* Melbourne: Big Box Publishing.

Collins, J. and Kunz, P. (2007) Ethnic entrepreneurs, ethnic precincts and tourism: The case of Sydney Australia. In G. Richards and J. Wilson (eds) *Tourism, Creativity and Development.* (pp. 201–214). London: Routledge.

Collins, J., Darcy, S., Jordan, K., Skilbeck, R., Grabowski, S., Peel, V., Dunstan, D., Lacey, G. and Firth, T. (2007) Cultural landscapes of tourism in New South Wales and Victoria. Sustainable Tourism CRC Technical Report, Brisbane.

Collins, J. and Jordan, K. (2009) Ethnic urban tourism in Australia. *Tourism Culture and Communication* 9 (1/2), 79–92.

Collins, J., Darcy, S. and Jordan, K. (2010) Multi-method research on ethnic cultural tourism in Australia. In G. Richards and W. Munsters (eds) *Cultural Tourism Research Methods* (pp. 87–103). Wallingford: CABI.

Conforti, J.M. (1996) Ghettos as tourism attractions. *Annals of Tourism Research* 23 (4), 830–842.

Conway, K. (2008) *Ecotourism, Poverty, and Conservation in Prek Toal, Cambodia.* Master thesis, Oregon State University. See http://ir.library.oregonstate.edu/xmlui/handle/1957/9530

Corijn, E. (2004) Matonge, centre multiculturel à Bruxelles. *Politique* 35, 32–33.

Cornet, A. (2004) Les Congolais en Belgique aux XIXe et XXe siècles. In A. Morelli (ed.) *Histoire des étrangers et de l'immigration en Belgique, de la préhistoire à nos jours* (pp. 375–400). Brussels: Couleur Livres.

Corrigan, G. (2001) *Miao Textiles of Guizhou.* London: British Museum.

Council of Europe (2014) European Commission against Racism and Intolerance (ECRI). See http://www.coe.int/t/dghl/monitoring/ecri/default_en.asp (accessed 26 February 2014).

Craven, P. and Wellman, B. (1973) The network city. *Sociological Enquiry* 43 (1), 57–88.

Crawford, D., Jackson, E. and Godbey, G. (1991) A hierarchical model of leisure constraints. *Leisure Sciences* 13, 309–320.

Creative City (2006) *Cultural Planning Toolkit.* See http://www.creativecity.ca/database/files/library/cultural_planning_toolkit.pdf (accessed 20 January 2007).

Crockett, D. and Wallendorf, M. (2004) The role of normative political ideology in consumer behavior. *Journal of Consumer Research* 31 (December), 511–528.

Croucher, S. (2011) South Africa: Opportunities seized in the post-apartheid era. In M. Tremblay, D. Paternotte and C. Johnson (eds) *The Lesbian and Gay Movement and the State: Comparative Insights into a Transformed Relationship* (pp. 153–167). Burlington, VT: Ashgate.

Cushner, K. and Karim, A. (2004) Study abroad at university level. In D. Landis, J. Bennett and M. Bennett (eds) *Intercultural Training.* London: Sage.

Dahles, H. (2002) The politics of tour guiding: Image management in Indonesia. *Annals of Tourism Research* 29 (3), 783–800.

Dann, G. (1996) Images of destination people in travelogues. In R. Butler and T. Hinch (eds) *Tourism and Indigenous Peoples* (pp. 349–375). London: International Thomson Business Press.

Davis, M. (2007) *Planet of Slums.* London: Verso.

Davies, L. (2012) Hungarian rightwinger denounced after calling for survey of Jews. 27 November. See http://www.guardian.co.uk/world/2012/nov/27/hungarian-rightwinger-call-survey-jews (accessed 13 January 2013).

Dawut, R. (2007) Shrine pilgrimage and sustainable tourism among the Uyghurs; Central Asian ritual tradition in the context of China's development policies. In

I. Beller-Hann, M. Cristina Cesaro, R. Harris and J. Smith Finley (eds) *Situating the Uyghurs Between China and Central Asia* (pp. 149–164). Aldershot: Ashgate.

De Certeau, M. (2002) *The Practice of Everyday Life*. California, CA: University of California Press.

De Clercq, D. (2001) Everyday urban space in Matonge/Alledagse stedelijke ruimte in Matonge. *OASE* 63–84.

Demart, S. (2007) De la distinction au stigmate. Matonge, quartier congolais à Bruxelles. *Les Cahiers de la Fonderie* 58–62.

DIAC (Department of Immigration and Citizenship) (2013) *Australian Migration Trends 2011–12*. See http://www.immi.gov.au/media/publications/statistics/australia-migration-trends-2011-12/ (accessed 6 June 2013).

Diekmann, A. (2013) Ethnic tourism. In G. Richards and M.K. Smith (eds) *Routledge Handbook of Cultural Tourism* (pp. 346–354). London: Routledge.

Diekmann, A. and Maulet, G. (2009) A contested ethnic tourism asset: The case of Matonge in Brussels. *Tourism, Culture and Communication* 9 (1), 93–106.

Diekmann, A. and Hannam, K. (2012) Touristic mobilities in India's slum spaces. *Annals of Tourism Research* 39 (3), 1315–1336.

Donaldson, J.A. (2007) Tourism, development and poverty reduction in Guizhou and Yunnan. *The China Quarterly* 190, 333–351.

Donham, D.L. (2013) Freeing South Africa: The 'modernization' of male-male sexuality in Soweto. In J. Lin and C. Mele (eds) *The Urban Sociology Reader* (pp. 278–288). Abingdon: Routledge.

Duffy, R. and Smith, M. (2003) *The Ethics of Tourism Development*. New York: Routledge.

Dürr, E. and Jaffe, R. (2012) Theorizing slum tourism: Performing, negotiating and transforming inequality. *European Review of Latin American and Caribbean Studies* 93, 113–123.

Durst, J. (2010) "What makes us Gypsies, who knows...?!": Ethnicity and reproduction. In M. Stewart and M. Rövid (eds) *Multidisciplinary Approaches to Romany Studies* (pp. 13–34). Budapest: CEU.

Duval, D.T. (2004) Cultural tourism in postcolonial environments. In C.M. Hall and H. Tucker (eds) *Tourism and Postcolonialism* (pp. 57–75) London: Routledge.

Dyson, P. (2012) Slum tourism: Representing and interpreting 'reality' in Dharavi, Mumbai. *Tourism Geographies* 14 (2), 254–274.

Efrati, D. (2012) Investment in the periphery: Not because I deserve it, but because it's worth it. *The Marker Business Daily*. 7 November. See http://www.themarker.com/opinion/1.1858884 (accessed 10 July 2013).

Elder, G.S. (2005) Somewhere, over the rainbow: Cape Town, South Africa as a "gay destination". In L. Ouzgane and R. Morrell (eds) *African Masculinities: Men in Africa from the Late Nineteenth Century to the Present* (pp. 43–60). London: Palgrave Macmillan.

Elishav, R. (n/d) Mitzpe Ramon: Visions of a Cooperative Town. Seminar thesis. Tel-Aviv.

Elliott, A. and Urry, J. (2010) *Mobile Lives*. London: Routledge.

Errol, J. (1986) Mama look a Mas. In Arts Council of Great Britain (eds) *Masquerading: The Art of the Notting Hill Carnival* (pp. 7–19). London: Arts Council of Great Britain.

Euronews (2013) Jobbik leads anti-Jewish rally in Budapest on eve of World Jewish Congress. 4 May. See http://www.euronews.com/2013/05/04/jobbik-leads-anti-jewish-rally-in-budapest-on-eve-of-world-jewish-congress (accessed 10 October 2013).

Eurostat (2012) Foreign citizens and foreign born population. *Eurostat Newsletter* July 11. See www.http://europa.edu/rapid/press-release (accessed 15 March 2012).

Evans, G. (2005) Measure for measure: Evaluating the evidence of culture's contribution to regeneration. *Urban Studies* 42 (5/6), 959–984.

Fainstein, S.S. and Campbell, S. (2002) *Readings on Urban Theory* (2nd edn). Oxford: John Wiley & Sons.

Fainstein, S., Hoffman, L. and Judd, D. (2003) Making theoretical sense of tourism. In L. Hoffman, S. Fainstein and D. Judd (eds) *Cities and Visitors: Regulating People, Markets, and City Space* (pp. 239–253). Oxford: Blackwell Publishing.

Feige, M. (2009) Midbar, Shmama, and garbage can. In A.P. Hare and G. Kressel (eds) *The Desert Experience in Israel: Communities, Arts, Science, and Education in the Negev* (pp. 27–32). Lanham, MD: University Press of America.

Fennema, M. (2001) *Persstemmingen na 11 september.* Amsterdam: Instituut voor Migratie en Etnische Studies (IMES).

Fenster, T. (2004) *The Global City and the Holy City: Narratives on Knowledge, Planning and Diversity.* Harlow: Pearson.

Ferdinand, N. and Shaw, S. (2012) The wide world of events: An introduction. In N. Ferdinand and P. Kitchin (eds) *Events Management: An International Approach* (pp. 5–22). London: Sage Publications.

Fitzgerald, S. (1997) *Red Tape, Gold Scissors.* Sydney: State Library of NSW Press.

Florida, R. (2002) *The Rise of the Creative Class.* New York: Basic Books.

Florida, R. (2005) *Cities and the Creative Class.* London: Routledge.

Follath, E. (2013) Europe's Capital of Anti-Semitism: Budapest Experiences a New Wave of Hate. See http://www.spiegel.de/international/europe/europe-s-capital-of-anti-Semitism-budapest-experiences-a-new-wave-of-hate-a-722880.html (accessed 10 October).

Fong, T.P. (1994) *The First Suburban Chinatown: The Remaking Of Monterey Park, California.* Philadelphia, PA: Temple University Press.

FRA (2012) Widespread Roma exclusion persists, find new surveys. 23 May. See http://fra.europa.eu/en/press-release/2012/widespread-roma-exclusion-persists-find-new-surveys (accessed 10 January 2013).

Freire-Medeiros, B. (2007) And the favela went global: The invention of a trademark and a tourist destination. In M. Valenca, E. Nel and W. Leimgruber (eds) *The Global Challenge and Marginalization* (pp. 33–52). New York: Nova Science.

Freire-Medeiros, B. (2009a) *Gringo na laje: produção, circulação e consumo da favela turística.* Rio de Janeiro: Editora FGV.

Freire-Medeiros, B. (2009b) The favela and its touristic transits. *Geoforum* 40 (4), 580–588.

Freire-Medeiros, B. (2012) Favela tourism: Listening to local voices. In F. Frenzl, K. Koens and M. Steinbrink (eds) *Slum Tourism: Poverty, Power and Ethics* (pp. 175–192). New York: Routledge.

Freire-Medeiros, B. (2013) *Touring Poverty.* New York: Routledge.

Freire-Medeiros, B., Vilarouca, M.G. and Menezes, P.V. (2012) Gringos no Santa Marta: quem são, o que pensam e como avaliam a experiência turística na favela. In A. Penalva dos Santos, G.J. Marafon, M.J. Sant'anna (eds) *Rio de Janeiro: Um território em mutação* (pp. 183–206). Rio de Janeiro: Gramma: FAFERJ.

Frenkel, S. and Walton, J. (2000) Bavarian Leavenworth and the symbolic economy of a theme town. *The Geographical Review* 90 (4), 559–581.

Frenzel, F. (2013) Slum tourism in the context of the tourism and poverty (relief) debate. *Die Erde* 144 (2), 117–128.

Frenzel, F., Koens, K. and Steinbrinck, M. (eds) (2012) *Power, Ethic and Politics in Global Slum-Tourism.* London: Routledge.

Fridgen, J.D. (1991) *Dimensions of Tourism.* East Lansing, MI: Education Institute of the American Hotel and Motel Association.

Gabaccia, D.R. (1998) *We Are What We Eat: Ethnic Food and the Making of Americans.* Cambridge, MA: Harvard University Press.

Gathercole, P. and Lowenthal, D. (eds) (1994) *The Politics of the Past.* London: Routledge.

Gay Net Cape Town (2013) *Exploring the Mother City.* See http://www.gaynetcapetown.co.za/places (accessed 3 December 2013).

Geertz, C. (1973) *The Interpretation of Cultures.* New York: Basic Books Inc.

Germain, A. and Radice, M. (2006) Cosmopolitanism by default: Public sociability in Montréal. In J. Binnie, J. Holloway, S. Millington and C. Young (eds) *Cosmopolitan Urbanism* (pp. 112–130). London: Routledge.

Ghebrihiwet, K. (2009) Cultural Diversity: An Asset For Tourism. See http://www.shabait.com/articles/nation-building/140-cultural-diversity-an-asset-for-tourism (accessed 5 November 2010).

Ghilardi, L. (2001) *Cultural Planning and Cultural Diversity*. London: Noema Research and Planning Ltd.

Gibson, C. (2009) Geographies of tourism: Critical research on capitalism and local livelihoods. *Progress in Human Geography* 33, 527–534.

Gilbert, D. and Hancock, C. (2006) New York City and the transatlantic imagination: French and English tourism and the spectacle of the modern metropolis 1893–1939. *Journal of Urban History* 33, 77–107.

Gill, A. (2013) Why Jewish life is thriving in today's Poland. June 21. See http://www.foxnews.com/opinion/2013/06/21/why-jewish-life-is-thriving-in-today-poland (accessed 10 September 2013).

Giulianotti, R. and Robertson, R. (2007) Forms of glocalization: Globalization and the migration strategies of Scottish football fans in North America. *Sociology* 41 (1): 133–152.

Gladstone, D.L. (2005) *From Pilgrimage to Package Tour: Travel and Tourism in the Third World*. New York: Routledge.

Gladwell, M. (2008) *Outliers: The Story of Success*. New York: Little, Brown and Company.

Goffman, E. (1963) *Stigma: Notes on the Management of Spoiled Identity*. Englewood Cliffs, NJ: Simon & Schuster.

Gold, M. (2012) *Taking the Township to the Tourist*. See http://www.atlas-webshop.org/ATLAS-Reflections-2012-re-creating-the-Global-City (accessed 15 June 2012).

Goldin, I., Cameron, G. and Balarajan, M. (2011) *Exceptional People: How Migration Shaped Our World and Will Define Our Future*. Princeton and Oxford: Princeton University Press.

Gordon, T. (2005) Global Villages: A Documentary Video. Tourist Gaze Productions.

Grabowski, S. (2013) Acculturation, re-entry and transformation: The story of a volunteer tourist. In Y. Reisinger (ed.) *Transformational Tourism: Tourist Perspectives* (pp. 183–198). Wallingford: CABI.

Graburn, N.H.H. (2008) Experiencing Xinjiang: Anthropologists and friends in Urumqi. In H. Song and K. Chon (eds) *Experiencing China* (pp. 41–65). London: Routledge.

Graham, B., Ashworth, G.J. and Tunbridge, J.E. (2000) *A Geography of Heritage*. London: Arnold.

Greenberg, Y. (1994) Utopia in the Negev: The Ramon cooperative town. *Iyunim Bitkumat Israel* (4), 299–324. In Hebrew.

Gruber, R.E. (2002) *Virtually Jewish: Reinventing Jewish Culture in Europe*. Berkeley, CA: University of California Press.

Gruber, R. (2009) The change has come to Jewish life in Eastern Europe. 19 November. See http://www.jewishjournal.com/travel/article/the_change_has_come_to_jewish_life_in_eastern_europe_20091119 (accessed 16 December 2013).

Gruber, R.E. (2008) Letter from Budapest: Reclaiming a heritage. *The New Leader* January/February, pp. 11–13.

Grunebaum, H. (2011) *Memorializing the Past: Everyday Life in South Africa after the Truth and Reconciliation Commission*. New Brunswick, NJ: Transaction.

Guaracino, J. (2007) *Gay and Lesbian Tourism: The Essential Guide for Marketing*. London: Elsevier/Butterworth-Heineman.

Gudykunst, W. (1998) *Bridging Differences. Effective Intergroup Communication*. London: Sage.

Gursoy, D. and Rutherford, D.G. (2004) Host attitudes towards tourism: An improved structural model. *Annals of Tourism Research* 31 (3), 495–516.

Gyárfás, K., Szegő, D. and Szőnyi, A. (2013) *Jewnior Guidebook: A Pocket Guide to Budapest's Jewish Quarter.* Budapest: Zachor Foundation.

Habermas, J. (1989) *The Structural Transformation of the Public Sphere.* Cambridge: Polity Press.

Hall, C.M. and Williams, A.M. (eds) (2002) *Tourism and Migration: New Relationships Between Production and Consumption.* Dordrecht: Kluwer Academic.

Hall, C.M. and Tucker, H. (2004) *Tourism and Postcolonialism.* London: Routledge.

Hall, D. and Brown, F. (2010) Tourism and welfare: Ethics, responsibility and well-being. In S. Cole and N. Morgan (eds) *Tourism and Inequality: Problems and Prospects* (pp. 143–161). Wallingford: CAB International.

Hamnett, C. (2003) *Unequal City: London in the Global Arena.* London: Routledge.

Hannam, K. and Diekmann, A. (2011) *Tourism and India: A Critical Introduction.* New York: Routledge.

Hannam, K. and Roy, S. (2013) Cultural tourism and the mobilities paradigm. In M.K. Smith and G. Richards (eds) *The Routledge Handbook of Cultural Tourism* (pp. 141–147). London: Routledge.

Hannerz, U. (1996) *Transnational Connections: Culture, People, Places.* London: Routledge.

Hannigan, J. (2007) From fantasy city to creative city. In G. Richards and J. Wilson (eds) *Tourism, Creativity and Development* (pp. 48–56). London and New York: Routledge.

Harper, K., Steger, T. and Filcak, R. (2009) Environmental Justice and Roma Communities in Central and Eastern Europe. Selected Publications of EFS Faculty. See http://scholarworks.umass.edu/cgi/viewcontent.cgi?article=1000&context=efsp_pub_articles (accessed 5 January 2013).

Harris, A., Henderson, G. and Williams, J. (2005) Courting customers: Assessing consumer racial profiling and other marketplace discrimination. *Journal of Public Policy and Marketing* 24 (1), 163–171.

Harvey, D.C. (2007) (Re)creating culture through tourism: Black heritage sites in New Jersey. In M.K. Smith (ed.) *Tourism, Culture and Regeneration* (pp. 59–68). Wallingford: CABI.

Harwood, R. (2013) *China's New Socialist Countryside: Modernity Arrives in the Nu Valley.* Seattle, WA: University of Washington Press.

Havas, G. (2002a) On sociological studies about the Roma. In E. Kállai (ed.) *The Gypsies/The Roma in Hungarian Society* (pp. 18–23). Budapest: Teleki László Foundation.

Havas, G. (2002b) The school as breakout point. In E. Kállai (ed.) *The Gypsies/The Roma in Hungarian Society* (pp. 79–106). Budapest: Teleki László Foundation.

Heap, C. (2009) *Slumming: Sexual and Racial Encounters in America Nightlife, 1885–1940.* Chicago, IL: University of Chicago Press.

Heidegger, M. (1996) *Being and Time.* London: Routledge.

Henderson, J. (2008) Managing urban ethnic heritage: Little India in Singapore. *International Journal of Heritage Studies* 14 (4), 332–346.

Henry, N., McEwan, C. and Pollard, J.S. (2002) Globalisation from below: Birmingham – postcolonial workshop of the world? *Area* 34 (2), 117–127.

Hester, J. (2002) Repackaging difference: The Korean 'theming' of a shopping street in Osaka, Japan. In A. Erdentug and F. Colombijn (eds) *Urban Ethnic Encounters: The Spatial Consequences* (pp. 177–191). London and New York: Routledge.

Higgins-Desbiolles, F. (2012) Resisting the hegemony of the market: Reclaiming the social capacities of tourism. In S. McCabe, L. Minnaert and A. Diekmann (eds) *Social Tourism in Europe: Theory and Practice.* Bristol: Channel View Publications.

Hitchcock, M. (2013) Souvenirs and cultural tourism. In M.K. Smith and G. Richards (eds) *The Routledge Handbook of Cultural Tourism* (pp. 201–206). London: Routledge.

Hoffman, L.M. (2003) The marketing of diversity in the inner city: Tourism and regulation in Harlem. *International Journal of Urban and Regional Research* 27 (2), 286–299.

Hollinshead, K. (2004) Tourism and new sense. In C.M. Hall and H. Tucker (eds) *Tourism and Postcolonialism* (pp. 25–42). London: Routledge.

Howe, A. (2001) Queer pilgrimage: The San Francisco homeland and identity tourism. *Cultural Anthropology* 16 (1), 35–61.

Hughes, H.L. (2002) Marketing gay tourism in Manchester: New market for urban tourism or destruction of 'gay space'? *Journal of Vacation Marketing* 9 (2), 152–163.

Hughes, H.L. (2006) Gay and lesbian festivals: Tourism in the change from politics to party. In D. Picard and M. Robinson (eds) *Festivals, Tourism and Social Change: Remaking Worlds* (pp. 238–254). Clevedon: Channel View Publications.

Hugo, G. (2008) Immigrant settlement outside of Australia's capital cities. *Population, Space and Place* 14, 553–571.

Huntington, S. (1993) The clash of civilisations? *Foreign Affairs* 72 (3), 22–49.

Hyde, S. (2007) *Eating Spring Rice: The Cultural Politics of AIDS in Southwest China*. Berkeley, CA: University of California Press.

Jackson, E.L. (1993) Recognizing patterns of leisure constraints: Results from alternative analyses. *Journal of Leisure Research* 25, 129–149.

Jaguaribe, B. and Hetherington, K. (2006) Favela tours: Indistinct and maples representations of the real in Rio de Janeiro. In M. Sheller and J. Urry (eds) *Mobile Technologies of the City* (pp. 155–166). London/New York: Routledge.

Janky, B. (2004) The Income Situation of Gypsy Families. *TÁRKI Social Report Reprint Series No. 22*. See http://www.tarki.hu/adatbank-h/kutjel/pdf/a738.pdf (accessed 5 January 2013).

Jayne, M. (2006) *Cities and Consumption*. London and New York: Routledge.

Jennings, G. and Weiler, B. (2004) Mediating meaning: Perspectives on brokering quality tourist experiences. Working paper 20/04, Monash University.

Jewinform (2012) Jewinform Magazine (English Edition). See http://issuu.com/jewinform/docs/jewinform_magazin_eng_2012_1 (accessed 15 December 2012).

Jewish Virtual Library (2013) Virtual Jewish History Tour. See http://www.jewishvirtuallibrary.org/jsource/vjw/Hungary.html (accessed 13 January 2013).

Jordan, K., Krivokapic-Skoko, B. and Collins, J. (2011) Immigration and multicultural place-making in rural and regional Australia. In G. Luck, R. Black and D. Race (eds) *Demographic Change in Rural Australia: Implications for Society and the Environment* (pp. 259–281). Dordrecht: Springer.

Jordan, K. and Collins, J. (2012) Symbols of ethnicity in a multi-ethnic precinct: Marketing Perth's Northbridge for cultural consumption. In V. Aytar and J. Rath (eds) *Selling Ethnic Neighborhoods: The Rise of Neighborhoods as Places of Leisure and Consumption* (pp 120–137). New York: Routledge.

Judd, D.R. and Fainstein, S.S. (1999) *The Tourist City*. New Haven and London: Yale University Press.

Kállai, E. (ed.) (2002) The Hungarian Roma population during the last half-century. In E. Kállai (ed.) *The Gypsies/The Roma in Hungarian Society* (pp. 35–50). Budapest: Teleki László Foundation.

Károlyi, J. (2002) The Roma, poverty and culture. In E. Kállai (ed.) *The Gypsies/The Roma in Hungarian Society* (pp. 157–160). Budapest: Teleki László Foundation.

Katz, J. (1990) The identity of post-emancipatory Hungarian Jewry. In D. Yehuda and V. Karády (eds) *A Social and Economic History of Central European Jewry* (pp. 13–31). New Brunswick: Transaction Publishers.

Kelly, J.R. (1987) *Freedom to Be: A New Sociology of Leisure*. New York: Macmillan.

Kemény, I. (2002) The Roma/Gypsies of Hungary and the economy. In E. Kállai (ed.) *The Gypsies/The Roma in Hungarian Society* (pp. 51–77). Budapest: Teleki László Foundation.

Keresztély, K. and Szabó, J.Z. (2006) Budapest: Regaining multiculturalism? *The Budapest Observatory.* See http://www.budobs.org/pdf/Regaining_multiculturalism. pdf (accessed 14 January 2013).

Kieti, D.M. and Magio, K.O. (2013) The ethical and local resident perspectives of slum tourism in Kenya. *Advances in Hospitality and Tourism Research (AHTR)* 1 (1), 1–21.

King, J. (2002) Destination marketing organizations: Connecting the experience rather than promoting the place. *Journal of Vacation Marketing* 8 (2), 105–108.

Kinkead, G. (1993) *Chinatown: A Portrait of a Closed Society.* New York: Harper Perennial.

Klepsch, L. (2010) A critical analysis of slum tours: Comparing the existing offer in South Africa, Brazil, India and Kenya. Unpublished master's thesis, Université Libre de Bruxelles.

Koens, K. (2012) Competition, cooperation and collaboration in township tourism: Business relations and power in township tourism. In F. Frenzel, K. Koens and M. Steinbrink (eds) *Slum Tourism. Poverty, Power and Ethics* (pp. 83–100). New York: Routledge.

Kováts, A. (2002) Local and international views on the migration of the Hungarian Roma. In E. Kállai (ed.) *The Gypsies/The Roma in Hungarian Society* (pp. 126–148). Budapest: Teleki László Foundation.

Koven, K. (2004) *Slumming: Sexual and Social Politics in Victorian London.* Princeton and Woodstock: Princeton University Press.

Kraske, M. (2007) Fighting for Tradition: Budapest's Jewish Quarter under Threat. 19 April. See http://www.spiegel.de/international/europe/fighting-for-tradition-budapest-s-jewish-quarter-under-threat-a-478207.html (accessed 13 January 2013).

Kugelmass, J. (1994) Why we go to Poland. Holocaust tourism as secular ritual. In J.E. Young (ed.) *The Art of Memory: Holocaust Memorials in History* (pp. 175–183). Berlin: Prestel.

KultUnió (2013) Budapest's Multicultural Quarter. See http://kultunio.hu/index.php (accessed 14 January 2013).

Kurtz, D. (2013) Burning the books, shattering the statue, of poet and holocaust victim Miklós Radnóti, 19 November. See http://www.mhpbooks.com/burning-the-books-shattering-the-statue-of-poet-and-holocaust-victim-miklos-radnoti (accessed 1 December 2013).

Ladanyi, J. and Szelenyi, I. (2001) The social construction of Roma ethnicity in Bulgaria, Romania and Hungary during market transition. *Review of Sociology* Vol. 7. See http://www.szociologia.hu/dynamic/RevSoc_2001_2_LadanyiJ_The_social_construction_of_romaa_ethnicity.pdf (accessed 5 January 2013).

Lafaye, C. and Thévenot, L. (1993) Une justification ecologique? Conflits dans l'amenagement de la nature. *Revue Francaise de Sociologie* 34 (4), 495–524.

Lamont, M. and Thévenot, L. (eds) (2000) *Rethinking Comparative Cultural Sociology: Repertoires of Evaluation in France and the United States.* Cambridge: Cambridge University Press.

LB Tower Hamlets (1999) *Brick Lane Retail and Restaurant Policy Review,* 1 March , London.

Lebor, A. (2008) Budapest quarter wins a reprieve from the demolition man. *The Jewish Chronicle,* 17 February. See http://www.eurojewcong.org/article.php?id_article=1103 (accessed 13 January 2013).

Ledwith, S. and Seymour, D. (2001) Home and away: Preparing students for multicultural management. *International Journal of Human Resource Management* 12 (8), 1292–1312.

Lefèbvre, H. (1974) *The Production of Space.* Oxford: Blackwell.

Lehrer, E. (2007) Jewish? Heritage? In Poland? *Bridges: A Jewish Feminist Journal* 12 (2), 36–41.

Lemée, C. (2009) Processes of identity reconstitution for descendants of Jewish emigrants from the Baltic and Central European post-Holocaust situations. *Identity*

Politics: Histories, Regions and Borderlands, Acta Historica Universitatis Klaipedensis XIX. Studia Anthropologica 111, 131–146.

Li, J. (2003) Playing upon fantasy: Women, ethnic tourism, and identity politics in Xishuang Banna, China. *Gender and Tourism*, Special issue of *Tourism Recreation Research* 28 (2), 51–65.

Li, Y. (2000) Ethnic tourism: A Canadian experience. *Annals of Tourism Research* 27 (1), 115–131.

Li, W. (2009) *Ethnoburb: The New Ethnic Community in Urban America*. Honolulu, HI: University of Hawaii Press.

Lichrou, M., O'Malley, L. and Patterson, M. (2008) Place-product or place narrative(s)? Perspectives in the marketing of the tourism destinations. *Journal of Strategic Marketing* 16 (1), 27–39.

Lim, F.K.G. (2009) Donkey friends' in China: The Internet, civil society and the emergence of the Chinese backpacking community. In T. Winter, P. Teo and T.C. Chang (eds) *Asia on Tour: Exploring the Rise of Asian Tourism* (pp. 292–301). London: Routledge.

Lin, J. (1995) Ethnic places, postmodernism, and urban change in Houston. *The Sociological Quarterly* 36 (4), 629–647.

Lin, J. (1998) *Reconstructing Chinatown: Ethnic Enclave, Global Change*. Minneapolis, MN: University of Minnesota Press.

Lin, J. (2010) *The Power of Urban Ethnic Places: Cultural Heritage and Community Life*. London and New York: Routledge.

Linke, U. (2012) Mobile imaginaries, portable signs: Global consumption and representations of slum life. *Tourism Geographies* 14 (2), 294–319.

Lukács, A. (2005) Save the Jewish Quarter in Budapest! October. See http://www.levego.hu/sites/default/files/stjqb.pdf (accessed 13 January 2013).

Maoz, D. (2006) The mutual gaze. *Annals of Tourism Research* 33 (1), 221–239.

MacCannell, D. (1973) Staged authenticity: Arrangements of social space in tourist settings. *American Sociological Review* 79, 589–603.

MacCannell, D. (1976) *The Tourist: A New Theory of the Leisure Class*. New York: Schocken.

Macleod, D.V.L. (2013) Tourism, anthropology and cultural configuration. In M.K. Smith and G. Richards (eds) *The Routledge Handbook of Cultural Tourism* (pp. 195–200). London: Routledge.

Macleod, D.V.L. and Carrier, J.G. (eds) (2010) *Tourism, Power and Culture: Anthropological Insights*. Bristol: Channel View Publications.

Maitland, R. (2007) Cultural tourism and the development of new tourism areas in London. In G. Richards (ed.) *Cultural Tourism: Global and Local Perspectives* (pp. 113–128). New York: Haworth Press.

Mallinson, C. and Brewster, Z. (2005) "Blacks and Bubbas": Stereotypes, ideology, and categorization processes in restaurant servers' discourse. *Discourse and Society* 16 (6), 787–807.

Markwell, K. and Waitt, G. (2009) Festivals, space and sexuality: Gay pride in Australia. *Tourism Geographies: An International Journal of Tourism Space, Place and Environment* 11 (2), 143–168.

Marx, K. and Engels, F. [1848] (1952) *The Manifesto of the Communist Party*. Moscow: Foreign Languages.

Massey, D. (ed.) (2010) *New Faces in New Places: The New Geography of American Immigration*. New York: Russell Sage Foundation.

Mayne, A. (1993) *The Imagined Slum: Newspaper Representation in Three Cities, 1870–1914*. Leicester: Leicester University Press.

Mazor, E. (1992) Introduction into the Ramon National Geological Park. *Israel Journal of Earth Sciences* 42, 103–114.

McDonald, D.A. (2008) *World City Syndrome: Neoliberalism and Inequality in Cape Town*. New York: Routledge.

McDonald, S.M and Murphy, P. (2008) Utilizing and adapting leisure constraints models to enhance 'short-break' vacations: Case study of Melbourne, Australia. *Journal of Vacation Marketing* 14 (4), 317–330.

McEvoy, (2003) The evolution of Manchester's "curry mile": From suburban shopping street to ethnic destination, paper presented to Metropolis Conference, Vienna, September.

McIntosh, A. and Prentice, R. (1999) Affirming authenticity: Consuming cultural heritage. *Annals of Tourism Research* 26 (3), 589–612.

McKercher, B. and Cros, H. (2002) *Cultural Tourism: The Partnership between Tourism and Cultural Heritage Management*. New York: Haworth Hospitality Press.

McKhann, C. (2001) The good, the bad, and the ugly: Observations and reflections on tourism development. In T.C. Beng, S. Cheung and Y. Hui (eds) *Tourism Anthropology and Chinese Society* (pp. 147–166). Bangkok: White Lotus Press.

McLaughlin, M. and Jesilow, P. (1998) Conveying a sense of community along Bolsa Avenue: Little Saigon as a model of ethnic commercial belts. *International Migration* 36 (1), 49–65.

McMillan, D.W. and Chavis, D.M. (1986) Sense of community: A definition and theory. *Journal of Community Psychology* 14, 6–23.

Meethan, K. (2001) *Tourism in Global Society: Place, Culture, Consumption*. New York: Palgrave.

Meethan K. (2013) Performing and recording culture: Reflexivity in tourism In G. Richards and M. K. Smith (eds) *Routledge Handbook of Cultural Tourism* (pp. 156–164). London: Routledge.

Mekawy, M.A. (2012) Responsible slum tourism: Egyptian experience. *Annals of Tourism Research* 39 (4), 2092–2113.

Menezes, P. (2007) Gringos e câmeras na favela da Rocinha. Unpublished thesis, Universidade do Estado do Rio de Janeiro (UERJ).

Menezes, P. (2009) Interseções entre novos sentidos de patrimônio, turismo e políticas públicas: Um estudo de caso sobre o Museu a céu aberto do Morro da Providência. MA Thesis in Sociology, Instituo Universitário de Pesquisas do Rio de Janeiro.

Mercer, C. (1991) What is Cultural Planning? Paper presented to the Community Arts Network National Conference, Sydney, Australia, 10 October.

Meschkank, J. (2010) Investigations into slum tourism in Mumbai: Poverty tourism and the tensions between different constructions of reality. *GeoJournal* 76 (1), 47–62.

Miles, M. (1997) *Art, Space and the City: Public Art and Urban Futures*. London: Routledge.

Milstein, T. (2005) Transformation abroad: Sojourning and the perceived enhancement of self-efficacy. *International Journal of Intercultural Relations* 29 (2), 217–238.

Mingay, G.E. (1989) Introduction. In G.E. Mingay (ed.) *The Rural Idyll* (pp. 1–7). London: Routledge.

Ministry of Foreign Affairs Budapest (2004) Fact Sheets on Hungary: Gypsies/Roma in Hungary. See www.kum.hu (accessed 10 December 2012).

Moscardo, G. (1999) *Making Visitors Mindful: Principles for Creating Sustainable Visitor Experiences Through Effective Communication*. Champaign, IL: Sagamore Publishing.

Moufakkir, O. (2008) Destination revisited: The Dutch market perceptions of Morocco as a tourism destination. In P. Burns and M. Novelli (eds) *Tourism Development: Growth, Myths and Inequalities* (pp. 85–112). Wallingford: CABI.

Moufakkir, O. (2011) Diaspora tourism: Using a mixed-mode survey design to document tourism behavior and constraints of people of Turkish extraction resident in Germany. *Journal of Vacation Marketing* 17 (3), 209–223.

Mowforth, M. and Munt, I. (2008) *Tourism and Sustainability: New Tourism in the Third World* (3rd edn). London: Routledge.

Mullins, P. (1999) International tourism and the cities of S E Asia. In D. Judd and S. Fainstein (eds) *The Tourist City* (pp. 245–260). New Haven, CT: Yale University Press.

Mumford, L. (1968) *The Urban Prospect*. London: Martin Secker and Warburg Ltd.

Munk, V., Mader, M. and Csako, G. (eds) (2005) Magyar Agora. Romák és nem romák romákról és nem romákról. [Roma and non-Roma about Roma and non-Roma]. ELTE. See http://www.magyaragora.org/dinamikus/kozponti_dokumentumtar/magora2005.pdf (accessed 23 March 2013).

Murphy, C. and Roe, D. (2004) Livelihoods and tourism in communal area conservancies In S.A. Long (ed.) *Livelihoods and CBNRM in Namibia: The Findings of the WILD Project, Final Report* (pp. 119–122). Windhoek: Ministry of Environment and Tourism.

Nast, H.J. (2002) Queer partriarchies, queer racisms, international. *Antipode* 34 (5), 879–909.

NationMaster (2012) *Immigration Statistics*. See http://www.nationmaster.com (accessed 20 June 2012).

Nemasetoni, I. and Rogerson, C.M. (2005) Developing small firms in township tourism: Emerging tour operators in Gauteng, South Africa. *Urban Forum* 16 (2–3), 196–213.

Nkemngu, A.-A. P. (2012) Community Benefit from Tourism: Myth or Reality A Case Study of the Soshanguve Township, Tourism Hospitality, 1:5. See http://dx.doi.org/10.4172/2167-0269.100010

Noy, C. (2003) This trip really changed me: Backpackers' narratives of self change. *Annals of Tourism Research* 31 (1), 78–102.

Nuissl, H. and Heinrichs, D. (2013) Slums: Perspectives on the definition, the appraisal and the management of an urban phenomenon. *Die Erde* 144 (2), 105–116.

Nunkoo, R. and Gursoy, D. (2012) Residents' support for tourism: An identity perspective. *Annals of Tourism Research* 39 (1), 243–268.

Nyeck, S.N. and Epprecht, M. (2013) *Sexual Diversity in Africa – Politics, Theory, Citizenship*. Montreal, Quebec: McGill-Queen's University Press.

Nyíri, P. (2006) *Scenic Spots: Chinese Tourism, The State, and Cultural Authority*. Seattle, WA: University of Washington Press.

Oakes, T. (1998) *Tourism and Modernity in China*. London: Routledge.

Oakes, T. (2006) The village as theme park: Mimesis and authenticity in Chinese tourism. In T. Oakes and L. Schein (eds) *Translocal China: Linkages, Identities, and the Reimagining of Space* (pp. 166–192). London: Routledge.

Oakes, T. (2011) Laser tag and other rural diversions: The village as China's urban playground. *Harvard Asia Quarterly* 13 (3), 25–30.

Okely, J. (2010) Constructing culture through shared location, bricolage and exchange: The case of Gypsies and Roma. In M. Stewart and M. Rövid (eds) *Multidisciplinary Approaches to Romany Studies* (pp. 35–54). Budapest: CEU.

Ooi, C.S. (2002) *Cultural Tourism and Tourism Cultures*. Copenhagen: Copenhagen Business School Press.

Opsomer, H. (2008) *Matonge als capaciteit. Gesprekken over een transnationale stedelijke ruimte*. Master thesis in African langages and cultures, Universiteit Gent.

O'Reilly, C. (2006) From drifter to gap year tourist mainstreaming backpacker travel. *Annals of Tourism Research* 33 (4), 998–1017.

Oswin, N. (2005) Towards radical geographies of complicit queer futures. *Acme: An International E-journal for Critical Geographies* 3 (2), 79–86.

Oswin, N. (2007) Producing homonormativity in neoliberal South Africa: Recognition, redistribution, and the equality project. *Signs: Journal of Women in Culture and Society* 32 (3), 649–669.

Owen, K.A. (2002) The Sydney 2000 Olympics and urban entrepreneurialism: Local variations in urban governance. *Australian Geographical Studies* 40 (3), 323–336.

Oyatambwe, D.W. (2006) Matonge – Porte de Namur: un quartier africain au cœur de Bruxelles? Research report from NGO Congo Cultures. Commission Communautaire Française de Bruxelles, Brussels.

Palmer, A., Koenig-Lewis, N. and Medi-Jones, L.E. (2013) The effects of residents' social identity and involvement on their advocacy of incoming tourism. *Tourism Management* 38, 142–151.

Paolillo, T. (2012) *Analyse des dynamiques de l'offre touristique de Matonge, quartier ethnique de Bruxelles.* Master thesis (Unpublished), Université Libre de Bruxelles.

Papp, S.Z. (2008) Sok a dalom. [I have many songs]. *Népszabadság* 10 June 2008.

Pascal, B. (2010) *Pensées, opuscules et lettres.* Paris: Éditions Classiques Garnier.

Pearlstone, Z. (1990) *Ethnic Los Angeles.* Los Angeles, CA: Hillcrest.

Philipp, S.F. (1993) Racial differences in the perceived attractiveness of tourism destination, interests and cultural resources. *Journal of Leisure Research* 25, 290–304.

Phua, V.C., Berkowitz, D. and Gagermeier, M. (2012) Promoting multicultural tourism in Singapore. *Annals of Tourism Research* 39, 1242–1263.

Price, M. and Benton-Short, L. (2007) Counting Immigrants in Cities across the Globe. See http://www.migrationinformation.org/Feature/display.cfm?ID=567 (accessed 15 July 2007).

Pidd, H. (2012) Poor, abused and second-class: The Roma living in fear in Hungarian village. 27 January. See http://www.guardian.co.uk/world/2012/jan/27/hungary-roma-living-in-fear (accessed 10 January 2013).

Plog, S.C. (2001). Why destination areas rise and fall in popularity. An update of a Cornell classic. Cornell Hotel, Restaurant & Administration Quarterly, 42(3): 13–24.

Podoshen, J.S. and Hunt, J.M. (2011) Equity restoration, the Holocaust and tourism of sacred sites. *Tourism Management* 32, 1332–1342.

Pratt, M. (1992) *Imperial Eyes: Travel Writing and Transculturation.* London: Routledge.

Pritchard, A., Morgan, N.J., Sedgely, D. and Jenkins, A. (1998) Reaching out to the gay tourist: Opportunities and threat in an emerging market segment. *Tourism Management* 19 (3), 273–282.

Pritchard, A., Morgan, N., Sedgely, D., Khan, E. and Jenkins, A. (2000) Sexuality and holiday choices: Conversations with gay and lesbian tourists. *Leisure Studies* 19, 267–282.

Pritchard, A., Morgan, N. and Sedgley, D. (2002) In search of lesbian space? The experience of Manchester's gay village, *Leisure Studies* 21 (2), 105–123.

Ram, U. (2000) The promised land of business opportunities: Liberal post-Zionism and the glocal age. In G. Shafir and Y. Peled (eds) *The New Israel: Peacemaking and Liberalization* (pp. 217–242). Boulder, CO: Westview Press.

Rapport, N. (1998) Coming home to a dream: A study of the immigrant discourse of 'Anglo-Saxons' in Israel. In N. Rapport and A. Dawson (eds) *Migrants of Identity: Perceptions of Home in a World of Movement* (pp. 61–83). Oxford: Berg.

Rath, J. (ed.) (2007) *Tourism, Ethnic Diversity and the City.* London: Routledge.

Raymore, L.A. (2002) Facilitators to leisure. *Journal of Leisure Research* 34 (1), 37–51.

Reich, A.Z. (1999) *Positioning of Tourist Destinations.* Champaign, IL: Sagamore.

Reichel, A. and Uriely, N. (2003) Sustainable tourism development in the Israeli Negev desert: An integrative approach. *Journal of Park and Recreation Administration* 21 (4), 14–29.

Reichner, E. (2013) *There of All Places: The Story of the Social Settlers.* Tel-Aviv: Yedioth.

Reid, C., Collins, J. and Singh, M. (2014) *Global Teachers, Australian Perspectives: Goodbye Mr Chips, Hello Ms Banerjee.* Singapore: Springer Press.

Reisinger, Y. (2009) *International Tourism: Cultures and Behaviour.* Oxford: Elsevier.

Reisinger, Y. (ed.) (2013) *Transformational Tourism: Tourist Perspectives.* Wallingford: CABI.

Reisinger, Y. and Turner, L. (2003) *Cross-Cultural Behaviour in Tourism: Concept and Analysis*. Oxford: Butterworth Heinemann.

Reisinger, Y. and Steiner, C. (2006) Reconceptualising interpretation: The role of tour guides in authentic tourism. *Current Issues in Tourism* 9 (6), 481–498.

Reisinger, Y. and Crotts, J. (2010) Applying Hofstede's national culture measures in tourism research: Illuminating issues of divergence and convergence. *Journal of Travel Research* 49 (2), 153–164.

Reisinger, Y. and Crotts, J. (2012) An exploration of the flipside of international marketing: The acculturation of foreign born residents of the U.S. Special issue of *Tourism Review New Minorities and Tourism* 67 (1), 42–50.

Reisinger, Y., Kozak, M. and Visser, E. (2012) Turkish hosts gaze at Russian tourists: A cultural perspective. In O. Moufakkir and Y. Reisinger (eds) *The Host Gaze in Global Tourism* (pp. 47–66). Wallingford: CABI.

Requiem for Auschwitz (2012) Objectives. See http://www.requiemforauschwitz.eu/objectives.html (accessed 10 January 2013).

Rex, J. and Moore, R. (1967) *Race, Community and Conflict: A Study of Sparkbrook*. Oxford: Oxford University Press.

Richards, G. (2011) Creativity and tourism: The state of the art. *Annals of Tourism Research*, 38 (4), 1225–1253.

Richards, R. and Wilson, J. (2007) The creative turn in regeneration: Creative spaces, spectacles and tourism in cities. In M.K. Smith (ed.) *Tourism, Culture and Regeneration* (pp. 12–24). Wallingford: CABI.

Ritchie, J.R.B. and Crouch, D. (2003) *The Competitive Destination: A Sustainable Tourism Perspective*. Wallingford: CABI.

Robertson, R. (1992) *Globalization: Social Theory and Global Culture*. London: Sage.

Robinson, M. (2013) Talking tourists: The intimacies of inter-cultural dialogue. In M.K. Smith and G. Richards (eds) *Routledge Handbook of Cultural Tourism* (pp. 28–33). London: Routledge.

Rogerson, C.M. (2004) Urban tourism and small tourism enterprise development in Johannesburg: The case of township tourism. *GeoJournal* 60, 249–257.

Rogerson, C.M. and Visser, G. (2007) *Tourism Research and Urban Africa: The South African Experience*. New Brunswick, NJ: Transaction.

Rolfes, M. (2010) Poverty tourism: Theoretical reflections and empirical findings regarding an extraordinary form of tourism. *GeoJournal* 75 (5), 421–442.

Rolfes, M. (2011) Slumming – empirical results and observational – theoretical considerations on backgrounds of township, favela and slum tourism. In R. Sharpley and P. Stone (eds) *Tourist Experience: Contemporary Perspectives* (pp. 59–76). London: Routledge.

Rolfes, M., Steinbrink, M. and Uhl, C. (2007) *Research Group Township Tourism*. Potsdam: University of Potsdam.

Rolfes, M., Steinbrink, M. and Uhl, C. (2009) *Townships as Attraction: An Empirical Study of Township Tourism in Cape Town*. Potsdam: Universitätsverlag Potsdam (Praxis Kultur- und Sozialgeographie).

Roodhouse, S. (2006) *Cultural Quarters: Principles and Practice*. Bristol: Intellect Books.

Rosello, M. (2001) *Postcolonial Hospitality: The Immigrant as Fuest*. Stanford: Stanford University Press.

Ross, E. (2007) *Slum Travellers: Ladies and London Poverty, 1860–1920*. Berkeley, CA: University of California Press.

Ruethers, M. (2013) Jewish spaces and Gypsy spaces in the cultural topographies of a New Europe: Heritage re-enactment as political folklore. *European Review of History* 20 (4), 671–695.

Rugh, J. and Massey, D. (2010) Racial segregation and the American foreclosure crisis. *American Sociological Review* 75 (5), 629–651.

Russo, A.P. and Quaglieri-Dominguez, A. (2012) From the city to the tourist dual creative melting pot: The liquid geographies of global cultural consumerism. In M. Smith and G. Richards (eds) *Routledge Handbook of Cultural Tourism* (pp. 324–331). London: Routledge.

Ryan, J. and Hellmundt, S. (2005) Maximising international students' 'cultural capital'. In J. Carroll and J. Ryan (eds) *Teaching International Students: Improving Learning for All* (pp. 13–16). London: Routledge.

Said, E. (1978) *Orientalism.* London: Routledge and Kegan Paul.

Said, E. (1994). *Orientalism,* New York: Vintage Books.

Salamensky, S.I. (2013) Culture, memory, context: Reenactments of traumatic histories in Europe and Eurasia. *International Journal of Politics, Culture, and Society* 26, 21–30.

Salazar, N. (2006) Touristifying Tanzania. Local guides, global discourse. *Annals of Tourism Research* 33 (3), 833–852.

Salazar, N. (2010) *Envisioning Eden. Mobilising Imaginaries in Tourism and Beyond.* New-York and Oxford: Bergham Books.

Salazar, N. (2013) The (im)mobility of tourism imaginaries. In M.K. Smith and G. Richards (eds) *Routledge Handbook of Cultural Tourism* (pp. 34–39). London: Routledge.

Sandercock, L. (1998) *Towards Cosmopolis.* Chichester: John Wiley.

Sandercock, L. (2000) When strangers become neighbours: Managing cities of difference. *Planning Theory and Practice* 1 (1), 13–30.

Sandercock, L. (2003) *Cosmopolis II: Mongrel Cities in the 21st Century.* London and New York: Continuum.

Sandercock, L. (2006) Cosmopolitan urbanism: A love song to our mongrel cities. In J. Binnie, J. Holloway, S. Millington and C. Young (eds) *Cosmopolitan Urbanism* (pp. 37–52). London and New York: Routledge.

Sandri, O. (2013) City heritage tourism without heirs: A comparative study of Jewish-themed tourism in Krakow and Vilnius. *European Journal of Geography.* See http://cybergeo.revues.org/25934 (accessed 16 December 2013).

Santos, C.A., Belhassen, Y. and Caton, K. (2008) Re-imagining Chinatown: An analysis of tourism discourse. *Tourism Management* 29, 1002–1012.

Sarajeva, K. (2010) You know what kind of place this is, don't you? An exploration of lesbian spaces in Moscow. In C. Gdaniec (ed.) *Cultural Diversity in Russian Cities: The Urban Landscape in the Post-Soviet Era* (pp. 138–164). New York: Berghahn.

Saunders, D. (2010) *Arrival City.* London: Heineman Publishers.

Savener, A. (2013) A host gaze composed of mediated resistance in Panama: Power inversion in Kuna Yala. In O. Moufakkir and Y. Reisinger (eds) *The Host Gaze in Global Tourism* (pp. 67–80). Wallingford: CAB International.

Schein, L. (2000) *Minority Rules: The Miao and the Feminine in China's Cultural Politics.* Durham, NC: Duke University Press.

Scheyvens, R. (2002) *Tourism for Development: Empowering Communities.* Harlow: Prentice Hall.

Scheyvens, R. (2011) *Tourism and Poverty.* New York: Routledge.

Schnell, S.M. (2003) The ambiguities of authenticity in Little Sweden, USA. *Journal of Cultural Geography* 20 (2), 43–68.

Scission (2010) Future Bleak for Hungarian Roma and Jews. 18 May. See http://oreaddaily.blogspot.hu/2010/05/future-bleak-for-hungarian-roma-and.html (accessed 10 January 2013).

Seetaram, N. (2008) Where the bloody hell are we? Immigration and tourism demand: Evidence from Australia (1992–2006). Cauthe 2008 Conference.

Selby, M. (2004) *Understanding Urban Tourism: Image, Culture & Experience.* New York: I.B. Tauris.

Selinger, E. and Outterson, K. (2009) *The Ethics of Poverty Tourism.* Boston, MA: Boston University.

Shadid, W. (2005) Berichtgeving over moslims en de islam in de westerse media: Beeldvorming, oorzaken en alternatieve strategieën. *Tijdschrift voor Communicatiewetenschap* 33 (4), 330–346.

Shapira, A. (2012) *Israel: A History.* Waltham, MA: University of Brandeis Press.

Sharpley, R. (2014) Host perceptions of tourism: A review of the research. *Tourism Management* 42, 37–49.

Shaw, S. (2007a) Ethnic quarters in the cosmopolitan-creative city. In G. Richards and J. Wilson (eds) *Tourism, Creativity and Development* (pp. 189–200). London and New York: Routledge.

Shaw, S. (2007b) Ethnoscapes as cultural attractions in Canadian 'world cities'. In M.K. Smith (ed.) *Tourism, Culture and Regeneration* (pp. 49–58). Wallingford: CABI.

Shaw, S. (2008) Hosting a sustainable visitor economy: Messages from London's Banglatown. *Journal of Urban Regeneration and Renewal* 1 (3), 275–285.

Shaw, S. (2010) Marketing ethnoscapes as spaces of consumption: 'Banglatown – London's Curry Capital'. *Journal of Town and City Management* 1 (4), 381–395.

Shaw, S. (2012) Faces, spaces, and places: Social and cultural impacts of street festivals in cosmopolitan cities. In S. Page and J. Connell (eds) *Routledge Handbook of Events* (pp. 401–415). London and New York: Routledge.

Shaw, S., Bagwell, S. and Karmowska, J. (2004) Ethnoscapes as spectacle: Reimaging multicultural districts as new destinations for leisure and tourism consumption. *Urban Studies* 41 (10), 1983–2000.

Shaw, S. and Bagwell, S. (2012) Ethnic minority restaurateurs and the regeneration of 'Banglatown' in London's East End. In V. Aytar and J. Rath (eds) *Selling Ethnic Neighborhoods: The Rise of Neighborhoods as Places of Leisure and Consumption* (pp. 34–51). New York: Routledge.

Sheller, M. and Urry, J. (2006) The new mobilities paradigm. *Environment and Planning A* 38 (2), 207–226.

Sklarewitz, N. (2012) Rebirth of Jewish life in Berlin. 5 June. See http://www.jewishjournal.com/travel/article/rebirth_of_jewish_life_in_berlin_20120605 (accessed 16 December 2013).

Smith, M.K. (2003) *Issues in Cultural Tourism Studies.* London: Routledge.

Smith, M.K. (2009) *Issues in Cultural Tourism Studies* (2nd edn). London: Routledge.

Smith, M.K. (2010) *Cultural Planning for Urban Regeneration: A Thirdspace Approach.* Saarbrücken: Lambert Academic Publishing.

Smith, M.K. and Carnegie, E. (2006) Bollywood dreams? The rise of the Asian Mela as a global cultural phenomenon. *Public History Review Journal* 12, 1–10.

Smith, M.K. and Robinson, M. (eds) (2006) *Cultural Tourism in a Changing World: Politics, Participation and (Re)presentation.* Clevedon: Channel View Publications.

Smith, M.K., Hart, M. and MacLeod, N. (2010) *Key Concepts in Tourist Studies.* London: Sage.

Smith, M.K. and Richards, G. (eds) (2013) *The Routledge Handbook of Cultural Tourism.* London: Routledge.

Smith, V. (2001) The nature of tourism. In V. Smith and M. Brent (eds) *Hosts and Guests Revisited: Tourism Issues of the 21st Century* (pp. 53–68). New York: Cognizant Communication Cooperation.

Soja, E.W. (1996) *Thirdspace: Journeys to Los Angeles and Other Real-and-Imagined Places.* Malden, MA: Blackwell.

Sonmez, S. and Sirakaya, E. (2002) A distorted destination image? The case of Turkey. *Journal of Travel Research* 41, 185–196.

Sonneborn, L. (2010) *The End of Apartheid in South Africa.* New York: Chelsea House.

Sorkin, M. (ed.) (1992) *Variations on a Theme Park: The New American City and the End of Public Space.* New York: Hill and Wang.

SouthAfrica.info (2013) Taking South Africa's Pink Route. See http://www.southafrica.info/travel/cities/pink-route.htm#.Up2o-M3Rfbo (accessed 3 December 2013).

Souros, G. (2012) Chinese New Year a boost for NSW tourism. See http://www.destinationnsw.com.au/__data/assets/pdf_file/0009/62010/Chinese-New-Year-boost-for-NSW-tourism.pdf (accessed 12 January 2014).

Spenceley, A., Relly, P., Keyser, H., Warmeant, P., McKenzie, M., Mataboge, A., Norton, P., Mahlangu, S. and Seif, J. (2002) *Responsible Tourism Manual for South Africa.* Pretoria: Department for Environmental Affairs and Tourism. See http://www.gov.za/documents/download.php?f=164725 (accessed 3 December 2013).

Statistics Netherlands (2005) *Statistical Yearbook of the Netherlands 2005.* See http://www.cbs.nl (accessed 10 June 2006).

Steinbrink, M. (2012) 'We did the slum!' Urban poverty in historical perspective. *Tourism Geographies* 14 (2), 213–234.

Steinbrink, M. (2013) Festi*favel*isation: Mega-events, slums and strategic city-staging – the example of Rio de Janeiro. *Die Erde* 144 (2), 129–145.

Stephenson, M. and Hughes, H.L. (2005) Racialised boundaries in tourism and travel: A case study of the UK black Caribbean community. *Leisure Studies* 24 (2), 137–160.

Stephenson, M.L. (2004) Tourism, racism and the UK Afro-Caribbean diaspora. In T. Coles and D.J. Timothy (eds) *Tourism, Diasporas and Space* (pp. 74–78). New York: Routledge.

Stevens, J. (2012) *The Urban Ecology of Matonge. A Research on Porosity.* Master thesis in human settlements (Unpublished), Katholieke Universiteit Leuven.

Stewart, M. (2010) Introduction. In M. Stewart and M. Rövid (eds) *Multidisciplinary Approaches to Romany Studies* (pp. 1–9). Budapest: CEU.

Steyn, D. (2006) *Queering the City: A Social and Spatial Account of the Mother City Queer Project at the Cape Town International Convention Centre in 2003.* MPhil thesis, University of Cape Town. See https://open.uct.ac.za/handle/11427/3569.

Stier, O.B. (1995) Lunch at Majdanek: The march of the living as a contemporary pilgrimage of memory. *Jewish Folklore and Ethnology Review* 17 (1–2), 57–62.

Sudgen, J. (2013) The Rights and Wrongs of Slum Tourism. *Indiarealtime*, blog. See http://blogs.wsj.com/indiarealtime/2013/05/03/the-rights-and-wrongs-of-slum-tourism/ (accessed 20 February 2014).

Swain, M.B. (1990) Commoditizing Ethnicity in Southwest China. *Cultural Survival Quarterly* 14 (1): 26–29.

Swain, M.B. (2001) Cosmopolitan tourism and minority politics in the stone forest. In T.C. Beng, S. Cheung and Y. Hui (eds) *Tourism, Anthropology, and China* (pp. 125–146). Bangkok: White Lotus Press.

Szerszynski, B. and Urry, J. (2002) Cultures of cosmopolitanism. *Sociological Review* 50 (4), 461–481.

Szuhay, P. (2002) Self-definitions of gypsy ethnic groups. In E. Kállai (ed.) *The Gypsies/ The Roma in Hungarian Society* (pp. 24–27). Budapest: Teleki László Foundation.

Tacoli, C. (1998) Rural–urban interactions: A guide to the literature. *Environment and Urbanization* 10 (1), 147–166.

Tadajewski, M. (2012) Character analysis and racism in marketing theory and practice. *Marketing Theory* 12 (4), 485–508.

Tan, S. and Yeoh, S.A. (2006) Negotiating cosmopolitanism in Singapore's fictitional landscape. In J. Binnie, J. Holloway, S. Millington and C. Young (eds) *Cosmopolitan Urbanism* (pp. 146–167). London: Routledge.

Tárki (2012) *Egy átlagos magyar szerint Magyarország éppen hogy a „magyaroké".* See http://www.tarki.hu/hu/news/2012/kitekint/20120709_magyaroke.html (accessed 14 January 2013).

Tavori, I. (ed.) (2007) *Dancing in a Thorn Field: The New Age in Israel*. Tel-Aviv: Hakibutz Hameuchad. In Hebrew.

Tebje, M. and Ozinsky, S. (2004) The Pink Route – Cape Town, South Africa. Insights, Volume 15, British Tourist Authority, London, pp. C31–C38. See http://www.insights.org.uk/articleitem.aspx?title=The+Pink+Route+-+Cape+Town%2C+South+Africa (accessed 3 December 2013).

Telfer, D.J. and Sharpley, R. (2008) *Tourism and Development in the Developing World*. London: Routledge.

The Economist (2014) The more the merrier. See http://www.economist.com/news/americas/21594328-debates-over-immigration-are-often-toxic-not-canada-more-merrier accessed 21/1/14 (accessed 18 January 2014).

The Malaysian Insider (2012) Hungary Roma restaurant eases prejudice through food. 24 April. See http://www.themalaysianinsider.com/litee/food/article/hungary-roma-restaurant-eases-prejudice-through-food (accessed 14 January 2013).

Thévenot, L., Moody, M. and Lafaye, C. (2000) Forms of valuing nature: Arguments and modes of justification in French and American environmental disputes. In M. Lamont and L. Thévenot (eds) *Rethinking Comparative Cultural Sociology: Repertoires of Evaluation in France and the United States* (pp. 229–272). Cambridge: Cambridge University Press.

Timothy, D. (2002) Tourism and the growth of ethnic islands. In C.M. Hall and A.M. Williams (eds) *Tourism and Migration: New Relationships Between Consumption and Production* (pp. 135–152). Dordrecht: Kluwer.

Todeschini, F. and Japha, D. (2013) Cultural identity and architectural image in Bo-Kaap, Cape Town. In N. Alsayyad (ed.) *The End of Tradition?* (pp. 187–209). London: Routledge.

Topbudapest.org (2012) Hungarian Restaurants with Gypsy Music. See http://restaurants.topbudapest.org/hungarian/hungarian-restaurant-with-Gypsy-music (accessed 14 January).

Torgovnick, M. (1990) *Gone Primitive: Savage Intellects, Modern Lives*. Chicago, IL: University of Chicago Press.

Tosun, C. (2002) Host perceptions of impacts: A comparative tourism study. *Annals of Tourism Research* 29 (1) 231–253.

TripAdvisor (2013) Holocaust Memorial Center Reviews. See http://www.tripadvisor.co.uk/Attraction_Review-g274887-d601982-Reviews-Holocaust_Memorial_Center-Budapest_Central_Hungary.html (accessed 20 May 2014).

Tsai, E. and Coleman, D. (1999) Leisure constraints of Chinese immigrants: An exploratory study. *Society and Leisure* 22 (1), 243–264.

Tuan, Y.F. (1977) *Space and Place: The Perspective of Experience*. Minneapolis, MN: University of Minnesota Press.

Tucker, A. (2009) *Queer Visibilities: Space, Identity and Interaction in Cape Town*. Malden, MA: Wiley-Blackwell.

Tucker, H. (2005) Narratives of place and self-differing experiences of package coach tours in New Zealand. *Tourist Studies* 5 (3), 267–282.

Tunbridge, J.E. and Ashworth, G.J. (1996) *Dissonant Heritage: The Management of the Past as a Resource in Conflict*. London: John Wiley & Sons.

Tzur, N. (2013) Budapest mayor rethinks anti-Semitic street name, 6 February. See http://www.jpost.com/Jewish-World/Jewish-News/Budapest-mayor-rethinks-naming-of-road-after-anti-Semite-315125 (accessed 10 October 2013).

UNESCO (2012) www.whs.unesco.org/en/lost/1223 (accessed 27 December 2012).

United Nations World Tourism Organization (UNWTO) (2012) *Global Report on LGBT Tourism* (AM Reports Vol. 3). Madrid: UNWTO.

UNWTO (2010) *The Role of the Media in the New Operating Model of Global Tourism*. United Nations World Tourism Organization. See http://pub.unwto.org?WebRoot/store/Shops/Infoshop/Products/1293/1293-1.pdf (accessed 26 May 2010).

Urry, J. (1990) *The Tourist Gaze*. London: Sage Publications.

Urry, J. (2002) *The Tourist Gaze* (2nd edn). London: Sage Publications.

Urry, J. (2007) *Mobilities*. Cambridge: Polity Press.

US Census Bureau (2012) *Office of Immigration Statistics*. See https://www.census.gov/population/intmigration (accessed 15 November 2013).

Vági, Z., Csősz, L. and Kádár, G. (2013) *The Holocaust in Hungary: Evolution of Genocide*. Plymouth: AltaMira Press.

Vajda, I. (2002) The Gypsies – the Roma and scientific research. In E. Kállai (ed.) *The Gypsies/The Roma in Hungarian Society* (pp. 149–156). Budapest: Teleki László Foundation.

Valladares, L. (2005) *A invenção da favela: Do mito de origem a favela.com*. Rio de Janeiro: FGV Editora.

Van der Duim, R., Peters, K. and Wearing, S. (2005) Planning host and guest interactions: Moving beyond the empty meeting ground in African encounters. *Current Issues in Tourism* 8 (4), 286–305.

Van Doorn, J. (1989) A critical assessment of socio-cultural impact studies of tourism in the third world. In T.V. Singh, J. Kaur and D.P. Singh (eds) *Studies in Tourism Wildlife Parks Conservation* (pp. 71–92). New Delhi: Metropolitan Book Co.

Van Egmond, Antionius Nicolaas (2007) Understanding Western Tourists in Developing Countries, Cabi.

Van Hoof, H.F. and Verbeeten, M. (2005) Wine is for drinking, water is for washing: Student opinions about international exchange programs. *Journal of Studies in International Education* 9 (1), 42–61.

Vargas-Sanchez, A., Porras-Bueno, N. and Paza-Mejia, M. (2011) Explaining residents attitudes to tourism: Is a universal model possible? *Annals of Tourism Research* 38 (2), 460–480.

Vidra, Z. (2010) "The Unhidden Jew": Jewish narratives in Romany Life-stories. In M. Stewart and M. Rövid (eds) *Multidisciplinary Approaches to Romany Studies* (pp. 196–208). Budapest: CEU.

Visagie, J. (2013) Race, Gender and Growth of the Affluent Middle Class in Post-Apartheid South Africa. Biennial Conference of the Economic Society of South Africa, University of the Free State, Bloemfontein, South Africa, 25–27 September 2013.

Visser, G. (2002) Gay tourism in South Africa: Issues from the Cape Town experience. *Urban Forum* 13 (1), 85–94.

Visser, G. (2003a) Gay men, leisure space and South African cities: The case of Cape Town. *Geoforum* 34 (1), 123–137.

Visser, G. (2003b) Gay men, tourism and urban space: Reflections on Africa's 'gay capital'. *Tourism Geographies: An International Journal of Tourism Space, Place and Environment* 5 (2), 168–189.

Visser, G. (2004) Second homes and local development: Issues arising from Cape Town's De Waterkant. *GeoJournal* 60 (3), 259–271.

Visser, G. (2007) Gay tourism in South Africa: The Cape Town experience. In C.M. Rogerson and G. Visser (eds) *Urban Tourism in the Developing World: The South African Experience* (pp. 101–126). London: Transaction Press.

Vörös, K. (2001) How Jewish is Jewish Budapest? *Jewish Social Studies* 8 (1), 88–125.

Waitt, G. and Markwell, K. (eds) (2006) *Gay Tourism: Culture and Context*. Binghampton, NY: Haworth Hospitality.

Walsh, E.R. (2005) From Nü Guo to Nü'er Guo: Negotiating desire in the land of the Mosuo. *Modern China* 11 (4), 448–486.

Wang, Y. (2008) *Naturalizing Ethnicity, Culturalizing Landscape: The Politics of World Heritage in China*. Doctoral dissertation in anthropology, Duke University.

Wang, Y. (2007) Customized authenticity begins at home. *Annals of Tourism Research* 34 (3), 789–804.

Warde, A. (1997) *Consumption, Food and Taste*. London: Sage Publications.

Warde, A. and Martens, L. (2000) *Eating Out: Social Differentiation, Consumption and Pleasure*. Cambridge: Cambridge University Press.

Weingrod, A. (1966) *Reluctant Pioneers: Village Development in Israel*. New York: Ithaca Press.

Wellman and Gulia (1999) *Networks in the Global Village*. Boulder, CO: Westview Press.

Wels, H. (2004) About romance and reality. In C.M. Hall and H. Tucker (eds) *Tourism and Postcolonialism* (pp. 76–94). London: Routledge.

Whyte, K.P., Selinger, E. and Outerson, K. (2011) Poverty and the problem of consent. *Journal of Global Ethics* 7 (3), 337–348.

West, D. (2008) Geert Wilders on 'Glen Beck'. In D. West (2008). 26 September. See http://www.dianawest.net/Home/tabid/36/EntryId/485/Geert-Wilders-on-Glenn-Beck.aspx (accessed 23 April 2013).

Williams, C. (2008) Ghettourism and voyeurism, or challenging stereotypes and raising consciousness? Literary and non-literary forays into the favelas of Rio de Janeiro. *Bulletin of Latin American Research* 27 (4), 483–500.

Williams, A. and Hall, M. (2010) Tourism and migration: New relationships between production and consumption. *Tourism Geographies* 2 (1), 5–27.

Wolff, M. (2006) The myth of the actuary: Life insurance and Frederick L. Hoffman's "Race Traits and Tendencies of the American Negro". *Public Health Reports* 121 (January–February), 84–91.

Wolfram, G. and Burnill, C. (2013) The tactical tourist – Growing self-awareness and challenging the strategists: Visitor-groups in Berlin. In M. Smith and G. Richards (eds) *The Routledge Handbook of Cultural Tourism* (pp. 361–368). London: Routledge.

Woosnam, K. (2012) Using emotional solidarity to explain residents' attitudes about tourism and tourism development. *Journal of Travel Research* 51 (3), 315–327.

World Bank (2007) *Strategic Environmental Assessment Study: Tourism Development in the Province of Guizhou*. Shanghai: Environmental Resources Management.

Yu, X., Weiler, B. and Ham, S. (2002) Intercultural communication and mediation: A framework for analysing the intercultural competence of Chinese tour guides. *Journal of Vacation Marketing* 8 (1), 75–87.

Yu, X., Weiler, B. and Ham, S. (2004) Cultural mediation in guided tour experiences: A case study of Australian guides of Chinese tour groups. Working paper 44/04. Monash University.

Zátori, A. (2012) A turisztikai élményteremtés módjainak feltárása vállalati szemszögből. [The exploration of the modes of tourism experience creation from a business point of view]. Unpublished PhD thesis proposal. Corvinus University of Budapest.

Zeiderman, A. (2006) The Fetish and the Favela: Notes on Tourism and the Commodification of Place in Rio de Janeiro, Brazil. University of California, International and Area Studies, Breslauer Symposium, Paper 17.

Zeppel, H. (2006) *Indigenous Ecotourism: Sustainable Development and Management*. Wallingford: CABI.

Zerubavel, Y. (2008) The desert and the settlement as symbolic landscapes in modern Israeli culture. In J. Brauch, A. Lipphardt and A. Nocke (eds) *Jewish Topographies Visions of Space, Traditions of Place* (pp. 201–222). London and Aldershot: Ashgate Press.

Zhang, J. (2009) Touristic encounter, identity recognition and presentation: The story of a Tibetan tourist driver. *Current Themes in Indigenous Tourism*. Special Issue of *London Journal of Tourism, Sport and Creative Industries*. 2 (1)

Zhang, X. and Liu, X. (2006) *Fu hao yu yi: Guizhou shan di wen ming tu dian*; 符号与仪式: 贵州山地文明图典/张晓松著;卢现艺摄影   [*Symbols   and   Rituals: An   Illustrated Introduction to the Civilization of the Guizhou Mountains*]. Guiyang: Guizhou ren min chu ban she.

Zhao, W. and Ritchie, J.R.B. (2007) Tourism and poverty alleviation: An integrative research framework. *Current Issues in Tourism* 10 (2–3), 119–143.

Zhao, W. and Getz, D. (2008) Characteristics and goals of rural family business owners in tourism and hospitality: A developing country perspective. *Tourism Recreation Research* 33 (3), 313–326.

Zhou, M. (1992) *Chinatown: The Socioeconomic Potential of an Urban Enclave*. Philadelphia, PA: Temple University Press.

Zhu, Y. (2012) Performing heritage: Rethinking authenticity in global tourism. *Annals of Tourism Research* 39 (3), 1495–1513.

Zukin, S. (1995) *The Cultures of Cities*. Oxford: Blackwell.

Zukin, S. (1998) *Urban Lifestyles: Diversity and Standardisation*, Urban Studies, 35(5/6): 825–839.

Index